NEARLY THERE

NEARLY THERE

Some Memoirs by

JOHN FROST
of
Arnhem Bridge

LEO COOPER · LONDON

First published in Great Britain in 1991 by
LEO COOPER
190 Shaftesbury Avenue, London WC2H 8JL
an imprint of
Pen & Sword Books Ltd.
47 Church Street
Barnsley, S. Yorks S70 2AS.

A CIP catalogue record for this book
is available from the British Library

ISBN: 0 852052 232 3

Typeset in 11/13pt Linotron Bembo by
Hewer Text Composition Services, Edinburgh
Printed and bound in Great Britain by
Mackays of Chatham PLC, Chatham, Kent

CONTENTS

B

I am very grateful Major-General Frost asked me to write a preface to this book about his life. It is the story of the life of a great soldier who does not hesitate to call a spade a spade.

I am particularly impressed by the last chapter and his description of the battle of Arnhem.

I only learned a few years ago that Montgomery had all the details about the German Panzer Division and had photographs of them taken by a Spitfire. I will never understand why he did not inform the gallant Airborne Forces about this.

When I asked his Chief of Staff, Freddie de Guingand, why Arnhem went wrong, he said: "It's very simple, I was sick." Had he been there, I think the operation could have succeeded and the Netherlands would have been spared the "Hunger-winter."

Prince of the Netherlands

INTRODUCTION

I started this book at the behest of my publisher who wanted me to record my life in the Army, other than my wartime experiences which I had previously described in *A Drop Too Many*.

After many vicissitudes it has become almost an autobiography. Rather difficult in many ways because the most important part of any professional soldier's life must be the wartime years when he is really put to the test. However, quite a lot seems to happen in peacetime and perhaps some of my experiences may be of interest. Most of the places in which I served are no longer available to today's soldiers, so perhaps it is useful to describe them.

Faced with the problem of a title for the book, I finally came up with *Nearly There*. Firstly, because at the age of 78 there cannot be all that more to come and, secondly, because although I achieved quite a lot, I never really hit the jackpot.

I owe much to Claire Attwater who did nearly all the typing and gave me encouragement when I was flagging, and give great credit to my wife who listened to the early drafts and finally took most diligent care over reading the proofs. Also to Captain Johnnie Coote who persuaded me to carry on when my first publisher packed up.

By far the best thing that happened to me was my marriage to Jean and it is to her that I dedicate this book.

JOHN FROST
Milland,
1991.

CHAPTER I

CHILDHOOD

I WAS BORN IN POONA on 31 December, 1912. My father, who
had begun his military service with the Yeomanry during the
Boer War, subsequently being commissioned into the Cheshire
Regiment, had transferred to the Supply and Transport Corps of
the Indian Army. He had been one of twelve children and very
little money could be spared to bolster his career so, when he fell
in love and wanted to get married, the additional income from the
transfer made sense.

The family had been ropemakers for three generations and lived
in Epping Forest, my grandfather had married a Dutton, which
family stemmed from Cheshire.

My sister, Betty, was born about one year after me and my
mother brought us back to England just before the Kaiser's War
began. My father spent most of the war in France where he gained
a certain amount of kudos for being involved with the development
of ultra-light railways as a means of bringing ammunition and
supplies to the forward positions. He was awarded an MC for
one particular episode and mentioned in dispatches five times.
I can just remember him when he came home from France on
sporadic occasions. Towards the end of the war he was posted to
Mesopotamia, as Iraq was then called, and as soon as it was possible
my mother brought us children out to India, with the intention of
going on to Mesopotamia as soon as that was practicable.

I remember little about India. Most of our time was spent up in
the hills at Simla. A Swiss governess joined us there and travelled
with us to Basra. By this time we had acquired a spaniel puppy.
There seemed to be no difficulties in arranging for it to come
everywhere with us, which was fortuitous, for during our one

night in Basra our hotel was burnt to the ground and it was the spaniel that woke us all, thus allowing us to escape in time.

Our house on the west bank of the River Tigris outside Baghdad was fabulous to my young eyes. It was built round a courtyard and had a splendid garden to one side. The grounds spread to stables and tennis courts, beyond which was agricultural land irrigated by mechanical means from the river. There were great numbers of staff in the way of indoor servants, gardeners, grooms and drivers for cars, mostly Model T Fords, they being the only vehicles that could cope with the almost complete lack of roads. Perhaps most attractive of all the assets was the *Sheerin*, a motor-engined, Arab craft which my father had had altered to his own specifications with a wheelhouse, sleeping cabins and a saloon for his use on his many expeditions up and down the river. When he was not using it, we children and Ma'mselle could be wafted where we would.

It was amazing that any families had been allowed into the country at all, for in 1920 a full-scale Arab insurrection was taking place. Mesopotamia for many years had been a Turkish Province. The Turks had been harsh taskmasters and the inhabitants were not pleased at having to accept another power to govern them. Britain had been given a mandate over the country at the peace conference but a decision over their future rulers was still in abeyance. All the tribes were well armed with rifles, which had come into their possession as a result of disasters to each side during the war.

Up to three divisions of British and Indian troops were needed to keep order. Frequently, our own columns would be beleaguered by greatly superior numbers, while attacks on all forms of communications were commonplace. My father, in the rank of Brigadier, was the Director of Labour and, as such, he organized an armed labour corps, who were able to defend themselves and their projects most of the time. Anyway, it was not the sort of situation in which women and children could move about in safety, although we were blissfully unaware of what was going on until much later.

There were several horses in our stables. Up to this time I had never ridden but I was now mounted on what was thought to be a fairly gentle beast and sent off with one of the Arab grooms to learn the business. As he had no English and I no Arabic, the instruction was basic. It really only consisted of how to get on and off and to steer or stop by pulling on the reins. However, I suppose that one has a certain amount of inborn instinct in such things because I very soon felt confident and, though I had a few falls, before long I was out with the Exodus Hunt. This was a pack of salukis that had been formed by the 110th Company of the Corps soon after the end of the war – 'Eck o Dus' being Hindustani for their number. The salukis chased any jackal that could be put on the move in front of them, hunting entirely by sight, and the pace was tremendous. Old Turkish trenches and irrigation ditches provided the obstacles and were the cause of many an empty saddle. I little thought then that a few years later I should be the master of a pack of English foxhounds, which were to succeed the salukis in due course.

Ma'mselle gave Betty and me lessons in all main subjects every day. She was an excellent teacher and we both made considerable progress but, unfortunately for me, my sister did much better, so Ma'mselle showed a certain amount of favouritism, which made me bolshy, and I often found myself in trouble as a result. Her normal punishment was to set me a number of lines to write and, when I was coping with these, she and Betty were free to go off somewhere. One seldom saw one's parents but I used to be able to think up some fairly subtle ways of getting my own back, which, in the end, caused Ma'mselle to lessen the line-writing ploy and we came to observe a state of armed neutrality.

The Commander-in-Chief was a delightful man, Lieutenant-General Sir Aylmer Haldane. Every now and then he would send his high-speed launch across the river to pick us up for a visit to the cinema in the town. He, himself, thoroughly enjoyed the flicks and was a marvellous host to the two young children involved. In fact, we very seldom went to Baghdad, which could hardly be described as a tourist resort in those days.

The RAF were very much in evidence. Indeed, Iraq was one of the parts of the Empire which, it was hoped, could, in the future, be controlled by them. However, as yet there had not been time to put this theory to the test. There was a squadron of DH bombers stationed at Hinaidi, just outside Baghdad, and I had a flight in one of the aircraft. I was absolutely entranced, feeling I could never have enough of it. Indeed, I determined that I would go into the RAF when I grew up.

The rivers were the mainspring of life in Iraq. Water from these was pumped up through most of the year to irrigate all the cultivatable land running alongside. With the water came incredibly rich silt, which settled on the fields over which the water flowed. Indeed, even if the water settled on bare, sandy desert, in no time at all it was possible to grow things on it and one could start a garden within a year of envisaging one. The level of the river varied considerably, depending on the time of the year. Spring coincided with the melting of the snows in the mountains in Turkey, which resulted in the arrival of great torrents of water lower down, with subsequent flooding wherever the water could find a way. Woe betide any man or beast that fell into the river at this time and woe unto all vessels that had to make their way upstream against the current. In fact, some of these, called Mahelas, had to be drawn by manpower, struggling along a riverside towpath.

As the summer advanced, the level of the river fell and mudbanks appeared to hinder navigation, which was never impossible, so quite large cargo-carrying barges were for ever on the go. No rain fell until well into the winter months, but this, when it came, had little influence on the river. It turned the hard-baked countryside into glutinous mud, but then only for a time, for the sunshine was never very far away. The midsummer temperatures were almost record-breaking, with 123 degrees as a norm. However, it was a dry heat and few people were inconvenienced thereby. Winter readings were definitely moderate and everyone wore clothes similar to those worn during the English summer. The authorities considered that the heat of the summer was too much for the British families and we were all sent up to the hills in Persian Kurdistan. A desperately bare piece of country was chosen for a tented camp and here we were dumped.

The nearest built-up place was a small town called Karind but there were practically no amenities of any kind. The hills were barren and rocky, with dry scrub bushes as the only form of vegetation. The local Kurdish people were not above pilfering and burglary; indeed, one man lost everything he possessed while leaving his tent for an evening walk. My father came up from Baghdad for a day or two and a marauder had a go at his clothing; however, he owned a dog, which was said to be a cross between a Persian Pushti-kooh sheepdog and a wolf, so the intruder was given very short shrift; in fact, the din he made woke up the whole encampment.

It was a very snaky place. I have always had a particular aversion to snakes, I think possibly because my father had shot one in the act of crawling up into my cot when I was only three weeks old. Anyway, one morning, when I was sitting on what was then known as a thunderbox placed in one of our tents, a medium-sized snake wriggled underneath the apparatus between my feet to coil up on the ground in front of me. I was too terrified even to make a noise, but fortunately, after pausing for a minute or two, the snake wriggled on and out through the other side of the tent.

Meanwhile, the insurrection was at its peak in Iraq and every possible resource was needed to contain it. The families had to be brought back to Baghdad where they could be more easily protected, which involved a fairly hazardous train journey, the railway being one of the principal targets of the rebels. I remember being quite fascinated by the make-up of the train, which had flat trucks in front, behind and interspersed between some of the carriages. These held soldiers with machine guns, protected with sandbags; I believe there were even some riflemen on the roofs of some of the carriages. Anyway, thus protected, we set off, a trolley with similar protection in front to examine all the bridges over the culverts, which might have been mined or weakened, so we did not move very fast. The train was attacked when we were quite near Baghdad. Mounted men moved from one vantage point to another, firing mostly ineffectually at the train and sometimes galloping alongside. I found it most exciting and was delighted to see how terrified Ma'mselle was. I do not believe there were any casualties.

Before long the train was brought to a halt by a blown bridge over a wadi and here we had to detrain to get into another, which was waiting on the far side of the demolition. The rebel attack now petered out but at least I had had my baptism of fire, of which I was inordinately proud.

We children were soon quite proficient in Arabic. At that age one has no self-consciousness and as none of the servants spoke English, we buckled down to using their lingo. This stood me in good stead in later years, for when I joined the Iraq Levies in 1938 I romped through the colloquial Arabic exam after a minimum of punching-up. I can still remember some of the servants, in particular one we called 'Wee MacGregor' as he was very small, and Abdul Fatah, who adored all children. The cook had a mongoose as a pet and I once watched it kill a snake, but as the snake was half in and half out of a hole in the ground, it did not seem to be a very fair match. I had more to do with the grooms or what were called *Sais* than any of the other servants. Stablewise, I most remember a terrible horse called Tommy, of which everyone was scared. When rustlers tried to steal the horses, Tommy made such a fuss that the thieves ran away empty-handed.

Towards the end of our time at Baghdad, my mother produced another daughter, who was christened Diana. There were a great many storks in and around Baghdad so the traditional story about the arrival of babies was readily believed by Betty and me. The difference in our respective ages was to mean that we saw little of our young sister until very much later in our lives.

The garden was a great pleasure to all of us. Once a week water was pumped up from the river to flow along the ditches there. It was lovely to watch it arrive and trickle into the sun-parched ground where it formed canals for a day or two, till it in turn was dried away. Oleanders provided most of the colour but there were many other flowers and shrubs. Most of the trees were figs, mulberries or eucalyptus. Among the birds, hoopoes and bee-eaters were the commonest, and swallowtails among the butterflies.

During the hot, dry weather we often slept on the great flat roof under mosquito nets which were apt to billow or almost take off in the sudden gusts of wind. The howling of the jackal pack could be a little unnerving when it started up close to the house. There was a platoon of Indian sepoys down below and sometimes one could hear the specially muted orders of the commander when the guard was being changed.

Towards the end of our time, during 1921, the insurrection was temporarily over, the recalcitrant tribesmen disarmed and some of the troops could be sent home. My father's job was finished and we all embarked at Basra on an Indian marine ship, called *The Harding* – fascinating from my point of view because it was armed and carried Indian marines with all the military trappings. General 'Tiny' Ironside was a passenger. He had just survived his umpteenth aeroplane crash. He was still covered in bandages and in a wheelchair. After he had been pushed up the gangway, for a moment the ADC and other attendants left him on the deck on his own. This was too much for Betty and me and we started to trundle him along the deck. As soon as he realized what was happening, he began to roar and very soon we were parted from our prey. My poor father was given a tremendous rocket and so was everyone else in view.

Several years later the General was inspecting the Wellington College OTC, stopping to ask boys their names at random. It chanced that he picked on me.

'You couldn't be that awful little boy who seized my wheelchair on *The Harding*, could you?' I had to admit it.

There was a sandbar across the mouth of the river in the Persian Gulf and here the ship got stuck for several hours. All the passengers were put into the lifeboats to lighten ship and eventually she could move. We stopped at Muscat, where we had a memorable swim, to be repeated many years later when I was next on my way home from Iraq.

At Suez we transferred to a British India Line boat, which was not nearly so interesting, arriving home for a very hot summer and a round of visits before Betty and I started on our prep school educations.

I began at what turned out to be a dreadful place at St Leonard's. The sons of a family called Hadow had done well there and recommended it strongly, and indeed it had a lovely position, but the staff, from the headmaster downwards, were second-rate. After we had been at school for one term, my mother decided to accompany my father out to India and we were left in the charge of a most formidable aunt. Ethel was the widow of a very high church clergyman and church and church-going were still her greatest interests, so that, when we had to spend our holidays in her sole charge, they were apt to be tedious. Fortunately we could spend some of them with relatives. Among them was Uncle Jim, the eldest of my father's family, whose son, Dick, became a lifelong friend. His elder sister, Rosemary, later married Geoffrey Legge, who was Captain of the Kent County cricket team. We spent one summer with our Aunt Jessica, who had a large house with its own farm at Ackworth near Pontefract – alas, all knocked down and built over now. Mostly we stayed with the Rowe family. Aunt Ethel's daughter had married a man we called Uncle George, who was a director of Rolls Royce, but above all he was a famous rowing man and had been the senior steward at Henley Regatta for several years. They were a big family with two boys, a girl and girl twins, who rejoiced in the names Grace and Glory. Ronnie, the eldest son, followed in his father's footsteps as regards the rowing world, representing Eton and Oxford, and Anthony, who was born some years later, not only achieved the like but won the Diamonds as well.

Anyway, the holidays with them were the greatest fun. Their house was at Cookham Dene. We children spent our time in the nursery wing, presided over by a wonderful nanny, who was supported by her own nursery maid. We three boys slept in an octagonal room at the top of the house, which seemed to us to be rather like the keep of a castle. One of the playrooms had a model railway laid on trestles round the room, which gave us much pleasure, but there seemed to be an infinite variety of things to do.

After a few unsatisfactory terms I left St Leonard's for Bigshotte Rayles, from which a lot of boys went on to Wellington, the public school for which I had been entered. The atmosphere was completely different. All the masters were thoroughly capable and the headmaster was devoted to his job. I can remember being amazed at seeing him playing ping-pong with the boys, something that the other school's headmaster would not have dreamt of doing. There was no shouting or blustering. Where, in the last establishment, there had been frowns or scowls, here there were smiles and laughter. There were no less than three matrons, as against none, and these went around the dormitories every night to make sure that all the boys were in good shape. Even the most sorrowful new boy was comforted and made to forget his longing for home.

Our parents came back from India when I was due to go to Wellington and they bought a house at Dibden Purlieu on the edge of the New Forest. This was heaven as far as Betty and I were concerned because at last we could put down roots and make friends with other children. Our parents then went back to India for another tour but now the formidable Aunt Ethel gave way to a more sympathetic régime in the shape of an aunt and uncle from my mother's side of the family. We were now able to keep ponies, had a grass tennis court, a small sailing dinghy on Southampton Water and I was able to start shooting. I played for the village cricket team and after a time organized an under-sixteen boys' team to play against the like in many of the other villages roundabout.

The New Forest was very different in those days from what it is now. There were no fences and the roads were of gravel, nearly always deeply potholed and exuding clouds of dust during the summer months.

There were two small estates nearby that gave me permission to carry a gun, both very much rough shooting, with pheasants a rarity, but as I was accompanied only by a very self-willed terrier I was happy enough with the pigeons and rabbits that occasionally fell to my gun. This developed from airgun to four-ten, to twenty-bore to eighteen. There were quite a few wildfowl on Southampton Water on the saltings near Hythe, where the dinghy lay, but I must confess to being singularly unsuccessful at shooting any.

My father came home from India for good after we had lived at Dibden Purlieu for about four years. His military career had ended in disappointment in that, after he had been definitely offered a job with promotion, it was rescinded. He found consolation by turning to religion, becoming secretary to an organization then called the Bible Churchman's Missionary Society. He never did anything by halves and now wanted his family to share his enthusiasm in his new-found faith so we children were put under considerable pressure in this respect. Family prayers after breakfast became a norm and these could last up to half an hour. Part of our holidays were spent under the auspices of an organization called the Officers' Christian Union, whose leaders were thoroughly genuine, likeable people of the 'Born Again' persuasion. They were so convincingly happy that I was almost persuaded, but the illogicality of it all always dissuaded me.

Meanwhile, I had not been doing very well at Wellington. There, you were in either a house or a dormitory and the latter consisted of a long corridor, from which some thirty-odd cubicles abutted. Every boy had his own cubicle with ten-foot walls giving privacy and these could be furnished and decorated to taste. They could, in fact, be made most comfortable. There was a gas ring at the end of the dormitories so that one could brew up hot drinks and there were cupboards where food could be kept. But in those days the house or dormitory was a closed society and one was actively

9

discouraged from having friends from elsewhere. This meant that friendships were limited to a very small number of one's own age group. Thus, if you did not happen to feel at home with those available, you could be lonely.

The houses or dormitories were named after Generals who took part in the Napoleonic Wars and I was in Blücher, named after the great Prussian leader. There was tremendous competition to excel and woe betide the boy who failed to pull his weight. During my time, the prefects in charge took their responsibilities with what might be called Teutonic zeal and if one happened to be somewhat backward, they could make life unpleasant. Failure to play well at a game or to run to the expected standard could bring retribution, while a succession of such might well earn a sound flogging. These were administered in the corridor so that all the preliminaries and the punishment itself were heard by everyone within earshot.

The standard of instruction varied considerably. The form classes consisted of thirty boys so the master's attention to the individual was necessarily limited. The man who taught geography was brilliant. He had evolved a system whereby each boy had actually to produce something during each lesson and he was able to congratulate or condemn. The language instruction was the worst, being reduced to the requirement to master the grammar, with no opportunities to converse.

I managed to get an upward move each term but always only just, and my reports were always just average. This was considered barely good enough at Wellington so, after three years there, I was moved to Monkton Combe. This school was best known for its Christian background and when my father heard of it, he could hardly wait to place me there.

It was very different from Wellington. As regards the buildings, whereas the former had been rather like a superior barracks, the latter was more like a collection of farm buildings. Wellington had stood on its own in its own splendid grounds; Monkton was almost in and indeed part of a village. At Wellington, one hardly ever saw anyone not connected with the College; at Monkton we were allowed bicycles and could even go to the city of Bath for restaurants and the cinema, if you wanted to. Although the fees at both schools were much the same, the types of boy were not, and at Monkton the masters were much more integrated with the boys. Monkton was a rowing school and sent its eight to Henley Regatta. The boat house was on a quite lovely stretch of the River Avon and here I was to spend many very happy hours.

No one at Monkton showed any surprise that I should have come from a major public school to a relatively minor one. Only one boy said, 'It must be simply awful for you.' I missed the privacy of having one's own cubicle, for now one slept in a dormitory with several others and preparation work was done in a classroom. Nevertheless, I felt much better, without the pressure one was exposed to at Wellington. To enjoy oneself there, you needed to be definitely above average and I was a late developer. Now, there was a much less demanding house system and one could make friends where and how one wished.

However, things religious were important and the Christianity was of the 'Born Again' variety. I had never really been able to believe and could not now declare myself. However well one did in other ways, one was most unlikely to be made a school prefect unless one was a professing Christian. This was inclined to lead one to make one's friends from those who were patently heathen. There is, of course, a half-way house to which most people probably belong. Many are prepared to kneel, shut their eyes and say the words, hoping that it will do them good, and, on the whole, people who do just this are nicer and better than those who do not. Very few people do not want to have their children baptised, married in church or have a Christian burial. It cannot be very ethical to only go to church for these occasions, for it costs money to keep the churches going and those who run them need support. I am glad to say that in later years I gave that support.

I soon became an enthusiastic oarsman and managed to get a place in the school eight. In those days the public schools competed against each other at Henley Regatta for a trophy called the Ladies Plate. Eton had won several times and Shrewsbury also, but the university colleges were able to enter teams and they were obviously very much stronger. Later, schools were able to compete more fairly in another event for the Princess Elizabeth Cup. Being a member of a crew propelling a racing eight through still water is almost unimaginable to those who have not done it, but infinitely more so is the excitement of racing alongside another crew, making every effort to go faster.

In the year that I rowed, we were beaten by the eventual winners of the event in the first round by barely a length. It was a tremendous thrill to have taken part and something one will never forget. Our stroke was Jack Bradley, who later stroked the winning Cambridge crew for more than one successful year. His younger brother, Malcolm, did likewise a few years later. The Bradley family lived quite close to us in Hampshire. Jack and I became great friends until he left the UK to live in the United States after the war. He spent most of that time in motor gun boats in the Burma seas. I believe that he stroked the Leander eight to victory in the Grand Challenge Cup in the first Henley Regatta after the war.

I became an enthusiastic member of the school OTC, rising to the dizzy height of Company Sergeant Major from being a corporal the term before. Few others shared my enthusiasm and the only person I can remember being involved was the ex-Regular Army Instructor, a Sergeant-Major Hannay. In addition to being a worthy old soldier, he was also a keen boxer and he persuaded me to introduce the noble art to the school, which up till then had desisted. I had done a certain amount of boxing at Wellington but never with any notable success. Anyway, we soon had a quorum and were able to stage a school tournament, which aroused considerable interest.

During my last term at Monkton, six boys were due to take the army exam. We were put together in a room which almost adjoined the prefects' room and, as we considered ourselves rather superior to the prefects, we found ways of tormenting them without going too far. Among our number was Hugh Olaf de Wet, a grandson of the famous Boer leader. He was always a rebel. So much so that at the end of his last term at Sandhurst, he still had several days of restrictions to serve and was told that if he wanted a commission, he would have to come back for another term to do them. He declined and joined the Deuxième Bureau in France. Caught in Germany by the Gestapo, he spent practically the whole war in concentration camps while under sentence of death.

I think that all the members of the army class passed the exam. I had trouble over the medical, which required me to have an operation for hydrocele before I could be accepted. This meant leaving the school a few days before the end of term. I had enjoyed my time at Monkton. It was much more like the school described by Kipling in *Stalky & Co* than a major public school. The religious background was disadvantageous to more normal boys for it led to a lack of magnanimity in some ways. For instance, although I had played for the 1st XV in every single match that I was there in my last term, except for missing one during the army exam and having to leave a week early, I was denied my school rugger cap. Anyway, I was given a great send-off when I left.

During this time, my parents had moved from the New Forest to Parkstone, which was a suburb of Bournemouth. Here, there were very different attractions for the adolescent. I always seemed to manage to have the use of a car of some sort, indeed, one of them was a Vanden Plas-bodied straight eight Bugatti. It was almost falling to bits. Heaven knows what it would be worth today. We soon had an amusing circle of friends of our own age, some of whom would be at Sandhurst while I was there. Much of our time was spent in social activities. Bournemouth could boast an abundance of fine hotels, many of which had excellent dance bands so that we could often dance the night away. Otherwise there were tennis parties – but most of our fun was on the sea. It was easy and cheap to hire boats of all sorts just to sail, to fish, or to explore and picnic. We got ourselves into trouble from time to time. I remember being stuck on the 'Broad Loo' in Poole Harbour for several hours and being suddenly engulfed in fog as we were lying off 'Old Harry'. On this occasion we had the lifeboat out looking for us.

I went to Sandhurst in January, 1930. I had heard a lot about it from other people who had been there so there were few surprises. I was unfortunate in that the operation I had undergone for hydrocele had gone slightly wrong and my testicles were so tender that even the slightest knock induced considerable pain. This ruled out my playing rugger or even hockey and I had to be very careful getting on a horse. This was a considerable disadvantage because those who do not take a full part in supporting the company are viewed with displeasure by those who do. Our Senior Under-Officer, the leading cadet of 5 Company, in which I was placed, was an outstanding man who set a tremendous example and I will never forget James Hill's address to our group of newly joined 'Gentlemen Cadets', as we were known. Some people said that we were, 'Almost officers but by no means gents'.

A dedicated body of non-commissioned officers ruled our lives for the first few weeks while we were marched up and down the square for several hours a day. No stones were left unturned to make us the smartest soldiers in the world. Perfection was the watchword and woe betide he who failed to come up to scratch. These men were mostly guardsmen, who had been specially selected. One had to address them as 'Staff', the one exception being the Regimental Sergeant Major, who was 'Sir'. One did not often meet this exalted person but if one failed to say the right word, he was said to be quick with, 'Now, Sir, I Sir you, Sir, and you Sir me, Sir. Do you see, Sir?'

The Staff addressed cadets with the prefix Mr, so it was as Mister Frost, Sir, that I would be named. Even Royalty were 'Mister Prince Henry, Sir'. 5 Company Sergeant Major was Hughes, commonly known as 'Windy Hughes'. He used to inspect the company every morning before breakfast at what was known as the 'Shaving Parade'. He had one stock question for every new intake. Pausing before some particularly hirsute youth, he would demand in staccato crescendo, "Av you shaved today, Mr Jones, Sir?'

'Yes, Staff.'

'Then, Mr Jones, Sir, are you sure you didn't shave somebody else's face?'

All the staff were presided over by a truly magnificent officer, the Adjutant. In my day he was a Coldstreamer, Norman Gwatkin, quite incredibly handsome and immaculate. His voice and his bearing were out of this world. It was nice to see that his performance during the war was just as impeccable. Our Commandant was likewise suitably cast. Major-General Sir Eric Girdwood was the epitome of his rank, quite delightful and full of fun. Rumour had it that he had once helped a newly joined cadet back into his quarters after giving him a lift after lights out and had then, while inspecting a parade, said, 'I am so glad you got back safely the other night'. He was a Cameronian and was dearly loved by all the members of that regiment.

One great bonus was the riding instruction, for here we were all given proper grounding in the art of equitation. I had to unlearn all the dreadful faults that I had assimilated from my Arab teachers, which had been confirmed while riding New Forest ponies. Now we began at the beginning. Just when one thought what fun it all was, the instructor would call, 'Quit and cross your stirrups. Trot.'

Those with uncomfortable mounts would then be in for an unpleasant few minutes. However, the instructors were most perceptive and more difficult animals were allotted to the more skilful. During my last year I was selected to train for the Modern Pentathlon Competition. One of the events was a cross-country ride over two and a half miles of made-up fences on a strange horse; so I was given a lot of extra instruction. The other events were cross-country running, swimming, fencing and pistol shooting. I got a half-blue.

We played a lot of tennis in the summer months but my only other sporting venture was to enter for the boxing. I was a light heavyweight and there were not many entries. I was drawn against Tony Cartland in the first round. He did his best to psyche me beforehand, saying that he had been a weight winner at Charterhouse and was much looking forward to this fight. However, when we got into the ring, it was obvious that he was not formidable at all. I failed to knock him out but the referee stopped the fight in the second round. In the process, I broke my thumb so was unable to fight again.

There was much that was quite splendid about Sandhurst. In those days, one's parents had to pay a quite hefty fee for their sons. Most of the entrants were from the major public schools, Eton providing more than any other. The setting, particularly of the old buildings dressed in shining white, with the lakes in front, was unforgettable. The standards attempted and achieved were of the very highest. The precision, dignity and pride we felt when slow marching for the last time to the immortal strains of *Figaro*, up the steps into the main building, will always enable us to say, 'I have marched and drilled with the very best in this world.'

CHAPTER II

JOINING

ONE EVENING IN SEPTEMBER, 1932, as my train slowed down in the gathering gloom of dark and fog on the outskirts of Glasgow, my spirits sank. I was on my way to join the 2nd Battalion of the Cameronians (Scottish Rifles) and my travelling companion was a man called Peter Featherstonhaugh. We had been in the same company at Sandhurst and we had not been particular friends. He was a good ball games player, achieving blues at tennis, squash and racquets. I had always thought that he would become a cavalryman. Now we were both destined for Maryhill Barracks and a regiment about which neither of us knew very much.

As a boy I had always wanted to fly. When my father asked me what I wished to do in life I said that I would like to go into the RAF, and with that in mind I sat for the examination. However, I think that in those days the qualifying marks gave entry to either Cranwell or Sandhurst and my father steered me into the latter. While there, I had opted for his old Regiment, the Cheshires, but he had great admiration for the Scottish and the Rifle Regiments and, having made his own inquiries, it seemed to him that the Cameronians, being both Scottish and Rifle, would be just the thing for his one and only son. In those days one was entirely dependent on one's parents for living expenses and had little or no option about doing what Father wanted, and so, rather late in the day, the strings were pulled and my destiny fixed.

I had been brought up in the South of England, Dorset and the New Forest, so now I was to find the massive, solid buildings with the cobbled streets and tramway lines intersecting the groups of houses rather depressing. The noise of the traffic was exacerbated by the trams and at the railway station entrance there seemed to be hundreds of paper-boys shouting for custom and the air was heavy with the actuality and smell of smoke.

On arrival at the Officers' Mess in the barracks by taxi, we were shown to our rooms. Mine was on the ground floor at the back with a view restricted by a ten-foot high barrack wall. A small fire sputtered in a small grate, the fuel mostly dross. A very young soldier took charge of my effects. He had been detailed as my batman, without any option, but it was considered to be a fairly cushy job. He had been in the army for a few weeks only, so knew little about officers and seemed to be a bit out of his depth. Although he had a runny nose, he appeared to be willing and I was glad he was there.

Once we had partially unpacked, I left him to finish and went to the ante-room in the mess. Here, I found that there were no fewer than six newly-joined subalterns and that we almost outnumbered the other officers. The large room was furnished with leather chairs and sofas. There were exciting pictures on the walls, massive curtains over the windows, the whole dominated by a roaring fire, which was surrounded by a 'bumwarmer' on which several people could perch at the same time. Now and then a waiter in livery appeared, bringing drinks for those who ordered them. Someone said, 'Just ask for whatever you want. This is your home now.'

The older members seemed to be a trifle perturbed by such a large influx and conversation was stilted, to say the least, for that first evening. We more or less introduced ourselves, for the senior subaltern and the adjutant who should have taken charge seemed to be withdrawn and rather vexed about the whole thing. The Colonel, Thomas Riddle-Webster, who later became Sir Thomas and Quartermaster-General, kept out of the mess as much as he could and Dick Hunter, the Second-in-Command, was diffident and shy. Anyway, we drank our drinks, ate a meal and all found our way back to our dismal quarters for baths and bed.

Our first introduction to regimental duty was to attend a training cadre for junior NCOs, which would show us the details of the weaponry we would have to handle, the minor tactics we would use on manoeuvres or in battle and the drill, which was rather different from that which we had been taught at Sandhurst. The instruction was all much more detailed than the teaching that we had been accustomed to. Now we actually had to strip the weapons and reassemble them; moreover, having done so, we had to be able to teach others how to do it. The minor tactics and the drill came fairly easily to most of us, but the mystery of the minutiae of the weaponry needed much concentration and homework to master. However, the hours of work and the general tempo were geared to an army which was very much at peace, so we were not unduly stretched.

That first morning, having woken to the dismal surroundings, I put on my Cameronian uniform for the first time. This had been made in something of a hurry, as my regimental destiny had been finalized so late; now I pushed and pulled myself into it with some trepidation. In Service Dress, we wore plus-four trousers with puttees and a jacket that was designed to be worn with tartan trews or a kilt. The result was a trifle incongruous. The black buttons did nothing to detract from any misfitting as brass buttons might have done, and the whole effect was not helped by our belts which had straps over each shoulder as opposed to the more normal arrangement. The only item denoting relationship to things Scottish was the glengarry headgear and it would take time before we learnt how to wear this in the prescribed manner.

We, the newly joined, walked across the sports ground outside the Mess to the barrack square, where we were detailed off to our various squads for instruction. We came back to the Mess for our meals and morning coffee, so perhaps we missed opportunities of getting to know our instructors and other members of the squads better. Some of us had some difficulty in mastering the 'lingo', which was very different from what we were accustomed to. Actually, most British Army NCOs are nothing if not articulate, so it was easy to get their message. It was not quite so easy to understand the conversations of the soldiers when we were off parade and even to this day I have to get tuned in to receive really broad Glaswegian with confidence. When it rained, as it often did, the instruction was given in the gymnasium or perhaps an empty barrack-room.

Not one of us was a real, bona fide Scot. David Jebb, who had passed out of Sandhurst very near the top, was a Northumbrian. Eric Baume, who had come up from the ranks and also passed out near the top, was patently English, although his parents lived in Renfrewshire. Critchley was from the South Coast. Featherstonhaugh was a Gloucestershire man and my family's roots were in Essex. Our last but not least member, bespectacled Gus Coldstream, was a university entrant who was a real eccentric but certainly not Scottish.

Very few of the soldiers were not proper 'jocks'. On the whole, they were small in stature and came from a very different background from that to which we had been accustomed. Many came from the poorer districts of the great city of Glasgow or the Lanarkshire coal-mining area. Most were tough in body, mind and spirit and it was obvious that they were not the easiest soldiers in the world to command. They were quick to notice peculiarities in the way of weakness and strength in their officers and attempts at familiarity were by no means welcome. Officers were meant to be officers and ought to be somewhat apart. In all, there was an innate sense of friendliness and kindness, which made service with the Regiment a business that could be thoroughly enjoyed.

At this time infantry regiments consisted of two regular battalions, a depot and three or four territorial battalions. One of the regular battalions was stationed abroad, usually in India, and this was maintained at full strength. The depot received and trained raw recruits who were fed into the home service battalion for further training. This battalion was often well below full strength, but it could be filled up with reservists in an emergency. These were men who had spent seven years in the army so they were very effective and readily available. Each year a draft of about one hundred men went from the home to the foreign service battalion, which left the home unit very below par until it gradually filled up from the depot.

The Cameronians originated from two very different sources. The 1st Battalion were the old Covenanters, the followers of Richard Cameron, who reputedly went into battle with weapon in one hand and Bible in the other. The 2nd Battalion had been formed in Perthshire by Thomas Graham, later Lord Lynedoch. His very beautiful wife had died in the south of France 'and French revolutionaries had interfered with her coffin when it was being brought back to England. This determined him to raise a regiment, largely from his own resources, to fight against his country's enemies. Anyway, the two battalions had been linked for many years, though by now nearly all the men came from the area round and about the Clyde.

One cannot help but say that those first few weeks were a trifle grim. I had never lived in a room without some sort of a view before, and now the barrack wall was a symbol of deprivation. The rooms in the Mess were of fine proportions and well furnished; indeed, the whole precincts were gracious. But they looked out across the sports field and barrack square to a group of the most hideous buildings that can ever have been designed. These were the barrack blocks for the soldiers. It was said that a mistake had been made between the outer and inner measurements, for the net result had been erections that looked as though they had been sliced in half. Anyway, few corrective establishments have looked more forbidding than Maryhill Barracks, Glasgow, with its massive, ten-foot high wall around it.

To leave the barrack gates was no relief, for they opened on to mean, tramwayed streets, and as soon as one reached areas that had shops and pubs, these were peopled with vacant-looking men seemingly with nothing to do but stand, hands in pockets, unkempt and unshaven and infinitely depressing. The actual effect of wide-spread unemployment in the northern cities was far more notice-able in those days and the actual hardships very much greater.

Conversation in the Mess was limited. All the older members seemed to be engrossed while eating their food at meals or reading the papers in the ante-room between whiles. There was a fine sports ground just outside the Mess and this was laid out for rugger. One day, I asked, 'Do we play rugger fairly often?'

'Good God, no! What an awful idea!' was the response, followed by silence.

However, there was a regimental rugby football team and it did play at home and away nearly every Saturday and I soon found myself embroiled. Some of the teams we played against were uncouth and then it was not much fun. But our team was captained by 'Brickie' Brickman, who was a fine leader and we always ended our matches having gained mutual respect with our opponents. Brickie later became Secretary of the Royal and Ancient Golf Club at St Andrews, where he became famous as an organizer throughout the golfing world.

All officers were expected to be able to dance reels, so once a week we were given lessons by the Pipe Major. In any Scottish regiment, this appointee has considerable authority and woe betide the newly joined subaltern who was clumsy and inept on his feet. Four of us made the grade in reasonable time but two could never manage it. One was given endless extra instruction with no success; the other managed to make the whole thing seem so ridiculous that he was forbidden to ever even attempt to dance again.

The dullness of the ordinary nights in the Mess were relieved by band nights and regimental guest nights. On these occasions, when all the silver was displayed, mess kit worn, strirring music played, fine wine drunk and good food accentuated, a wonderful feeling of camaraderie obtained. Stuffy old majors unbent, pompous captains relented, and we, the newly joined oddities, were almost clasped to their bosoms.

Like puppies in a new kennel, we instinctively found our way around and soon I was reasonably happy, until the weekends. It was then that one realized how much one needed affordable other activities if life was to be anything else but tedious. It soon became obvious that the financial and other resources of my brother officers were uneven. The parental homes of two of them were within easy reach; two of the others were well off and two of us not. The regiment had always enjoyed and encouraged officers to play polo and hunt and there were several chargers in the stables able to take their place in the hunting field. It was made easy for any of us who wanted to hunt to do so and the horses were often available for hacking. I found that I could afford to turn myself out in rat-catcher without much difficulty and so came the day when I joined the glad throng and from then on I was hooked on fox-hunting, until I gave up for several reasons many years later.

Among the older subalterns in the Mess were two whom one could not help but notice. One was a lanky, red-headed Scotsman called David MacEwen, known to all and sundry as 'Loopy', and the other a large, burly man called Smerger Drought, who was Officer Heavyweight Champion of the Army. He seldom fought or won any fights; there was very little opposition at the time but he was always able to give a very good account of himself. Loopy MacEwen affected to dislike all newly joined subalterns, especially Englishmen, and he was often heard muttering 'dreadful Sassenachs' as he went about his business.

There was very little social life with the inhabitants of the great city in which we lived, but we fairly frequently used to ring up Luigi, who was the head waiter of the Malmaison Restaurant, which was part of the Central Hotel. We would say, 'Have you got something rather special for some extremely hungry young officers tonight?' and he would often offer special terms, which made it well worth our while to drive down and dine there.

The traffic in Glasgow, although extremely noisy, was very much lighter in those days and Christmas itself a very different sort of festival. Indeed, two officers rode down to Sauchiehall Street on horseback at that time, with horse-holders in attendance, to do their final shopping and caused no embarrassment to anyone else thereby.

Gus Coldstream had managed to get himself appointed as the horse transport officer. He claimed to know everyone worth knowing at the Remount Depot and sure enough he got them to send three excellent remounts while we were there. After Christmas some of the officers went off to Switzerland with their families and so their chargers became available for those of us who were left behind. Lanark and Renfrew was very sporting country in those days, very little wire, and stone walls everywhere to jump. I managed to go out once on a great-hearted horse called Polly and some people thought we might have a very good chance in the regimental race at the Lanark and Renfrew point-to-point. Unfortunately, just before this was due, Polly showed signs of weakness in a tendon and we had to scratch. In the event, the race was won by Donald Campbell on a horse called Crossword.

After we had finished our NCO's cadre, life in the barracks became humdrum. Once a week the whole battalion paraded in battle order and went out for a ten-mile march in the countryside. At that time there was an internal security problem in the great city and on one occasion, when three Glasgow policemen had been thrown into the Clyde, the battalion had to stand by in case it was needed to back up the civilian police. Meanwhile, life consisted of routine inspections, visits to rifle ranges from time to time and so on, but most of the soldiers available were required to spend their time doing mundane fatigues just to keep the barracks running.

★

The regiment had suffered severe officer casualties during the 1914 war and some who had survived to be company commanders at this time were inclined to be eccentric.

My immediate superior was a Captain R. G. Hogg, generally known as 'Hoggie' or 'The Marshal'. He strolled around in a military manner but carried out his duties with a lack of enthusiasm that I found depressing, and most of my questions were answered with a glare and a harsh clearing of his throat. But he was great fun to be with when off parade. He was a keep sportsman and confirmed bachelor who appeared to much enjoy life in the Officers' Mess. He had once overstayed his leave while serving in India and, on return, when told that he would be in serious trouble, said, 'Ah, but I shot a tiger, a man-eater.'

And so indeed he had. Instead of a reprimand, he received high commendation all the way up, from the colonel to the general, and all misdemeanours were forgiven him for many weeks to come.

The duties of Orderly Officer came round to each of us every so often and in those early days one welcomed any opportunity for duty, however tedious. In a good regiment the routine was well-established and there was little that the Orderly Officer had to do except be present at various minor parades and mealtimes, so it was perhaps only tiresome at weekends. The Orderly Sergeant and Corporal accompanied one and it was reassuring to have the advice of these more experienced men.

However, Gus Coldstream, our university entrant, had done his preliminary service with one of the Regiments of Foot Guards and he was inclined to try to make something of this whenever possible. There was to be no leisurely saunter round the barracks when it was his turn to do the duty. The Orderly Sergeant and Corporal were ordered to parade outside the Officers' Mess, when Gus would fall himself in between them. He would then shout, 'Orderly Officer. Orderly Sergeant. Orderly Corporal. Right turn. Party Quick March.'

Whereat the party moved off sharply at rifle pace. Any soldiers within view who failed to salute this strange cortège had their names taken. On each occasion, the party had to be halted and the Orderly Sergeant dispatched to do the necessary, so that Gus's progress round the barracks could take a considerable time.

Eventually this unusual procedure was noticed by superior authority and Gus was advised that his methods were not part of his present regiment's customs. However, he persisted till an exasperated Orderly Sergeant led the cortège across a previously opened manhole over which he skipped to let the short-sighted Gus fall in.

All young officers had to go on a musketry course at the Small Arms School at Hythe in Kent during the first year of their service. This was conducted by instructors of the Small Arms Corps, a highly efficient body of men who were experts with all the smaller weapons of the Army and superbly efficient at passing the knowledge on. I went there in the late spring of 1933 to meet again many others with whom I had been at Sandhurst. Six months with their regiments had transformed most of them. At Sandhurst, one was reckoned to be 'almost an officer but not quite a gentleman'. Already the great regiments to which they had been gazetted had groomed them into better mould. Now most felt that they were representatives of something more important than they themselves and were much pleasanter to live with than they had been a few months before.

That particular spring and summer produced warm and balmy days with cloudless skies. The rifle ranges were set by the sea. The instruction hinged on the method whereby the students had to be able to give the lessons themselves, it being a fact that if you need to teach something you have to know a great deal about it. It was difficult to match the performance of the Small Arms School instructors, but gradually the standards improved until the final tests at the end of the course. Most people found it necessary to do much homework to achieve a reasonable standard so temptations to spend time doing other things had to be restricted.

There were several 'characters' on the course, among them Neville Crump, who was to become one of the most successful National Hunt trainers; Bobbie Petre, who rode many steeplechase winners including the Grand National, Shimi Lovat of Commando fame, to name but a few. I was in the same squad as Eric Hay of the Gordons and Dick Fyffe of the Rifle Brigade, both of whom I was to meet fairly often in the years to come.

As the end of term drew nigh, a sense of relief brought thoughts of celebration, which in those days tended to include a desire to break things and be a nuisance in other ways, and so after the requisite destruction of glass on the last evening, the final rites. Our leaving was even enlivened by the introduction into the grounds of a small flock of sheep and a steam-roller, while two light aircraft flew overhead, bombing the school with lavatory bumf.

I rejoined my Regiment at Stobs Castle near Peebles, on the borders, where they were carrying out their annual summer training programme. This was a heavenly place compared to Maryhill Barracks. I much enjoyed most of the exercises on the moors and over the hills. Training was never really strenuous in those days. The company commanders, our seniors by many years, set the pace so everything was well within our capacity. The nights were short, indeed there was always a glow of light from the northern sky and the weather continued fine.

It was with no sense of joy that I found myself back in Maryhill Barracks at the end of July. The battalion almost shut down for the main leave period. The draft of some hundred men would be due to sail to India in the autumn so they now went off. We also had to find the guard for Balmoral Castle. The royal family would be there for much of August and September and each Scottish regiment took it in turns to do the duty.

It was a great privilege to be chosen as one of the party and fulfilment of a heart's desire for those who would stalk, shoot or fish. The soldiers, when not on guard duty, would spend their hours beating for the guns, so there was little work for the officers to do. This year command devolved on Donald Campbell, who was a gifted sportsman and an enthusiastic socialite with few inhibitions.

The officers were invited to dine with Their Majesties from time to time. King George V and Queen Mary, though very kind and welcoming on these occasions, seemed fairly formidable to those unaccustomed to life at this level, but not to Captain Donald Campbell.

Early during their stay, he had lost the fore-end of his gun and when sitting next to the King he had taken his monarch minutely to all the places where he might have left it. The King was perhaps much amused, for on his leaving in the royal train, he said, 'Captain Campbell, I have been so worried about the fore-end of your gun and so much regret that you have never found it.'

Meanwhile I remained one of a mere handful of officers and men at Maryhill. We shared the barracks with the depot of the Highland Light Infantry who were still going full tilt. Their officers wore white spats with their tartan trews. These must have been a nuisance to maintain in bad weather but looked most elegant. However, nothing looked nicer than our own pipes and drums and military band in full dress. It was then that the black buttons merged so successfully with dark green tunics and trews. The glint of silver accoutrements added the lustre to make our number one turnout the most tasteful of all.

By this time I had got to know people living in the country round about. In those days nearly all daughters lived at home and very few sought jobs in London or elsewhere. The girls ran the social life of the county and pressingly prevailed upon parents to pay for the parties that they were prepared to organize.

So there were lunch parties before race meetings, dinner parties before shows and elaborate arrangements for going to dances. One of the great annual events in the west of Scotland was the Western Meeting at Ayr. All the big houses were full of guests. All the gallantry and beauty were assembled. And this year, among them were Loopy MacEwen and myself.

A magnificent ball set a seal on the meeting. For some reason we both had to be on duty that same morning so we drove off towards Glasgow in a hired car at daybreak. Our hostesses were somewhat reluctant to let us go for we were both tired out and would have liked to have been able to go to sleep there and then. We tried to keep each other awake. We decided to take turns in driving and I was at the wheel in the middle of Paisley when there was an almighty crash as our hireling hit an electric light standard with the near front wheel. We clambered out unhurt. Not so our carriage, which was firmly fixed to its light standard. Within moments, people arrived from the nearby flats, some still in dressing gowns.

We were in full evening dress, buttonholed still, and our cry was for a taxi at any price. Nothing had been damaged except our pride and the front of our vehicle. We must have seemed like creatures from another world to the inhabitants of the tenements now surrounding us. However, one of them was on our side, because soon there came a taxi and off we went.

I was Orderly Officer. My first duty was the issue of rations at 7 am. I could only do it if I appeared as I was in my 'tails', and this I did. I think the attending soldiery approved for I heard nothing further of it.

It would perhaps have been strange if I had not been affected by any of the girls I met and sure enough I found my *femme fatale*. It happened at a point-to-point. There were many ladies present and three were lining the rope around the ring as two of us approached from behind. They were all known to my companion so he announced our presence and they all turned.

The one in the middle made an immediate impact on me and from that moment on for many years she was seldom far from my thoughts. I soon got to know and love her family too and it was almost my greatest pleasure to visit them, which I did as often as possible.

It was difficult to reconcile oneself to the plain fact that there would be no possible chance of marrying her in any foreseeable future. Even the age of thirty was considered almost too young in an impecunious officer in those days. I was but twenty and the lady two or three months my senior in any case. There was no sympathy for me within the regiment. 'Don't be a bloody fool,' they said. 'The girl you will marry eventually is hardly out of her pram right now!'

Anyway, perhaps it was salutary to have to yearn and pine. At least one had an ideal. A really rather lovely actuality for whom to try to improve.

Towards the end of the summer, we saw the draft off to India. These were the young soldiers who had enlisted at the age of eighteen and thereabouts and, after initial training at the depot in Hamilton, had served for some months or weeks with the battalion. They would be in India for six years without any home leave or chance to see their parents. It was perhaps quite a long sentence so there was 'weeping and gnashing of teeth' as the troop train drew out of Maryhill railway station. Whenever possible on these occasions, the train was drawn by an engine named 'The Covenanter' or 'The Cameronian'. With the band playing on the platform, the Colonel of the Regiment and the GOC to see them go, it was quite a send-off. Most of my own platoon went too and three of the subalterns who had joined with me.

Maryhill Barracks had one redeeming feature, which was the setting of the barrack square. On parade days one could see the battalion being formed up from the windows of the Officers' Mess and at the right moment the company officers would walk across the sports field to join the troops. When the preliminary inspections had been carried out, the parade would await the arrival of the Commanding Officer, who could be seen approaching from afar. When he had taken his place the battalion was complete. One felt oneself to be a part of something quite splendid and capable of anything.

It was said that on one occasion an officer, who had dined much too well at a dinner night before a parade to mark a great regimental occasion, came into the ante-room, where all officers assembled, still in his mess kit. He was hustled off to his quarters but not locked in and, just as the battalion received the Commanding Officer, a figure was seen to burst out of the large mess doors, doing up his tunic as he ran, waving a sword and shouting, 'Wait for me, wait for me'.

Then it was our turn to get into the troop train to England and the South. The Black Watch took over at Maryhill. I was not sorry to think that I would never again enter my horrid little room on the ground floor.

CHAPTER III

BORDON

BORDON GARRISON in the Aldershot command in Hampshire could hardly have been more different from our own battalion station at Maryhill. Here there were four other infantry battalions and two artillery regiments. The training areas were adjacent to the barracks, as were several playing fields, and the rifle ranges were some minutes' march away.

Our barracks were in fact wooden huts, but they were warm and cosy. Single officers' quarters comprised two rooms with one bathroom for three of such. Grass and shrubs separated each small block, all quite close to the mess, which, though looking awful from the outside, was snug and easy to run from within.

A London to Portsmouth road ran through the garrison, and there was a small village tacked on with shops providing almost everything a soldier could want. There was even an Officer's Club and, though it was seldom used for social purposes, it had squash courts, tennis courts and an excellent cricket ground.

There were several small towns within reach, each with hostelries able to provide the meals that hungry subalterns often preferred to the more formal feeding in the Officers' Mess, and the bright lights of London were just fifty miles away.

With the change of station also came a change in the command of the battalion. Thomas Riddle-Webster went away on promotion. He was not the sort of colonel a subaltern could easily get to know. Conventional and straight-laced, he did everything very properly. Perhaps he was a little too aloof but nevertheless a great soldier, who rose to the top of the Army through the test of several years of war.

Now came a very different character in the shape of Lieutenant-Colonel Baynes. He had served in West Africa for many years but had no particular wartime reputation, nor had he qualified at the Staff College. There was tremendous competition to command then as now and to many it seemed strange that he had been preferred to others who could have been made available. The Army is a great institution for nick-names and perhaps it is relevant to note that Baynes was known as 'Bingo', whereas Riddle-Webster was 'Tiddly-pom'. However, to us subalterns it seemed unlikely that there would be much change in the even tenor of our lives. Nor was there, for a while.

Aldershot Command and its Commander would provide the Expeditionary Force if or, indeed when, war came to Europe. And two infantry divisions with all the necessary support were based in and around it. The barracks there were occupied by such soldiers as the 1st Cavalry Brigade and the 1st Guards Brigade, 2nd, 3rd and 4th Infantry Brigades and so on. Squadrons of the famous cavalry regiments, companies of immaculate guardsmen, batteries of horse-drawn artillery, were all to be met with in the environs. In the streets one would see Highlanders, riflemen and representatives of all the great regiments going about their own or official business and in the evenings trumpeting from the cavalry and bugle calls from all other units were very much part of environmental noise.

All the administrative chores were made possible by the use of horse-drawn transport. There were hardly any heavy lorries and few units had mechanical vehicles of any sort. So the clip-clop of horses' feet, the jingle of harness and the rumble of wagon wheels accompanied the troops wherever they went.

However, it ill behove a commanding officer who failed to realize that close proximity to other units and superior commanders led to competition and comparison. Four years in Maryhill Barracks, Glasgow, well away from the rough hurly-burly of the outside military world, induced a feeling of false confidence and now failure to achieve high standards at everything brought frequent criticisms from experts in each particular. First came advice, then cajolery and finally threats. Behind loomed the hierarchy all the way up the chain of command.

I was to become the battalion Signals Officer. This entailed a fairly intensive effort to actually qualify as a trained signaller able to read Morse and semaphore at so many words a minute. One spent most mornings practising with the signal platoon and had to try to think in terms of those two codes just as one would when learning a language. Like many other people, I found the Morse buzzer was the most difficult and it was alarming to discover that one had 'on' and 'off' days. The Army Signals School was run by the Corps of that name at their depot at Catterick in Yorkshire and I spent three months there learning to be an instructor. High standards were required and one aspiring student was sent straight back to Hong Kong on failing to get good enough marks at the passing-in test. He sent us a long and involved message from his regiment when he returned and after puzzling over it for a while, we found that the first letter of each word spelt out 'Fairly castrated'.

There were many advantages to being Signals Officer, the main one being that one had the best platoon in the battalion. It took several months to train a signaller, so once trained they were kept together. Moreover, if insufficient time was given for training, the communications would fail and the battalion would become uncontrolled on training or operations. So with the business side of things looking tidy, one could attend to other things.

★　★　★　★　★　★

Bordon lay on the edge of the HH (Hampshire Hunt) country and much of the local area had been given over to the Royal Artillery Drag Hunt. The best of the HH could boast some fine stretches of open farming land with good going for horses and every type of jump. However, massive coverts were never far away and these provided shelter for fair numbers of foxes, so that, once hounds went in, they were liable to come out behind or be confused by several choices. Considerable skill and then direction were needed by the huntsman who was going to get hounds away across country. In our day, a famous character, George Evans, was the master. It was said that he had had a pack of hounds ever since he began with the Eton Beagles. Now, though still highly skilled, he did not seem to be over-fond of a gallop, and many of our days ended with a sense of frustration.

The Drag had the worst of the country, mostly the Army

training areas and unattractive patches adjacent to the barracks. When hunting fox, the aim was to kill as many as possible, so there was much marking to ground and digging out. This was popular with the local small farmers, and if one wanted actually to see and hear hounds working, it was great fun for the field too. Members would often be given various tasks and even though these may have been glorified sentry-go, it was exciting to be fully involved.

Every Wednesday afternoon a drag line was laid over one of the best bits of country, which included the cream of the HH and their point-to-point course. The total length was about four miles with a check in the middle and usually included some twenty-four obstacles. This was 'meat and drink' for those who really loved a gallop and a ready-made school for those who hoped to point-to-point at the end of the season.

In addition to the ten chargers which were on the strength of every infantry battalion, it was possible to hire troop horses from the cavalry in Aldershot for a very small sum. Moreover, with an abundance of stabling and the availability of soldier grooms, it did not cost a great deal to keep a privately owned hunter. So getting oneself mounted was no problem. During most of my time at Bordon, I had the use of a very strong mare called Sally. She was as bold as brass and perhaps a bit too willing. A great 'doer' and, whenever she smelt the stable at the end of the day, she was for home. Both horse and rider would end up in a muck sweat, for there was no way she was going to walk quietly back. How one used to curse and cajole her, even get off and walk. But one could forgive her anything for her performance across any country whenever hounds ran.

A fair proportion of our officers hunted and quite often five or six of us would be out together. Grooms would take horses on to the meets to which we drove and we hacked to all nearby ones. Quite a lot of the officers from the other infantry battalions would be out. In those days, they were Inniskilling, Irish or Northumberland Fusiliers and the 43rd Light Infantry, together with nearly all the gunner officers from the garrison.

Meeting nearer Aldershot would attract officers from there and among them came Major-General Kennedy, our Divisional Commander. He was a bit of a thruster and caused the Field Master trepidation, for who wants to rebuke a serving general of the Aldershot Command within his own domain, more or less? However, Gus Coldstream was never a man to miss a chance of tweaking authority, so when he saw the General overstepping, he would shout, 'Hold hard, Sir, can't you? Let hounds have a chance. Hold hard.' The General wondered who on earth Gus was, but we told his ADC that Gus was an important businessman and most generous subscriber. Gus wore horn-rimmed spectacles and was the most unobvious-looking soldier imaginable. So the General sighed and kept a tight rein whenever he saw Gus in the offing.

Came the day when the General visited the battalion unheralded and was sitting in the ante-room of the Mess when Gus, all unsuspecting, blundered in. Gus, who looked imposing in pink, was a pretty dreadful sight dressed as a second lieutenant, and on seeing him, the General leapt to his feet, saying to the Colonel, 'Is this thing actually one of yours?' He then marched Gus out into the billiard-room. We never heard what was said, but Gus kept his horses and hunted far away in Oxfordshire from then on. The General was, in fact, a very good man to hounds and was sometimes invited to act as Field Master, which was perhaps salutary.

Donald Campbell was probably out more often than anyone else. His wife, May, was a great performer on her mare, Miss Murphy, and together they were an indomitable pair. Among the subalterns, 'Loopy' MacEwen, 'Monkey' Stephen and Dick Villiers were the most regular and I managed thirty-three days in one season. Nigel Hendricks was our top performer, having been invited to whip in to the Drag, and actually hunted hounds himself several times with great success.

Donald Campbell and I laid out and organized a new drag line which began at Frithend House and ran past Malthouse Farm to the other side of Kingsley. My signal section provided the labour and we opened up a piece of country that had been quite unrideable before. The local farmer entered into the spirit of the thing and it was hard to persuade him from adding bits and pieces to the obstacles we so carefully prepared. Nine officers from the regiment presented themselves on the appointed day and I now quote from the hunting diary kept at the time.

'There were all kinds of jumps to contend with, timber, water, cut-and-laid, open ditches, banks and brush. Enough to make the most adventurous gunners cry, 'Capevi'. However, we ourselves suffered most grief. Three down at the first water, two at the timber, one of whom was so overcome that he remounted the wrong horse. In fact the whole of the first line seemed to be littered with spare horses, bodies, bowler hats, bridles and whips. However, the second line was better and after the final water, many a gallant officer turned to a friend to say, "Flew it all like a bird." But there's many a gap in every fence that will have to be mended tomorrow.'

At the end of each season came the Regimental Race at the Crawley and Horsham Hunt point-to-point, which was held at Knowle Park, Cranleigh. Each year, 1934, 1935, 1936, I rode Sally and each year Jeremy Fisher, the Adjutant, won on a very fast chestnut mare called Miss Vanity. The first year Sally was not really fit. The next I was a rather poor second and the last only beaten on the run-in after a great race which was only a few seconds slower than the nomination race.

This was great consolation to me because in 1935 I had ridden a horse called U.C. in the farmers' race immediately after the Regimental; U.C. took the fourth fence by the roots and we turned a most spectacular somersault. I came to in the Aldershot Military hospital. After a bold attempt to escape, which was only just foiled, I spent four weeks in bed nursing a fractured skull.

★   ★   ★   ★   ★   ★

I rode in other races with no success, except for a second place in the HH Farmers' Heavyweight, and there were hunter trials before each season.

Although the local people were friendly enough, we never got to know them as we had in Scotland. Here, all the daughters were away working in London and none were busy organizing parties for the likes of us. All units took turns in entertaining the Drag at lawn meets and as there was a certain amount of competition, these could be quite splendiferous. At the RA Mess on one occasion, hounds got out of control and, having bolted down most of the food provided, they invaded the Officers' Mess, and one even leant out of an upstairs window to give tongue.

The 1936–7 season was more or less a washout as the battalion had to spend the last two months of 1936 in Palestine. Although no one could claim that the hunting was top-notch, we managed to have enormous fun. Indeed, there were times, when hounds ran over the best of the HH, that one could not have wished to be anywhere better.

The shooting over the training areas was available to the officers. This was arranged on a 'pottering' basis with each unit syndicate being allotted an area in turn. Some of the areas emerging on to farmland held a fair amount at the beginning of the season and there were bits of water for the duck to flight to. With a well-trained, hard-working spaniel, some days could be rewarding. In any case, it was another nice thing to do. Nearly all the best shooting was let to syndicates, so invitations to the local soldiery were few and far between.

The Cameronians, like most of the other Scottish regiments, were predominantly soccer-playing and the production of teams for this held priority. Nevertheless, we could field a useful rugger side and we played our part in the Command fixture list. We boasted a fairly formidable scrum, which included Smerger Drought, the Army officer heavyweight boxing champion, Sergeant Wallis, the all-ranks heavyweight champion, Sergeant Pickles, the welterweight champion and some other largish men. Any team that tried any dirty work was apt to finish the game with depleted numbers.

We were not a cricketing regiment and probably the most important match of the season was the Officers v Sergeants. For the rest of the time, we were represented by some of these and the opposition was limited to local village teams. The band provided the hockey team and this could give an excellent account of itself. However, it was at boxing that the regiment really shone and here the team was often in the championship class, both at home and abroad.

For most of the time, for most of the year, life moved on at a leisurely pace. Each autumn the draft would leave for India and the time-expired men from India would come home to be absorbed or discharged, so there was a period of adjustment, reorganization and leave. My parents lived on the Thames at Moulsford in a capacious bungalow with river frontage, boathouse and a nice large garden with a tennis court. It almost backed on to the downland. I spent much of my spare time there for we had many friends around. There was a stable with hirelings available and one could hack nearly all the thirty miles to Newbury without crossing a road. Sometimes we would collect as many dogs of all kinds as possible to chase some of the many resident hares. We liked to call our collection the 'Moulsford Harriers' but we were never able to claim victory.

Autumn and Christmas were succeeded by the individual training season, but battalion strength would be so weak that a large proportion of the men would be on fatigue, ie doing the chores necessary to keep the barracks going. As the year advanced and numbers increased, training would step up from individual to section, platoon and then company. The annual weapon classifications were fitted in and woe betide the unit that failed to achieve reasonable standards. So for a time the whole battalion's first parade was devoted to musketry, with the aim of familiarizing all ranks and trades with their weapons, and this measure effected much improvement in our standards.

The signal platoon was part of headquarters company, which included the regimental band, the pipe band, the horse transport, the clerks, the cooks and the police, with all others rudely classified as odds and sods. Most looked after themselves and were billeted in odd corners through the barracks, but still they all had to be paid once per week and have their kits inspected. Often the only officers available for this would be the transport officer and me. Sometimes I found myself commanding this heterogeneous body of men and might find that I had to make do with the Pipe Major in place of the Company Sergeant-Major to get the routine done.

The Army took religion rather more seriously in those days, for there was a Church Parade on most Sundays. Our Church of Scotland service was at 10 o'clock and all available paraded in time to march behind the pipers to the garrison church. The regimental band played during the service, which was pushed through at a fair speed with ten minutes being the maximum the padre was allowed for his sermon. Our riflemen's pace would be emphasized to the full on the way home and sometimes we would meet the 43rd Light Infantry coming in the opposite direction.

I can still remember the impression of the bandsmen leaning inwards to take the corners, such was the pace maintained by all.

We had enough contacts in London to bring invitations from time to time. In those days one could dance the whole evening away at a club called the Florida which had a revolving floor and telephones to every table. People dressed up to go to the theatre and all the big hotels had their own dance bands. Rosa Lewis at the Cavendish Hotel gave a warm welcome to subalterns who were in her good books. Champagne was often freely served and *mirabile dictu* with no accompanying bills. The Caledonian Ball was a must for young officers of the Scottish regiments and they far outshone their partners in glamour by reason of the full regimentals everyone wore. The set reels were often rehearsed beforehand, for any mistakes brought much shame.

My 'soulmate' from Aryshire descended on London from time to time and then I would try to dance attendance as often as possible, but I was by no means the only applicant.

It was thought proper that all officers should attend a levee and on one occasion eight of us were presented to the Monarch by Major-General Sir Eric Girdwood, the Colonel of the Regiment. I think that we were perhaps the biggest single contingent from any one regiment and looked very different from the others in their pervading scarlet. Anyway, it was said that King George V gave a special nod of acknowledgement as we went by. On that occasion, all four of his sons stood behind him. Two years later, some of us were to parade for the second son, then George VI, as we, as part of the street-lining troops, saw him drive past with his consort on their way to the coronation. Our contingent was opposite the Dorchester and it was tantalizing to see the bottles of champagne being poured down the throats of those on the balconies while we stood for several hours hemmed in by dense and curious crowds.

Dressed in string chain mail, we took part in the 'Battle of Bannockburn' at the Aldershot Tattoo in 1935. The Royal Scots Fusiliers were our opponents and they were armed with long, wooden pikes which were more than a match for our short claymores. The Royal Scots Greys took part, so we arranged to have a small tent with a bar that we could use in between our particular act and the finale. The repetition of our act for several nights in succession was boring in the extreme and any diversion was welcome. One evening, this was provided by the reigning King Edward VIII, who walked in as though it was the most natural thing in the world and sat down on the table that served as our bar to accept the proferred whisky and soda. He seemed deeply interested in what we had to do, yet managed to drink up quickly and readily accepted another, but, alas, at that moment there was a 'clatter clatter' of anxious attendants arriving. Our monarch rose: 'Blast. They've found me and I'll have to go now,' and off he went.

The troops taking part in the Tattoo camped nearby but had to spend most of the daytime on the rifle ranges. Friends who knew where our camp lay were apt to call in after the show to stay until the early hours, so, as we had to start shooting at 8 am, there was never much time to sleep.

It was always nice to get back to our cosy little garrison at Bordon. All the married officers had pleasant, secluded, rented houses scattered among the villages and hamlets nearby and many of them were wide open to the young bachelors of the mess. All the old company commanders were married so the mess was very largely what we subalterns made it. We often entertained our opposite numbers from the other regiments and sometimes a quite impromptu party would start up. The Irish Fusiliers owned four Bentleys between them and there was always a risk of being hijacked to London at short notice whenever they were around. For one short period, a senior subaltern on his way through from one staff job to another thought to clip our wings and tried to introduce uncalled-for rules and obstacles. However, he lowered his guard at a guest night and, having drunk unwisely, swallowed four vegetable laxatives given him in the guise of aspirins late that night. He behaved all right thereafter.

Our elderly company commanders were never going to 'set the Thames on fire' and the congenital lack of numbers in all the home service battalions mitigated against anyone turning them into fighting fit storm troops permanently poised for a sudden alert. Everyone knew that the Germans were re-arming and that the time would come, but we also knew that there would be a considerable period of tension first. At this time the Spanish Civil War was raging and this occupied the Axis powers, while giving them a most valuable proving ground for their new weapons and tactics. Mussolini's campaign in Abyssinia seemed to give no cause for alarm. In the meantime, it was decided gradually to replace horses with mechanical transport and this happened while we were at Bordon.

Every August or September Corps or Army manoeuvres would be held somewhere in the south of England. Salisbury Plain was the usual venue and then the two divisions in the Aldershot Command would march there. It took most units three days. The complete brigade would bivouac for the night in fields outside small country towns like Alresford or Stockbridge and many of the officers would besiege the local pubs for baths and beer to counteract the effects of prodigious sweating on the march. There was usually a summer leave period just before the manoeuvres and most people were a long way from being hard and fit when they began.

We marched in column of fours by companies, or perhaps platoons, on the left-hand side of the road and traffic had to take pot-luck in passing in either direction. We halted for ten minutes in every hour and it was then that any holdups would dissolve. At one such halt I was sitting beside the machine-gun officer, Smerger Drought, the army officer heavyweight champion boxer of that time, when a large earthworm wriggled along the edge of the road. He turned to his batman, Joe MacLaughlin, also a great boxer, and said, 'Bet you ten bob you won't swallow that worm.'

'Done,' said Joe, and without hesitation picked it up and dropped it down his throat.

As a Scottish regiment, we had at least one piper per company and he was expected to play for at least half of the total time of the march. While the piper rested, we often sang. Some of the songs were rudish and if we happened to be passing a built-up area at the rudery time, the naughtier words would be mouthed only. I was the battalion Signals Officer and had to walk beside the Colonel and the Adjutant and we were not meant to know about some of the things the songs were about. The population

39

turned out en masse along the route, especially if our unit was in the van. Apart from those men suffering from sore feet or with crutches, everyone enjoyed the march in fine weather and gradually you could feel a growing togetherness being engendered. We were so much an established order of things, so much a part of old Britannia.

As Signals Officer, I was allotted a horse, and on our first outing I had very much looked forward to riding for part of the way. However, I didn't think I should get on until the Colonel did, and now no amount of veiled suggestions on my part had the effect of getting him off his feet. Every now and then the Adjutant would make an excuse to ride back to the rear to see the form, but the Colonel plodded on regardless. He had been a keen man on a horse in his younger days but by now golf was his pervading joy so that his legs and feet were in excellent nick. I had spent most of my spare time on a horse.

The camps on the plain were pretty basic but we saw them for only a few hours between the exercises, which usually lasted for three days. These exercises were conducted in an atmosphere of such intense wind-up as to bring some officers to a state of terror. The presiding genius who directed most of the exercises was known as 'Stop Me and Buy One', or King Kong. It was felt that anyone who chanced within his orbit would be seized upon and chewed into ribbons. I can well remember seeing a collection of some twenty umpires being lambasted with such unadulterated vehemence that the soldiers marching by rose on tip-toe with bated breath. The ferocity spread the whole way down. The Brigadier became beastly to my Colonel, who became beastly to the Adjutant and me. He still would not get on his horse and was furious with me whenever I came to see him on essential business riding mine. He insisted on my laying a telephone cable to all the companies, when often a signal lamp would have provided the necessary communication. As a result, whenever we moved, I had to leave men behind to reel up cable while I went on ahead with diminished numbers to lay even more cable. In those days the rim of the wheel of a horse-drawn limber was sharp enough to slice a cable and once when a loose end of cable got caught up among the horses' legs in the dark, I was in dire trouble.

I remember that on one of our exercises there was no one left to lay the cable but me. It was well after 3 am when a heavy mist came down and I had no compass. I staggered on in what I thought was the right direction until I ran out of cable before reaching the forward company. I was exhausted and lay down beside the empty drum to sleep. Dawn woke me and to my horror, who should I see asleep beside me but the Colonel. I buzzed the headquarters who wanted the Colonel at once as the Brigadier was after him. I woke him and as I had no horse there he was quite polite. I explained my problem and we set off down the line in the fog to headquarters. Suddenly the fog dispersed and there was my cable crossing over itself in a most abandoned way in full daylight for all to see. I had been full circle. The Colonel became impolite again.

After the annual manoeuvres we romped home. Our three-day march could have been done in two, indeed this is what we accomplished in later years, singing all the way. During our time in the Aldershot Command we became mechanized and lost the horses. I was given a motor bicycle instead of my charger and no longer marched behind the piper. Map reading now became a real problem, for mistakes made by the leader of the column had far-reaching effects. I so well remember leading the battalion up the Great North Road, the A1, all embussed, when I saw the advanced guard, in trucks, coming south in the opposite direction with the officer-in-charge's nose buried in his map regardless of all else.

The last time I saw horses on an exercise was in Sussex when my regiment was grouped with the Life Guards against a normal infantry brigade. Operations had gone according to plan during the day and we were holding a river line for the night. To my surprise the Life Guards had not, like ordinary cavalry of the line, disappeared at eventide, and just before midnight, when I was once again laying a cable up to the forward companies on the river, the enemy decided to attempt a surprise crossing. I was able to phone straight through to Force HQ, which was the Life Guards, and to my delight two squadrons cantered forward in the moonlight, till they completely overbore our opponents, who nipped back across the stream and were not seen again.

The most magnificent finish to any exercise was 'Stop Me and

Buy One's' last. After several days, all four divisions of the Army were in position near Micheldever. We had been mucked about good and hearty in bad weather. Wireless control was in its infancy and never really worked. After a dull night during which all concerned thought that everything that could be squeezed out of the exercise had been squeezed, we were all 'Standing to' as dawn broke.

Then in the stillness we heard the noise of someone galloping a horse towards us. It was the transport officer of the Devons, who were on our immediate right, and as he saw us, he reined in and blurted out, 'Have you got a Stand-to?'

Without hesitation, our transport officer, Gus Coldstream, said, 'Don't be so disgusting,' at which we all burst into laughter and the man of Devon trotted off.

Then somewhere along the line a bugler played the 'No Parade'. This was taken up by all the buglers and trumpeters of all the units of the army. Immediately there were shouts of 'Pack Up', 'Fill in Trenches', 'Send for the Transport', 'O Group in ten minutes', and in just no time at all some hundred thousand men were poised and ready to foot it for home. Breakfast would be eaten if it was available and if it was possible but the main thing was 'Home, Boys, Home'. No question of complicated march tables. The Army knew it could sort itself out.

There was uproar at 'Stop Me's' HQ. King Kong was said to have roared in agony. The umpires were adjured to get the troops back to their positions and keep the exercise going, but no amount of cajolery or cursing on their part could halt the determined men. Once the regiments were on the road towards Aldershot, Tidworth, Bordon or Bulford, from colonels downwards they were unstoppable and so, by the same night, we were all happily bedded in our barracky homes.

CHAPTER IV

PALESTINE

ON 2 SEPTEMBER, 1936, when we were in camp at West Chiltington in Sussex, the exercise we were ready for was cancelled. Most of us were told to make ourselves scarce for the day and, lo and behold, on our return the camp had been struck and that evening we were embussed to Bordon. The Arab rebellion in Palestine was out of hand and after a few hours' leave we were to sail to the Middle East, having taken unto ourselves the Class A reservists.

We embarked on the P&O *Naldiva* and left on the 15th. There had been no time to adapt our passenger ship in any way and some of the soldiers never tired of ringing the bell for the white stewardess. The food and service were impeccable so perhaps it was just as well for the state of fitness of all concerned that the voyage lasted no longer than the 25th, when we disembarked at Haifa, from which most basic of base camps we were whisked away to Bethlehem, 4000 feet above sea level.

The root cause of all the trouble was the Balfour Declaration, pronounced and endorsed by the British Government during the 1914 war. The relevant part stated:

'His Majesty's Government view with favour the establishment of a National Home for the Jews in Palestine.'

No one consulted the Palestine Arabs, who were the indigenous inhabitants. Nay, rather it was it implied that the British would do all in their power to back Arabs everywhere if they would help in the expulsion of the then ruling power, the Turks. At first things happened gradually. Much money was made available

43

to buy the Arabs' land. Good prices were paid for what had been regarded as second-rate and a good time was had by all on the proceeds. Then the fact that they had lost their land for good dawned on the erstwhile landlords and what made it worse was the improvement almost immediately effected by the new owners. The Arabs now demanded that further sales should be forbidden, all Jewish immigration stopped. If this was not done there would be a general strike. The Grand Mufti of Jerusalem, the chairman of the Arab Higher Committee, was the leader responsible. He was backed by a guerrilla fighter called Fawzi El Din Kawajki, who had brought armed bands with him from Trans-Jordan and Iraq.

The strike made things unpleasant for the mandatory power. The schools and public services were closed down. The rebel guerrillas distributed arms and explosives to anyone wishing to attack communications, Jewish settlements, police and British troops. In no time the equivalent of an infantry division was embroiled and the situation deteriorated to such an extent that the 1st Infantry Division from Aldershot was dispatched.

The contents of the military hospitals at Jerusalem and Sarafand bore testimony to the success of some rebel operations and there was no delay in committing our battalion. B Company was sent to Hebron, a real hot-spot. C Company began picketing the railway from Jerusalem to where it left the hilly ground at Artap, and A Company, with the rest of the battalion, remained at Bethlehem. The headquarters were established within the monastery of the Church of the Nativity and, largely owing to the kindness of the Orthodox Archbishop of Bethlehem, most of us were billeted in hospice-type accommodation with all the facilities. My room was high up almost alongside one of the sets of bells that seemed to ring all day and night. I was fascinated by the antics of the diminutive Arab operator, who had a different rope attached to each of his limbs. Anyway, he could play quite a tune all by himself, which went 'Tiddeldy – Dink – Boong'. The only real problem was the bedbugs, which one can only describe as ferocious.

I was soon rushed off my feet providing communications for all concerned. Everyone in Bethlehem wanted a telephone, whilst the pickets on hilltops along the railway line had to have Aldis lamps or heliographs. This latter instrument really came into its own in the hills of Galilee where there was uninterrupted sunshine most of the day. Once, when I was visiting my signallers, we picked up a unit in Jaffa some eighty miles away. Shortly before leaving the UK, we had been issued with a prototype infantry wireless for use within the battalion. The range of these sets was limited to under a mile and they were difficult to operate. However, they had unique characteristics so far as we were concerned and we now experimented in their use by the fire controller of the mortar platoon. This was to make these weapons far more effective, as up till then we always had to lay telephone lines before fire orders could be delivered.

The hills all around were brown and bare at that time of the year but there were wonderful views in every direction. The drive down to Jerusalem was quite an experience, both environmentally and for danger to life and limb. The road soon took its toll of accidents. The Army was only just learning to drive and the twisty, narrow roads with hard stone walls bordering them were a harsh schooling ground. Road blocks and patrols were the methods used to make contact with the enemy and before long the Cameronians were in action. In the course of the first brush, one of the rebel leaders, Said El Aasi, was killed and futher casualties were inflicted without loss. B Company's billets in Hebron were often the targets for snipers but, despite this, football matches were arranged with the younger men. On one occasion, the opposition gave warning that a more serious move was planned against the Cameronians that night. Sure enough, a fusillade poured in on the billet area for perhaps an hour. This was returned in full measure. Next afternoon, when teams assembled for their game, the captain asked his opposite number, 'Did we get any of your chaps last night?'

'No. Did we get any of yours?'

'No. El Humdulillah. Let's toss up, then.'

Soon after this incident, the Battle of Bethlehem took place. Armed men penetrated between the billets and bullets flew in all directions. This was the one opportunity those who were normally anchored to the headquarters would have of seeing action and perhaps they contributed a greater threat to everyone than the insurgents themselves. I even found Leslie Seymour, the bandmaster, with a rifle on Manger Square and when I remonstrated with him, he said, with a huge grin, 'Bandmasters seldom have such fun.'

Soon after this, the strike was called off and life in the country went back to normal. We were able to see most of the holy places. Trips to Galilee and the Dead Sea were organized. There were shopping expeditions to Haifa or Tel Aviv and duck shooting at Lake Huleh. However, I was soon to be stuck.

As we left for Palestine, the battalion gained a real live Second-in-Command in the shape of Duzely Graham. He was a splendid soldier who became famous during the war still to come as the Commander of 50 Division. Monty used to refer to him as 'that fine old war-horse' but in addition to being good at war, he was also a great administrator. He now saw that unless adequate measures were taken to keep the soldiers fully employed during their working hours and amused during their free time, boredom would soon be responsible for all kinds of trouble. So, in addition to games, expeditions and excursions, we were to have evening entertainment, among them a Christmas pantomime. J.D. Frost was to run it.

This meant first of all writing a script. In the pantomimes I could remember, the actors flew. This was something I knew I could not manage, having nothing to begin with except a clean piece of paper. I decided to call it the *90 Crusade*. I developed a plot in which an officer and two of the shadiest characters in the battalion are detailed to unearth the unscrupulous machinations of a powerful chieftain, who is in a position to damage HM Government's interests in a small, unspecified country. A hostile agent is the next menace and the chief's daughter is a goodie being kept in subjection by a cruel stepmother. There are other characters to help thicken the plot. The pipe band, suitably accoutred, would effect a thrilling rescue to bring the proceedings to a happy end.

There were plenty of volunteers for the male parts from within the battalion, including Loopy MacEwen, and I managed to find six very presentable young ladies, who were either the wives or daughters of British people living in Jerusalem. The regimental band was the mainstay. We took the tunes from the stage hits currently running in London and wrote suitable words to fit the songs. We made up dances based on Highland reels and designed clothes simple enough to be run up by the unit tailor out of cheap material bought in the bazaar. I owed everything to Leslie Seymour, our bandmaster, and we spent endless hours edging our way into a production.

Fortunately, there was a ready-made theatre within the monastery precincts which would normally have been part of a children's school. Directing the ladies of the cast was my biggest headache. I had designed their dresses and there was one very leggy scene which I knew would bring the house down, but it took much persuasion, some of it with the gin bottle, to get them all to parade and dance with the confident abandon needed.

We put on three performances in Bethlehem and one at the police barracks on Mount Scopus. I think we provided quite a lot of amusement. Previous experience had taught me to avoid getting entangled with any such assignment. I found that I was perforce to breathe, think and live nothing else for the few weeks from start to finish. I really do not know what happened to my signallers meanwhile, which just goes to show how a well-organized sub-unit can look after itself. As for me, the time flew and almost before I knew it we were on our way back to England on the *SS America*, just missing Christmas in Bethlehem.

After a fair stretch of leave, things felt rather flat back at Bordon. It was considered too late in the season to get the horses fit to start hunting and the absence of it in the last months of winter left a gaping void. My signallers seemed to be getting a little bit stale. The Army was wise to move units to a fresh station every four years and I am not sure that four years is not one too long. The battalion was due to move up to Catterick in Yorkshire at the end of the year and people soon began to look ahead, leaving less enthusiasm for what they had now. Manoeuvres this year were in Hertfordshire and by then the whole of the Aldershot Command was mechanized. The very act of adopting mechanization was upsetting to many. The Army had to do it all absolutely properly. There must be drills for starting up and moving off. For getting in and out. Rigid convoys whenever possible. Exact loading, but above all documentation down to every item. Each journey, however short, had to be entered on a 'work ticket' and woe betide a driver caught moving without one. Fortunately some horses remained – all the chargers and a handful to pull limbers for in-station duties.

Loopy MacEwen, while attending a signals course at Catterick, was killed in a car accident. He was a great character, who would always have a stab at everything and the soldiers had a special regard for him. I missed him greatly. If one had had to write an obituary, after mentioning his nearest and dearest, it would have been necessary to say that he had left two terrible dogs behind him – Airedales, mother and son, who would, when covered in mud, get into a brother officer's room to sleep on his bed and chew up everything that came to mouth. Once, when their master and I were watching the final putt of the final of the Ladies' Golf Championship of Hampshire, one of them ran onto the green, picked up the ball and galloped off, and so did we.

Everyone had dogs in those days. I had inherited Nero, an old black labrador that had been with the battalion since being born in India several years before. He could not resist trying to copy a bugler. When I was Orderly Officer, he would, if possible, sneak after me down to the guardroom in the dark and when the 'Last Post' sounded, so would Nero. It was often quite a problem preventing the bachelor officers' dogs attending the parades, for they dearly loved the fuss and bother.

At the end of the year I was sent on a PT course at Aldershot. Here they measured one's performance at various physical feats both before and after and it was revealing to note how much even the least athletic specimens could improve. 'Deep breathing' and Prunella Stack were the two linch-pins in my day. Miss Stack had formed a Women's League of Health and Beauty, which persuaded the fair sex to exercise in a rhythmical routine which led them to achieve results never expected. It was thought that if such a simple formula could do so much for the girls, how much more could it do for the boys. I became an enthusiastic advocate and, when I returned to the battalion, greatly relished leading the early morning PT parade, without the need for giving words of command bar 'Follow me' and 'Rest'.

I went on my annual leave after the course and by the time that was over, the battalion had moved to Catterick and it was here I rejoined them for a few weeks. As a regiment, we often provided officers for the various Colonial Forces and I was fascinated to hear of their experiences when they returned. They had tales to tell of East and West Africa, the Sudan, Somaliland and Trans-Jordan. It seemed to be a completely different sort of soldiering to the normal

British Army. There was much more responsibility in the outposts of Empire and a completely different type of soldier to command, a real change of scenery and climate, with a considerable increase in pay. Above all a chance of active or semi-active service.

In addition to these possibilities, I had always had a penchant towards the Air Force. It was now or never as far as military flying was concerned so I tried for this first, only to be turned down on medical grounds. However, the RAF authorities happened to have a vacancy in the Iraq Levies, which they controlled by virtue of their overall command in that country. (Having been out there as a boy when my father was serving there just after the 1914 war. I had very happy memories of a big house set on the banks of the River Tigris on the outskirts of Baghdad, with every kind of expedition by boat, motor car and Arab pony, so I jumped at the offer of a secondment there.)

Thus it was that I saw very little of Catterick. The regiment were hunting with the Bedale and the Zetland and enjoying sport that was really rather beyond comparison with that down in the south. All the horses were hard and fit and raring to go in the Regimental Race to be held early in the spring. I was back in the saddle on my precious Sally and felt that I had a real chance of beating this Vanity for the first time. Then disaster struck. The local Army vet considered that our chargers were far too light. He wanted all horses under his charge to be fat and comely, caring nothing for fitness to racing. He ordered immediate suspension of further training, no more hunting and all exercise to be limited to one hour's walking a day. The Colonel appealed to the Brigadier with no effect.

I was held responsible as I had just taken over the duties of Horse Transport Officer on my return from leave and had not realized that the vet in a new station could be such a menace to our aspirations. Duzely Graham had taken over command from Bingo Baynes in my absence and it was terrible to feel that I had let down a man I so admired. Thus my last few weeks were blemished and I could hardly wait for the day when I could take my embarkation leave.

CHAPTER V

IRAQ

IN THE LATE SPRING of 1938 I embarked on a P & O liner, the *Rawalpindi*, in Tilbury Docks bound for the East. Naire Palat Sankaran, an Indian friend from Sandhurst days, was a fellow passenger. The boat was almost empty as most people got on at Southampton or went by train to Marseilles.

Naire said, 'Now one thing you will miss while abroad is good English bitter. When we get to Southampton, we'll go ashore for the last two pints you will have for many a day.'

And we did. When we had finished Naire said, 'When you come back, the first really enjoyable drink will be another two pints.' He was right.

Naire had an irrepressible sense of humour and when we were on the square as Junior Cadets at Sandhurst, was prone to see the funny side of things and was apt to be doubled off to the guard room for laughing on parade. After an interval the Company Sergeant Major would send a staff sergeant to see if 'that there Mister Sankaran had stopped laughing and if so to double him back'.

At least once Naire and his escort had almost reached his place in the ranks when he was again smitten with a sense of the ridiculous and back to the guard room would he go. However, he learnt to control himself and became a very useful soldier in later life, attaining the rank of brigadier. He was a most amusing companion.

At Southampton I teamed up with two naval sub-lieutenants to share a small table on the edge of the dining-room to which we could slink our way in after gin sessions at the bar before meals. We had to make our own fun for there were few people about going through the Bay of Biscay. We went ashore at Gibraltar which was a hive of activity as the Spanish Civil War was then at its height. We heard some interesting tales at the Rock Hotel and met Lord Rhidian Crichton-Stuart who was a non-intervention officer. We could not gather exactly what his duties were, but were left in no doubt as to where his sympathies lay. Indeed his views were shared by almost everyone and conflicted considerably with what was being published by much of the British Press at that time.

At lunch next day we were disconcerted to find a more elderly man at our table and we were not as polite as we should have been. He had had little if any tongue-loosening gin and his demeanour hardly fitted ours. At the end one of our naval officers said, 'Well, sir, and who and what might you be?'

'I am Captain So-and-So,' he said, 'and I am on my way to be Chief of Staff on the Yangtze.'

My two companions breathed heavily and bowed gravely. At dinner the Captain had moved to the Captain's table and we were more circumspect in timing our arrivals to meals.

The ship filled up at Marseilles, our next stop, where we had had a night ashore, which included an evening at a night club where I had no difficulty in cashing a cheque drawn on the Farnham branch of Barclay's Bank. Such was the honour of a British officer in those days.

Back on board among the passengers were the Maharajah of Rajpipla with his whole entourage, also the Baron Empain, reputedly the third richest man in the world. We were told that he owned the Paris underground and the Egyptian railways and that his yacht was following. Indubitably, he had a most beautiful, ex-Ziegfeld Follies girl as his wife.

Rajah and Baron vied with each other to give the better parties to which our little group were usually invited. Sailing through the Mediterranean in those circumstances was quite delightful. The standards of food and service of the old P & O liners at that time were remarkable. It was wonderful to think that one was actually being paid while travelling thus. There was a short stop at Malta which in those days was not considered worth a visit ashore!

Despite other attractions, there was no proper swimming pool and we all used a simple canvas bath temporarily erected on the foredeck. However, it was fun, if more for cooling off than for showing off.

I was sad to leave my shipboard friends at Suez – I was almost the only person to get off. I had to spend a day there by myself before getting on a train for Haifa in Palestine that evening. There was considerable unrest in that country at the time so it was an uncomfortable journey, both to Haifa and then on by car to Damascus in Syria. All the way my mind was taking me back to the comforts and company on the P & O ship now forging gracefully out of the Canal and down the Red Sea.

Never a one for sightseeing I was glad to leave Damascus on the huge Nairne air-conditioned multi-wheeler bus, which carried people in relative comfort across several hundred miles of Syrian desert, and eventually dropped me off at Falujah on its way to Baghdad. Thence I was taken to the RAF base at Habbaniya. It was a Saturday and most of my future bosses or companions were on their way to enjoy a pre-planned weekend. Anyway I could move into my bachelor bungalow in peace and quiet after the journey.

The base had been built within a loop of the River Euphrates some seventy miles west of Baghdad. It was dominated to the west by a plateau which was about one hundred feet above it and still further west was Lake Habbaniya, an expanse of brackish water suitable for flying-boats. The actual aerodrome was outside the perimeter of the enclosed cantonment, which had to be kept secure from the local tribesmen. Even within the cantonment there was an enclave for local civilian labour among whom were people who could jeopardize the working of the base.

The safety and effectiveness of the base depended on the goodwill of the Iraqi government and it had been relatively stable for many years. At this time Iraq, a constitutional kingdom, was headed by the Amir Abdulillah as Regent. He was Anglophile, but the political leaders were by no means all of like mind: Britain's greatest friend was Nuri Said Pasha, one of the original desert warriors of Lawrence's campaign.

The troubles in Palestine caused by Jewish immigration into that Holy Land by tacit British Government connivance meant that virtually all Arab opinion was tending against us and UK personnel had to tread warily; moreover the local tribe were the Dulaimi, noted for general unpleasantness and by no means on our side. So the main task of the Iraq Levies which I now joined was the guarding and security of what the RAF called HAB.

Huge aircraft hangars dominated the base which serviced the bomber squadrons, one ancient, one modern, a communication flight and all the ancillary support which included an RAF armoured car squadron and five companies of Levies. There was capacity for many more aircraft in emergencies and the administrative back-up for repair, supply, medical and relaxation was supreme. The whole complex had been planned with loving care so that there was room for everything and everything seemed to be in its proper place. Even while the buildings were being erected, gardens with lawns and trees were being made. The layout included a theatre, churches, clubs, playing-fields for all sports including a golf course, polo ground, and of course swimming pools. By the time I arrived our Levy Officers' Mess had a beautiful garden with pergolas, trees and shrubs. Even our bachelor bungalows boasted lawns sheltered by oleanders. All you had to do to make things grow was to make the water from the river flow temporarily across a bit of land and stick plants in for the water was always heavy with silt. As an ex-collector, I was thrilled by the butterflies, swallowtails two a penny, and enchanted by the bird life with hoopoes and bee-eaters galore. The crowing of black partridge brought promise of shooting days to come.

It was early summer and the temperature had not yet reached its daytime peak of 123°F in the shade, but still hot enough to shock a man newly out from home. However, it was a very dry heat and far from oppressive. It was nice to have to wear so little and delightful to be able to sleep out of doors during the much cooler nights. I had been introduced to Kinneas Khoshaba as a potential Assyrian bearer. We seemed to click. He spoke very adequate English and I liked his manner. I was to find that with him as my servitor I was fortunate indeed.

The next day I met most of the officers, including the Acting CO, a Major 'Tubby' Brawn. He was very much a ranker regular officer who was not averse to showing a dislike for 'gentlemen officers'. The real CO was a retired, re-employed last war officer, who spent as much time as possible in the Lebanon; he was away there now. There was a small coterie of the same ilk around the Force headquarters.

The Force consisted of seven infantry companies, six at Habbaniya, of which four were Assyrians, one Kurdish and one Arab with another Arab at Shaibara near Basra in the south. I was to command the Kurdish Company and also be responsible to the signal section which was part of a headquarter company in Habbaniya. Transport was almost entirely mule-drawn or pack.

The Kurds were reckoned to be the most difficult of our soldiers. No respecters of persons, they despised the Arabs, distrusted the Assyrians and took a rather poor view of the British. Most of them were dour mountain people from the north of Iraq who spoke only the Kurdish tongue. The second-in-command was a Turk who had fought against us in the 1914 war and been so well treated as a wounded prisoner that he had become Anglophile. Ahmed Effendi was a stalwart character, heavy of build and rubicund of face. After a walk round the company lines and a visit to the soldiers who were doing musketry training, he said that a groom would bring my charger to my quarters at 5 am the next day as I should be on the rifle range by 5.30. The company was about to fire the annual classification course.

Before lunch I met several of the other officers in the Mess, which was very well run and had every possible comfort in the way of furniture, an excellent staff, mostly Assyrians, an exemplary cuisine which provided infinite variety and a well-stocked cellar. Spirits cost twenty pence a bottle, but beer was much more expensive. There were some great characters among the officers, who had been seconded from their own regiments and continued to wear those uniforms.

Outstanding among them was Basil Fanshawe of the West Yorks. Fair-haired, blue-eyed, mustachioedly handsome, excellent horseman and ball-game player, a ready wit and raconteur, he was our unelected leader and exemplar. Noteworthy, too, was John Onslow from the DCLI, an ex-army quarter-miler. Also a fine horseman but exceptionally skilled with his pen, for his articles in *Blackwood's Magazine* brought him considerable fame. He was always great fun even if in a rather noisy way. There were many others.

The next morning when I arrived at the firing point on the range, Ahmed Effendi called the company to attention and a soldier took my horse. There were two tables with chairs just behind the firing

1 *Right*: The author as a Second
Lieutenant in the Cameronians
(Scottish Rifles), Maryhill
Barracks, Glasgow, 1933 (see
p. 16).

2 *Below left*: "We were married in
the Grosvenor Chapel" (p. 86).
The author with his wife, Jean, 31
December, 1947.

3 *Below right*: "Not the average
person's idea of a likeable man"
(p. 104). The author as GSO1,
17th Gurkha Infantry Division,
with General Sir Gerald Templer,
Malaya, 1953.

4 "I had to arrange and command a monster parade at which the salute
would be taken by the Sultan of Negri Sembilan" (p. 110). The Sultan and the
author, Coronation Parade, Seremban, 1953.

5 "We christened it the mobat" (p. 118). Netheravon, 1956.

point; one bore sheets of clean paper, copies of the firing practices to be shot and a thermos flask with a glass, the other a pile of stones. We began. I had not long to wait to see what the stones were for. Ahmed sat behind that table and before long a soldier missed his target twice, whereupon Ahmed hurled a brick at him amid a shower of invective.

In a pause after this incident, I said, 'Ahmed Effendi, I don't think I have ever seen this sort of thing done on the range before.'

'Ah, sir, but I am very strict mans,' he said.

The heap of stones on his table gradually decreased as he launched his missiles from time to time. I must confess that it made the proceedings much more interesting than any such I had attended before. Three other native officers were there and one was a young blue-eyed gallant, who reminded me of other light-hearted young officers one might find in many regiments at home.

Assyrians, who made up the bulk of the force including the signal section, are the descendants of the great warriors of Ancient Babylon and still have names such as Sennacherib, Nimrod and Tiglath. After their days of ascendancy in biblical times, they were gradually reduced to a tiny Christian nation living in Turkey. In 1917 they declared for the Allies which resulted in their expulsion from Turkey and a dubious exile in the Kurdish region of Iraq ever since. British officers in Mesopotamia, which became mandated to us after the war, realized their potential and soon had many of their menfolk recruited with the Levies to give outstanding service in the mountainous regions there in the troublous times arising after that First World War. Now the RAF was responsible for the Levies, whose main role had become the security of the airfields in Iraq. Most of what was left of the Assyrian nation still lived in Kurdistan, their villages alongside Kurdish villages in an uneasy yet tolerable state of neighbourliness.

The Arab companies were recruited from the tribes living in the Basra marshes. Most were very dark-skinned with negroid features, their ancestors having been intermingled with slaves from Africa brought over by Arab slave traders. They were a cheerful, carefree body of men, quite outstanding at foot drill on the barrack square but not so good at hitting the target on the range.

I was delighted and surprised to find a complete pack of English foxhounds kennelled in the cantonment. I had hunted in Iraq when

I was seven years old and was much the youngest member out. We galloped like mad, sometimes in a great cloud of dust, the hunt staff being hard put to it to keep hounds together for they were almost impervious to discipline. The salukis were finally replaced with English foxhounds. Now here they were, forty couple being looked after by a Kurdish kennelman called Aziz with a Master, who was also Adjutant of the Levies, called Le Mesurier. He was just about to go home for good when he heard that I was keen. I was quickly introduced to all the fraternity and before I could draw breath found myself appointed as first whip. Within a year I became Master and Huntsman, which, although it was an enormous pleasure, effectively bound me for nearly all my spare time and available leave to that particular pursuit.

A handful of enthusiasts kept a polo club going on locally bred Arab ponies, which could then be bought for as little as £20 apiece. They took to the game almost naturally and were easily schooled, but being entire were not averse to starting a fight so that line outs and mêlées could be anxious times. The big match of the year was Army v RAF. There were not many RAF officers who were interested in equestrian sports. Understandably they could get all the thrills they needed in the air.

By one means or another, I soon had a string of four ponies for polo and hunting and settled down to enjoy the life.

It was not an enthralling form of soldiering; much time was spent on the barrack square and one's most important duty was to ensure that all the guards and sentries were alert and efficient around the twelve-mile-long perimeter of the base. Blockhouses were sited at intervals and these had to be inspected at unexpected times during the night. This had to be done using a vehicle so each guard had warning of one's approach, but it was seldom that they could be faulted and if one tried to be clever and come on foot there was considerable risk of being shot. As one approached and was detected the challenge would ring out: 'Halt, who goes there.'

'Grand Rounds,' one would reply imperiously.

'Halt, Grand Rounds, to be recognized.'

And so halt one did till the guard commander had had a look and then 'Guard turn out' would be the next item and one would carefully inspect the men and their weapons.

Perhaps incredibly humdrum on the face of it. Yet if anything be done, if it be done really well, there is always a sense of satisfaction. I was inwardly delighted to feel that one could so seldom find fault, not only in this particular exercise but also in the turnout on parade and the near perfection of the barrack rooms and offices. Every single item that was 'on charge' to each company commander was inspected once per month. The soldiers' kit inspections were more frequent but the weapons, their spare parts, the barrack furniture, including electric light bulbs and basin plugs, were solemnly counted and marked as being present, which they almost invariably were. Not a very practicable procedure to a modern mechanical army but for us it was nice to know that everything was there.

Military crime was virtually non-existent. I cannot remember any cases of disobedience, absence or drunkenness, the normal offences in most armies. I can remember dealing with cases of men being marginally late for something or for a lessening of standard in drill or turnout. Then it was only necessary to suggest that the man's family would be ashamed of his delinquency for an almost tearful promise of rectitude in the future to be tendered.

The hot summer days passed pleasantly enough. One's morning work consisted of supervising a routine that was firmly established, either on the barrack square or the range. The standards of weapon handling and shooting were almost unbelievably high for lesser standards were just not accepted, and with this one was content, for ability to kill an enemy rests on these things. We were armed with air-cooled Lewis and water-cooled Vickers machine guns and we not only expected a high score on the targets but knew that any stoppages which might occur to the mechanisms would be corrected in the minimum possible time. While we were doing our business, we could hear the roar of the RAF Blenheim bombers taking off and circuiting. These were the most modern aircraft in service at that time and were a completely different generation from the Hawker Audaxes manned by one of the squadrons. George Stainforth, a previous winner of the famous Schneider Trophy, commanded a Blenheim squadron for a time and it was alleged that he could spin his undercarriage wheels on the roofs of lorries crossing the desert.

There were some intriguing characters in the Air Force, among them the commander of the Communication Flight who overflew Basra with a cricket team on board and had to land on the shores of the Persian Gulf. He took me up in a DH Moth for some unofficial dual instruction after a guest night. He allowed me to take off and I, having flown about happily for a time and having had no response to my remarks on the intercom for a while, turned round to see him fast asleep in the after cockpit. I had to throw the plane about all over the place to wake him as I had had absolutely no instruction as to how to land.

That autumn brought the Munich Crisis and I and others enjoyed a brief sojourn in the Syrian Desert through which RAF ground convoys would have to travel to and from Egypt if war began. But, flap over, we were back in time for the winter rains, which brought a completely different way of life. Heavy rain begat mud everywhere except on hard standing and metal roads. Lovely sunny days interspersed the downpours and the atmosphere was freshened.

We went out to shoot the never-ending stream of sand grouse moving near the lake, we dealt with flights of all kinds of duck coming in to newly filled shallows in various places and we walked up the black partridge in the tamarisk coverts which bordered the river. Quite exciting for they usually flew spasmodically to the end of each strip then broke backwards over the guns in a grand finale, coming at different heights and speeds.

We began hunting too. Here again the tamarisk coverts nearly always held 'jack'. Between them and their habitat on the edge of the desert was cultivated land intersected with ducts through which water was pumped from the river in the summer. Some of these took quite a bit of mastering for they were all of different shapes and sizes, so when the chase became fast and furious there could be considerable grief.

The opening meet was held at Air House, the house of the Air Vice-Marshal, and was quite an occasion. He usually invited the British Ambassador, the Major-General in charge of the mission to the Iraq Army and a few Iraqi notables. The Amir Abdulillah, the Regent, was a keen supporter. At Christmas time we took hounds to Baghdad for a week and then the field was swelled by officers of the Bodyguard and people of any nation who could put a leg across a horse. Normally meets were held in the open countryside as early as we could persuade members to attend. However, there was usually a white tablecloth with good things upon it.

We now wore clothes suitable for the summer in England and even had a fire in the mess in the evening, blankets on the bed at night and worked the same sort of hours as one would at home. Mosquitoes took the place of sandflies as a nuisance so one still had to sleep beneath a net. I remember best the long hot days of the summer from spring to autumn, when one slept on the verandah and was woken at dawn by Kinneas, my bearer, splodging an ice-cold sponge on my face and shouting, 'They are on parade. They are on parade.'

Sometimes one would be woken before that during the night when the 'jack' pack would howl mournfully, to be answered by hounds in the kennels with the crashing lingering chords that only they can sing.

Each spring brought the melting of the snows in the mountains to the north and the rivers would swell alarmingly. The Habbaniya base was particularly vulnerable, for the flood waters were only kept at bay by mud-banks, called bunds, and if the water overflowed these, everything in its path would be swamped. The year 1939 provided a crisis, for the threat resulted in the emergency move of everything that could be moved up on to the dry desert plateau above. We had spent nights and days working on the bunds with lorry-loads of already filled sandbags to bolster any weak places and one night I had managed to interpose a 'bellum', a local boat, into a nasty-looking gap which may have saved an immediate threat but not averted the danger. The Levies were fully extended in moving equipment up to the plateau and in subsequently guarding it there. Never before had the local tribe had such an opportunity of pilfering and they tried to make the most of it.

The sudden advent of so much equipment and so many people on to a small piece of desert churned the surface into a powder which flew into the air on the slightest provocation and apparently engendered local dust-storms. The whole exercise was absolute hell for all concerned and though the base was deemed to be evacuated, everyone who could sneaked back to do their work and sleep there in comfort. The hounds had to stay there in kennels so I always had an excuse for going back, as did most people with anything really important that could not be moved.

After a week or so of intense discomfort on the plateau, everything and everybody moved back into the base. I can so well remember the noise our Levy working parties simply had to make when they were loading and unloading things into vehicles. The shouting, hubbub, imprecations and exhortations filled the air until the lorries were loaded or emptied. Then there was a sudden hush and if one looked up you would see the fatigue party poised, tense and waiting for fresh instructions, like gun dogs eagerly expectant.

The handful of nursing sisters from the hospital, the Air Vice-Marshal's wife and one other RAF wife comprised the total female population so the social life in the base was limited to male drinking parties at the Officers' Club. The competition for the favours of the ladies was quite considerable and you really had to get into the hospital as a patient to have a chance with one of the nurses. Weekends in Baghdad could make a pleasant change, for there there was female company of all sorts but still in relatively short supply. We would stay at the Alwiya Club and dine at one of the riverside hotels on a diet of caviar and champagne.

During the winter I said goodbye to the Kurds and took over No 2 Assyrian Company from John Onslow who went home. This was a much easier assignment for most of No 2 were veterans, many of whom spoke or understood English. The Rab Emma Gewergis, my second-in-command, was a most experienced and intelligent officer. We became firm friends.

So-called point-to-points were held in the last months of the winter. In the first one, I was fairly successful winning the heavyweight race, for a cup presented by the British Ambassador, on a truly terrible horse called Why Not. His pasterns were so stiff that there was no flex in his forelegs and he bumped his rider up and down in the saddle as if motivated by a piston, added to which he pulled like the proverbial train. The Royal Exodus Hunt depended on these meetings for most of its income. They were very popular with everyone in the garrison and also the locals who were allowed in for the events. Short polo scurries were part of the programme intermingled with the longer races over the sticks. Knowing the form of both the jockeys and their mounts, I never ceased to be amazed at the way people placed their bets, but at least they all had a run for their money, for hope springs eternal in the human breast.

I took over the hunt from Flight Lieutenant Clifford Ash in the spring. He was a dedicated MFH and managed well without all the advantages of equine and human back-up that I as a Levy officer could enjoy. Drafts of hounds were brought out free from the UK by the Stryx Line and I already had a promise of ten couple from the Eglinton in Ayrshire. Bryce Knox, who later became Master, was to manage this for me and this influx was a tremendous shot-in-the-arm. In the event, they arrived in midsummer at Basrah. Their disembarkation, during which they ripped the clothes off two Arab stevedores whom I had engaged to help the subsequent kennelling for the day, the train journey to Baghdad and lorry drive to Habbaniya was a nightmare so akin to fiction that even now I sometimes wonder if it really happened. I looked and smelt so horrible when we eventually arrived at the main gate manned by RAF police that I had the devil of a job to convince them of my identity.

I grabbed a fortnight's leave in the mountains soon after. The RAF had a rest camp at Ser Amadia as a change of station for some of their people in the heat of the summer, and just below it was an annexe available for such as me. Kurdistan's upper parts are like those regions all along the Himalaya Massif: lovely fertile little valleys with poplars, flowering shrubs, vineyards, running streams, cosy villages, no roads, telephones, adverts, railways nor any modern trappings. No police either but a fairly quarrelsome population.

Rab Emma Odisho, the second-in-command of No 1 Assyrian Company, had come up on leave at the same time and we set off on trek together. I had my Assyrian bearer Kinneas also. Very soon we became a party of a dozen or so. We were all armed for there were no police there then, and there were characters who would take advantage of easy pickings so it was best to be prepared. Each village we came to had sour milk or wine cooling in their streams and their hospitality could be taken for granted. Everyone wanted to hear any news we had so it all took quite a long time. It was hot in the daytime and much of the going was steep and stony. We would spend the nights on the roof-tops of Assyrian villages where wine and arak flowed while we coped with the abundance of food on offer. This was mostly mutton with rice and vegetables, followed by all kinds of fruit. We usually got merry enough to sing by the end of the evening and finish by shooting the tops off the trees.

At one village the Assyrian and Kurdish populations were almost adjoining and there happened to be a wedding at which the bride-groom was a fairly important young chieftain, Tewfic Beg. The party escorting the bride was welcomed by a fusillade of rifle fire aimed just above their heads. Ammunition cost a lot so this particular ploy was regarded as a great compliment and everyone was highly delighted. Odisho and Tewfic were old friends and after the ceremony the latter came over to sample my whisky, which we all enjoyed so much that he had to be summoned somewhat peremptorily to carry out his nuptial duties.

The next morning an impromptu rifle meeting was held and here the targets were eggs suspended on string about a hundred yards from the firing point. One evening I was invited to sit up for bear known to be in the area where we were staying. I was taken up to my hide in the dark and given very vague instructions, then firmly wedged into the fork of a tree. In the morning when I saw where I was I was horrified. I have no real head for heights and had not a hope in hell of getting down by myself. Fortunately Odisho recognized my predicament and, realizing that I was no mountaineer, guided my footsteps down to safety. Not surprisingly I had no success when going after ibex but managed to shoot a few chukor and si-si. One will always be haunted by the lilting songs of little men as they worked their land in the mountains, which accentuated the general peace and quiet.

Back at Habbaniya there was near disaster in the kennels. Hounds were vulnerable to a disease called surra. This was thought to be initiated in the tse-tse fly areas of Africa and transmitted through jackals and carrion right through to the Middle East. It was a horrible wasting disease but there was a vaccine which had to be given intravenously. Unfortunately a local vet had treated the pack with intra-muscular injections and these had caused dreadful-looking ulcers in several animals. Accommodaton for sick hounds was limited and it did sometimes happen that they were attacked and killed by their brethren, so we had a real crisis. Like all such, we managed to overcome it after losing some three couple and struggled on to keep the rest fit and well through the heat of the summer.

There were water troughs in the kennels where hounds could wallow and each evening we took them down to the river for a change of scenery. It always rather amazed me how well in lact they kept.

Meanwhile, it was obvious that war was inevitable and when it came I was out in the desert with a staging post. It was an amusing interlude which I have described elsewhere, as also the reasons which pressured me to get myself posted home and back to my own regiment. There was in fact another reason that I have not mentioned before and that was a letter from Ayrshire which implied that the lady had still not yet met anyone she preferred to me and that it was time I came back to see her. Anyway, so encouraged, I finally got my posting orders and having addressed all my heavy baggage to her parents' address, I set off.

A few weeks afterwards, troubles came to a head in Iraq. Senior Officers of the army took control and the Iraqi Prime Minister made unacceptable demands to the British authorities. This was followed by the investment of Habbaniya by an Iraqi Brigade which included artillery. The base was shelled and bombed and in view of its vulnerable position could have been easy meat. However, three companies of the King's Own Regiment which had arrived from India were flown in and the RAF mobilized every possible aircraft with which to strafe the enemy on the plateau. At the right moment two companies of King's Own, with two Assyrian companies, executed a brilliant sortie and drove the Iraqi forces back to a place called Falujah on the way to Baghdad. An enemy counter-attack nearly regained a crucial bridge at Falujah but highly skilled and gallant fighting by No 1 Assyrian Company, commanded by Alastair Graham, set matters to rights.

Soon afterwards a relieving column, mainly comprised of the Life Guards, went on through to rescue the beleaguered British Embassy in Baghdad and there was no more trouble in Iraq for the duration. The inherent disciplined fighting skill of the Assyrian was a notable feature of this so little known but remarkably successful small campaign. Thereafter the Levies were considerably expanded and even produced a company of parachutists which later very nearly joined my own 2nd Parachute Battalion in North Africa. All the rest of one's life it was nice to remember the exemplary standards set and maintained by those we most affectionately called 'the Little Brown Men from the Mountains'.

Travelling through the Persian Gulf in a small liner in the autumn is quite an experience. We stopped at every possible port, which added interest, and as we had the top decks full of local passengers who lived, slept, cooked and did everything else in full view of the first class passengers, we were never short of entertainment. There was a cargo of dried fish and a permanent list to starboard. Even after a cold shower in the evening, the clothes one put on were wet with sweat in minutes and it was difficult to look nice for dinner.

Among the passengers was Houston-Boswall, the late Chief Counsellor at the Embassy in Baghdad. Known to everyone as Hoosty-Boo, he was a great character who made this particular voyage much more fun than it would have been. There were only a handful of first-class passengers and we had only one steward to look after us. We nicknamed him 'the poor relation' as we always seemed to have to help him getting our drinks. Muscat was the only place at which we could go ashore and here we joined two Russian cabaret girls from Teheran for a swim. Unfortunately, a rather nasty looking sea-snake appeared which forced an early end to the party.

Out in the Indian Ocean, along the South Coast of Iran, the sea was full of snakes and sting-rays. Perhaps it was a special time of the year for them but the thought of falling in among them was particularly disturbing. Looking at the barren coast beyond, it seemed difficult to imagine a more horrible part of the world.

Then there was Bombay and the Taj Mahal Hotel. All officers in transit were billeted there and it was a very pleasant change from the comparatively austere way of life in Iraq. One of the Australian divisions had recently passed through Bombay on their way to Egypt and some of them had taken the town apart. I was wearing a slouch hat rather similar to the Aussies' and some small shopkeepers were apt to bolt their doors when they saw me coming and taxi-drivers would sheer off. I quickly changed to my glengarry. We were made honorary members of various clubs and found plenty of ways of passing the time. Fortunately I by now had a substantial bank balance, because life could be expensive.

Whenever one sat down to have a drink, others would join and inevitably the wretched business of standing rounds would begin. I have never understood how like sheep people can be over this.

The movement authorities could not give us any idea of when we were likely to get a passage home. However, they were insistent that we should be available in Bombay at immediate notice to take up any berths that became available and that if we missed a chance for any reason, we would be put back to the end of the queue. At that time, my parents were living near the North-West Frontier at Quetta and I applied for the means to visit them. The movements officer was not only not prepared to help but advised me not to encourage my parents to come to me because I might well be on my way before they arrived. The Services are all very different now and I am sure that today one would be flown up to see one's next of kin in such circumstances.

In the event, a small group of us were embarked from Karachi on the *City of Hongkong* some four weeks after arrival in Bombay. We had a very uneventful voyage to Durban where there was a restrained welcome from the locals. They had done so much for so many already and we were an undistinguished bunch of men from the Services, but there was a wonderful atmosphere there. I spent a night ashore at the Hotel Edward and was delighted to read in the local paper that Captain J. D. Frost had arrived and was staying there.

A day or two out from Durban, for some reason I had an early lunch and went up to the top deck. The temperature suddenly dropped and in the distance I saw a wave coming towards us. Immediately behind it the sky was dark and then came the howl of a wind. The wave hit the ship's bows which rose to meet it, but behind it were other waves, not so big but less smooth. The ship rose to the second one but the third came aboard and the water surged down into the saloons and wherever it could reach. The canvas swimming pool on the foredeck was pulverized and that water did not help. However, the ship rose to meet all the following waves and we sailed on. It was quite an experience.

The inhabitants of Cape Town were not so welcoming. At that time the Afrikaners were almost pro-Hitler and there were some who would as readily assault a British Serviceman as befriend him. We were glad to leave on the long leg to Freetown. We were a very mixed bunch on board, mostly RAF, some with their wives. Pamela Urquhart, the wife of the future commander of the 1st Airborne Division, was among the passengers setting the high standard one would expect from such and there were several kindred spirits, among them Squadron Leader Bobbie Peel, an accounts officer of the RAF who had been the treasurer of the Royal Exodus Hunt in Iraq. Despite his age, he qualified as a pilot after returning to the UK and much distinguished himself thereafter.

Freetown was our last stop before setting out into the Atlantic for the perilous part of our journey. Here we met people who had been bombed at home, who regaled us with tales of such savage destruction that we almost wondered if it was wise to go home at all. When we mentioned parts of England that we were interested in they were apt to say, 'Flat. Flat as your hat.'

We were not allowed ashore. I gathered that we did not miss much, but with the prospect of another four weeks at sea it would have been nice. Out at sea we were apprised that there were no potatoes left and the bar had run out of everything except Dutch gin, and there were only limited supplies of that. It was amazing how much one missed the potatoes. Rice was served in lieu. We all found it difficult to forgive the Captain and his staff for allowing the drink situation to occur. We were routed out into the Atlantic beyond the Azores so this leg of the journey was to last some time. We were in a slow convoy of tramps and the City of Hongkong took pride of place, with the Convoy Commodore on board. By now it was January and the seas rose. Before long we seemed to be in perpetual stormy conditions. This brought pros and cons. Our escort, such as it was meant to be, only arrived in part but it was reckoned that enemy submarines would not be able to operate.

However, the enemy air was active for the 'Flying Pencils' or Dorniers were able to reach and shadow us.

Perhaps they were short of fuel and bombs, for they never stayed long but usually hit one of the last ships in the convoy. We were able to see their final pathetic messages, 'Fires out of control. Taking to the boats.' 'Good luck and God bless,' was the only possible response.

Our own officers unofficially advised us to fill our pockets with the heaviest possible stuff to help us to sink quickly and get our suffering over as soon as possible if we were hit and had to take to the boats, because they would have no chance of staying upright in the prevailing conditions. Not a very cheerful prospect, but it was quite amazing how little perturbation there was. Most of us were much more upset at the lack of booze and potatoes than at the thought of a watery grave.

Anyway, a few days nearer home, the bulk of the escort arrived and there would then have been a chance of being picked up. Then came Liverpool just as it was getting dark. From the stories we had heard, I imagined that it would take several hours in the train to reach London as the line would have been out of action, but now we romped down to our destination at the normal peacetime speed. Grabbing a taxi, I said, 'Cabbie, please take me to the hotel nearest to Piccadilly Circus that is still standing.'

'OK, Guv,' said he, and drove me to the Regent Palace.

CHAPTER VI

WARTIME

AFTER ONE NIGHT IN THE HOTEL, I went to the War Office to see an old Regimental friend, John Law, who might be able to tell me where my next appointment would be. Having found him, his first remark was, 'And what do you think about FF getting married?'

'Impossible,' said I. 'I have just come all this way home to do that very thing.'

'Too late. It was not very long ago. But everyone knows about it.'

It would be wrong to say I felt broken-hearted; in fact there had never been any kind of firm understanding between us. Nevertheless something that I had always rather hoped might happen was now not on at all and it took a bit of getting used to.

John told me about the newly formed Commandos, saying that that might be just the thing for me. But I now wanted to rejoin my own regiment and so it was going to be the Infantry Training Centre up at Hamilton in Lanarkshire in about three weeks' time.

He introduced me to the United Hunts Club in Upper Grosvenor Street where he was staying and I moved in from the Regent Palace straight away. It was quite like staying in a prolonged country house party presided over by most meticulous and thoughtful hosts, who were in fact John and Daphne Slee. At that time it was their business, also their hobby, and they were experts. Staying there was enormous fun. Most of the other guests were kindred spirits, one being just about the right age and sex to help me surmount my matrimonial disappointment. Most people staying there appeared for a drink before dinner and table companions were often changed. At that time a splendid night club, called the Suivi, was thriving and some of us would go on there. Unfortunately this was closed down by the police, for some very good reason I have no doubt.

Meanwhile the bombing of London continued each night. It made little difference to one's life or plans. Before the war, I had often been to a restaurant in Panton Street known as Stone's Chop House. It was unique in many ways, not least for the vast helpings of food and the strength of the beer, but also because the waiters wore brown knickerbockers and red waistcoats.

I meant to renew my acquaintance one evening but for some reason decided not to. The next morning when I did go there, there was nothing left. A bomb in the night had demolished it.

Re-introduction to my regiment was at what was then known as the Infantry Training Centre at Hamilton in Lanarkshire. From here I contacted FF and went to her home to pick up my luggage. Only a little of the fascination had diminished but I felt no bitterness. She was a couple of months older than me and I think it better if the man is the senior partner. Anyway it was lovely to see her again. During my four months' journey home she had sent me four cables, none of which I had received.

The First: 'Have got engaged to So and So. Don't Hurry Home.'
The Second: 'Have broken off engagement. Hurry.'
The Third: 'Have got engaged again. Don't hurry.'
The Fourth: 'Have married. Very sorry.'

Her first fiancé was an up-and-coming soldier, who later became a member of the Army Council; her second a Commando and peace-time stockbroker with whom she has been happy ever since. But there were to be only four days of honeymoon, during which she had measles, and he then sailed round the Cape to take part in a raid on Bardia and went straight into the bag for the rest of the war.

I was soon posted to the 10th Battalion of the Cameronians. That and the rest of my wartime experiences are told elsewhere, but therein I neglected to mention the meeting I had with the Regimental Sergeant-Major of that battalion when I went to see him about supplies of ammunition for the company I had joined. I found one of the smartest, brightest and liveliest Warrant Officers I have ever met.

'You do not recognize me, sir,' he said.

'No, Sergeant-Major, I do not think that we have met before.'

'Well, sir, I was your first batman.'

It did not seem possible that this could be the same person as the batman with the runny nose at Maryhill Barracks. It was nine years before that I had last seen him. What a wonderful tribute to the Regiment and the Army he had turned out to be.

The rambling house called Scots Hall which was our Officers' Mess was often short of hot water so I used to go to a pub in the outskirts of Leiston, a small country town, for a bath. One morning I booked in for midday but when I arrived I had been preceded by a sneak enemy bomber and the bath lay hanging in the open air in the midst of the ruin of the room, being kept in place by the plumbing. In fact such attacks were rare. This incident should have made me realize that I was being preserved for a more spectacular disaster later on.

Soon after that, I left to join the 2nd Parachute Battalion for the rest of the war.

My 1939–45 war activities have been fully described in my book *A Drop Too Many*, so I do not propose to retell those tales, but I will try to summarize the events and make comments about some of them which I hope may be useful to others. I fear that many of these may be critical but, if they be valid, it is wrong to withhold what one sees as the truth. Many splendid lives were lost through the mistakes and shortcomings of others and these could all recur if ignored. Being myself a recipient of the consequences of certain errors, I have always been somewhat perturbed at the complacency displayed by most of the perpetrators and the reluctance of others to apportion blame.

The endemic trouble with British Airborne Forces was that the Army never really believed in them. When 'Archie' Wavell, later to become a famous though not very successful General and Field-Marshal, returned from seeing the Russians carry out a massed parachute exercise a few years before the war began, he gave a lecture to the officers of the Aldershot Command about this, finishing with the words, 'I advise you when you go home to forget all about it.'

Despite the successes of the German Army's invasions in Europe at the beginning of the war, some of which were certainly boosted by their use of airborne troops, the effectiveness of these was downgraded by nearly all the commentators and even derided by much of the popular Press. Had it not been for the insistence of Winston Churchill, the war-winning Prime Minister, it seems doubtful if our airborne forces would ever have been formed.

Having joined the 2nd Battalion of the Parachute Regiment in the autumn of 1941, I was appointed Adjutant with responsibility for the regulations, enforcement of discipline, and general arrangements for life and duty within the battalion. We knew that all the infantry battalions throughout the UK had been enjoined to send only their most willing, physically fit, adventurous men of known good conduct when the call for volunteers went out. In the event, although undoubtedly some of the arrivals were in the described category, many were in the reverse, as though some of the battalions had taken the opportunity of unloading mostly those men who would be missed the least. Much time was wasted in sending many back to their parent units, but as far as I know, none of the guilty units were ever brought to book. Later, when there was criticism of airborne forces, it was said that we had creamed off the best of other units, thus contributing to their failure to stand the test when the time came.

It never seemed to me that much serious thought was given to producing the type of leaders or their staff needed to head a completely new force who would be pioneering a new means of introducing soldiers into battle. As a mere Captain and Adjutant, I had no knowledge of those who ran our affairs at the War Office. I knew of 'Boy' Browning, a Grenadier Guard, who had made a great name for himself as Adjutant at Sandhurst, who had been an Olympic hurdler and was the husband of Daphne du Maurier, the brilliant novelist. He was to be our first divisional commander when the division formed. He was a quite splendid personality, a man whom everyone could put on a pedestal. He had won his spurs as patrol officer with the impeccable Guards Division during the First World War. But was this the right background for someone who ought to be able to think quite new thoughts and realize that airborne forces would have to rely entirely on air forces, not only to enter battle, but thereafter, to be supported and supplied?

Brigadier Richard Nelson Gale was nominated to command 1st Parachute Brigade. He had spent much of the First World War as a machine gunner and there could be no doubt that this weapon had come to dominate infantry fighting. But it was a very different form of infantry fighting from what was now being considered. He, in turn, nominated Ted Flavell, his old machine gun company commander as the CO of the 2nd Parachute Battalion. Ted was not even a regular soldier and had been with a TA Battalion of the Middlesex Regiment during the inter-war years. He was already beyond the age recommended as the limit for those who would have to undergo the stresses and strains required of the would-be parachutist, yet he was now our CO.

Through a great stroke of luck and a certain amount of perseverance on my part, I was the Commander of C Company of the 2nd Battalion when it was decided that it would carry out a night raid at Bruneval on the coast of France in February, 1942, with the aim of dismantling and bringing back the innards of the latest German radar equipment.

I was presented with a plan by a liaison officer from the 1st Airborne Division HQ, which involved splitting up the normal company organization into different-sized and armed parties, each with a different task. I was to command a party which had to assault and capture a villa which overlooked the radar equipment, while another party, which included engineers and a radar expert, dealt with the radar. Another party was to take the enemy beach defences from the rear and another was to be a reserve. There was no provision for an HQ, it being presumed that after I had dealt with the villa, I could then assume control of the whole operation.

Such a plan can look all right on paper but if things went wrong, as they almost inevitably do in real life, I would be involved, in my attack on the villa, with a secondary duty to establish an HQ from which to exercise control. When I protested, I was told that if I did not accept the plan, divisional HQ would very soon find someone who would, so I shut up.

In the event, we found the villa almost empty, but the engineer party were delayed, which fact required urgent consideration. German prisoners were taken, with valuable information which had to be assimilated. German reaction was much faster than had been anticipated, for many of the local garrison happened to be on an exercise with all their weapons and vehicles readily available. Then, as we were moving down to the beach to be, as we hoped, taken off by the Navy, we heard that the beach assault party had been partially misdropped, so the defences were not yet in our hands. While we digested this unpalatable news, Germans attacked the rearguard defending our retreat to the beach, so a quick, immediate counter-attack was required. Fortunately, the misdropped party arrived in the nick of time to capture the beach defences but now there was no sign of the Navy. There was no reply to our wireless Morse lamp signals and we fired off 'last ditch' Verey lights. Then, just as I was most reluctantly making provisions for taking up positions at the base of the cliffs to be able to fight it out to the end, the boats came in.

As will be seen from the foregoing, there was a very considerable amount of commanding to be done and, as I had foreseen, there never had been any possibility of a cut-and-dried plan going like clockwork, and I felt the lack of a proper company HQ very much.

General 'Boy' Browning came over to see us the next day after we had returned to the camp at Tilshead, which we were sharing with the newly forming Glider Pilot Regiment.

'You have put airborne forces on the map,' said he. 'From now on we should be able to get all sorts of things that have been withheld up to now.'

He had not been so pleased the night before when Johnnie Goschen, his AA & QMG, had arranged for us to spend the night on board the *Prinz Albert*, the mother ship of the landing craft flotilla that had taken us off the beach at Bruneval. But by then we were whacked. There had been scant proper rest for us crossing the Channel within the very cramped living quarters of the motor gun boats which were towing the landing craft. We had all got wet through scrambling into these, while they were bobbing up and down in mounting seas and in danger of getting stuck with a falling tide. We had been very happy aboard the *Prinz Albert* when she was up on Loch Fine during one of our training periods. The alternative to sleeping there would have been a long, cold drive in the dark in the back of troop-carrying vehicles – not the acme of comfort.

We were somewhat amazed but delighted at the public acclaim accorded to our raid but this was rather spoilt by the need to suppress the real reason for our venture on security grounds. After extracting the required components of the enemy radar, the sappers had blown up as much as they could of what was left, so the Germans could not be certain about what we had got. Informed commentators wondered why it had been thought necessary to effect the destruction of the radar by a complicated raid, when this could probably have been achieved by conventional air action.

We were brought down to earth when it was known what our ration of gallantry awards was to be, for they compared unfavourably with those given to the other Services involved and later to all those taking part in other raids. To add to discomfiture over this, we were castigated for losing some equipment during the action, but anyone witnessing our evacuation in the circumstances obtaining would have been congratulatory rather than otherwise. One of the principal losses was sixteen pairs of binoculars, which we in fact never took with us at all.

Anyway, Richard Gale turned out to a very fine airborne divisional commander and was advanced to become Commander-in-Chief during peacetime. Ted Flavell followed him as Commander 1st Parachute Brigade, and under his tutelage the Brigade won undying fame during the Tunisian campaign in 1942 and 1943. However, no sensible, firm policy was emerging as to feasible roles which so manifestly required the full co-operation with all available air forces, and when the 1st Parachute Brigade embarked by sea to join and operate with the 1st British Army in French North Africa, after the reaction of the initial concept of a brigade drop to capture Tunis because the Axis forestalled the Allies, there seemed to be no ideas at all. One battalion had seized the small port of Bône, which required no subsequent action there on their part; another had been dropped up forward in an infantry reinforcing role and 2 Para had been kept in reserve.

Fervent though amateurish efforts were made to find us a suitable task because the maximum number of fighting units were badly needed up front, yet to waste our special characteristic now would obviously be a gross misuse of an opportunity to use at least one of the battalions in the way that was envisaged when airborne forces had been conceived. But what the way was, even at this stage, no one was able to say. Just as the tanks had been frittered away in the First World War, so now the new parachute battalions were in danger of being grounded to fight as normal infantry.

In the event, after I had had to undertake two quite useless aerial reconnaissances, 2 Para were dropped some forty miles into what was in fact enemy territory, with the task of destroying non-existent enemy aircraft on airstrips already evacuated by them. The Brigade operation order included instructions to salvage our parachutes, but as soon as the enemy located us, we had to operate for four days without any form of support, supply, evacuation of wounded, or even recognition.

In the end, we managed to get one third of the battalion back to the 1st Army lines at Medjez el Bab. We had had to leave our wounded behind with an escort, as they might be harmed by local Arabs, who were not particularly friendly. We now know that no fewer than two German parachute battalions with personnel carriers, tanks, armoured cars, artillery and aircraft were given the task of our destruction. Yet throughout this time neither 1st Army nor 5 Corps made, or caused to be made, even one gesture to find out where we were.

After this somewhat traumatic experience, we were given one day's rest before being given an operational task, which did not test us much because it was so futile. Soon after that we were withdrawn for re-equipping, reinforcement and general reorganization, but as soon as could be we were back holding a part of the line, which was much better than being out of things.

Early in January, 1943, the rest of the brigade went back to our base area near Algiers to prepare for an airborne operation that was to assist the newly arriving American troops to cut off the retreating Afrika Korps from the Axis forces in Tunisia.

2 Para were still so understrength that there was no possibility of our being able to parachute as a battalion. I was offered some two hundred reinforcements of redundant soldiers from AA Command. I had no opportunity of inspecting them but it was these or nothing. Many of them were horrified at being hijacked into Para, having no such thought in their minds, and we were not exactly delighted at being made up to strength with unwilling

men, some of whom had never even fired a rifle. I felt that it was the future of the battalion that mattered and went out of my way to welcome them wholeheartedly. We gave them red berets immediately, saying that we could leave the question of their qualification as parachutists till later. Shortly after their arrival, we went into a very quiet sector of the line above a place called Beja and here we taught them to shoot, using petrol cans as targets. It was quite remarkable how quickly they learnt, not only with the rifle, but the other weapons too. Feeling completely accepted, they were soon playing their part to the full. We then went through a period of unpleasant mucking about from pillar to post, followed by a most successful defensive battle, which induced a feeling of confidence. By now some parachute-trained reinforcements were arriving in dribs and drabs, but soon you could no longer tell the difference between these and our AA gunners, many of whom became casualties and most of whom stayed to the end of the war, qualifying as para as soon as they had a chance.

Although we always hoped for an airborne role again, we soon knew that we were likely to see this campaign through as infantry. The rest of the brigade came back in early February, when we rejoined them, and from then on we were in action almost constantly.

Although we were smaller and less well equipped than the normal infantry battalion, nearly anyone who was in a position to make a judgment in 1st Army agreed that we were more effective and this was amply verified by the enemy, who nicknamed us *Der Röte Teufel*. All the other nations engaged in the Second World War found that there was some mystique engendered within their parachute corps. The very genuine effort of fear-suppression needed to make men jump from aircraft together seemed to create an invisible bond, which held the paras together in almost all circumstances. There are far too many authentic examples of this for me to have to list them and it would be difficult for anyone to argue that this does not still hold good today.

Unfortunately, the planning with the support required from air forces still lagged grievously behind. In Tunisia the Germans, using pairs of fighter aircraft, were able almost to deny the use of the roads behind our lines to our own traffic by day, which meant that nearly all movement and supplying had to be by night. The effectiveness of light bomber and fighter aircraft on ground targets, which can be accurately described by the ground troops, is out of all proportion to the effort involved. Yet our brigade never had communications to give the RAF targets, although the cost would have been no more than one wireless set and perhaps one airman. During the recent campaign in the Falklands, it did not seem that there had been much improvement in that direction since the war of forty years before.

Most of the old members of the 1st Parachute Brigade look back on the few months spent fighting as infantry as the most memorable of their careers. No true soldier wants to be kept cocooned in comfortable surroundings while others do the fighting and it is not, in fact, very difficult to extract a unit from the forward area, take it to an airfield, emplane it and drop it back into operations. With the more sophisticated means of introduction available today, there should be countless opportunities. Lacking still is the brain-power of the planners and the services of the Air Force.

In the Tunisian campaign our army was so hard pressed that all the commanders and planners were understandably reluctant to forego the use of 1st Para Brigade as infantry, yet there were occasions when comparatively small and offensive air parties of para operating in the enemy's rear, targeting the guns accurately, laying mines on the very inadequate, vulnerable communications, could have achieved results out of all proportion to the effort and risks involved. If helicopter evacuation were feasible, which today it should be, the risks would be considerably lessened.

However, you have to have really forward thinkers and planners, who must be provided with information from the Air Force. Without the latter, you will not get the former. The main trouble with the Air Force is that since its inception it has been encouraged to imagine that it can and should win campaigns and wars on its own. Perhaps a trouble with British Airborne Forces was that each commander at every level wanted to command his own unit in battle *in toto*, which is of course most understandable. But this tendency led to another, which was for the planners to be looking for brigade tasks when there was a brigade available, and so on up to division and corps. Yet there may have been countless occasions when much smaller forces applied at the crucial time and place could pay dividends never yet conceived.

Perhaps it is a fallacy to think that the commander of an airborne operation should be on the ground sharing the dangers, discomforts and partial ignorance of all the relevant factors with those he commands. Would he not be much better able to command from a relatively secure position within friendly territory, with much more powerful radio to contact those necessarily being used by his subordinates? Moreover, with modern VTOL aircraft and helicopter lift available, he should be able to overfly or land amidst his own whenever really necessary.

Many people will think that helicopter-borne trooping has made parachuting from aircraft obsolete. They forget that surprise is one of the most important principles of war. With the development of free-fall accuracy, quite large numbers could be introduced into enemy territory undetected, supplied thereafter, supported when necessary and brought out if essential.

Other people will maintain that all such effort detracts from the main strength available to oppose the enemy frontally and defeat him face to face. Fair enough when your numerical strength matches that of your enemy and you are not concerned with casualties, which may finally govern your actions. But when, as a nation, you are always likely to be outnumbered, you should surely always be concerned with trying to succeed with the indirect approach, with guile and subtlety, rather than brute force.

If another world war starts, with both sides using tactical nuclear weapons, then the accurate targeting of the enemy concentrations and our avoidance of being so targeted will provide the only possible chance of success. The known available ground approaches to each other's positions will be vulnerable to nuclear strikes, so the unpredictable air approach should always be sought. Unexpected counter-attacks from the rear will be more likely to succeed than conventional frontal ones. But then who will hold the line?

Perhaps one should speculate no further and just hope that Gorbachev will continue to seek peace, but if I were a Russian planner, I would aim to capture London with my airborne forces while talking peace. And then who would nuclear bombard whom?

The capture of Sicily followed in the summer of 1943. By now the 1st Airborne Division, concentrated in Tunisia, was under the command of Major-General 'Hoppy' Hopkinson, another amateur soldier. He was a glider enthusiast and managed to insist that the glider-borne 1st Airlanding Brigade undertook the intitial assault. They were unlucky with the weather and offshore winds caused many of the gliders to come down into the sea. Many of those that made good the land had to put down in small stonegirt fields and came to grief. All in all, it was a needlessly expensive catastrophe for which no one was brought to book. Fortunately for them, the 2nd Parachute Brigade's drop was cancelled, as advancing ground troops forestalled the need for their operation.

By now it was obvious that the navigational ability of the airmen available was abysmal, yet in the absence of any guarantees of effective fighter support to the vulnerable air transport columns, it was accepted that the airborne operations would have to be carried out at night. Thus there was to be a near certainty that many of the pilots would fail to find the dropping zones. To compound this hazard, it was proving difficult to ensure that trigger-happy naval gunners would abstain from having a go at any aircraft within range, friend or foe. So when 1st Parachute Brigade left the airfields near Sousse for the Ponte Primasole on the southern edge of the Catania Plain on 13 July, few people expected that it would arrive intact. Nor did it. As described in my book and in many other accounts, we were scattered far and wide and only skeletal parties were available to carry out the task. Even at this stage of the war, absolutely no air support was provided. The Air Force was fighting the air battle, we were told, and not one single sortie of any kind could be spared for us, although the availability of the bridge giving entrée to the Catania Plain was then considered to be absolutely vital for future operations. Meanwhile, the Navy were prepared to risk valuable ships, and the 6-inch gun support provided by one cruiser off-shore made a crucial difference to the battle fought between 2 Para and a German parachute battalion.

With the absence of Gerald Lathbury, who had been wounded, I was in charge of the remains of the brigade when we returned to Africa, and I arranged to inform the United States Air Forces concerned of the outcome of the navigational errors. Division took virtually no interest in this and did not even send a representative to the conference we held with the Americans. But without improvement all future operations would be jeopardized and there could be no question that such improvement could, should or would be made. General 'Hoppy' now spent much time considering a reorganization of the brigades into a mixture of parachute and glider troops. Fortunately, the imminent collapse of Italy put an end to this, for the Division was urgently required to undertake an infantry role in that country.

At the end of the Sicilian campaign, despite the Allies' almost total naval and air supremacy, most of the very seasoned and skilful German soldiers managed to escape across the Straits of Messina into Italy, where they were able to continue to try and kill our soldiers throughout another campaign. As far as I know, the reason for this has never been explained. But if the initial plan for the capture of Sicily had had the Catania Plain as the objective for the two available airborne divisions, the whole campaign could have been won in a week. We were glad to leave Italy, where we had a minor role, but could not help taking note of the almost incredible performance put up by our opposite numbers in the German 1st Parachute Division throughout.

The success of the 6th Airborne Division in Normandy on D-Day for the invasion of Europe was a great boost to all concerned. The planning and the training had been under the control of the commander, General Richard Gale, in whom everyone had great confidence. We, in the 1st, now had to wait our turn under the command of a General new to Airborne Forces, but experienced in modern battle fighting, which was no bad thing. Roy Urquhart was a splendid, gallant and resourceful leader but was in no position to be able to prevail against the mistakes in planning which finally resulted in the destruction of the 1st Airborne Division at Arnhem, and nor would anyone else have been.

The story of that battle has been told many times. My version is in full in my book and I would not wish to go through it again. What happened to me thereafter is also described therein. But to provide continuity for the reader I will summarize as follows:

I was wounded and captured with most of my battalion during the battle for the main road bridge at Arnhem in September, 1944. I spent most of the following six months in the POW hospital at Obermaasfeldt, being released from there by the American Army in April, 1945. After a short period of leave, I went to Norway to join the 1st Airborne Division and ran the Battle School there until the autumn, when we returned home for the disbandment of the Division. I then reassumed command of 2 Para, part of the 1st Parachute Brigade, due to become a part of the 6th Airborne Division, which was to be stationed in Palestine. During this time, I met my future wife, Jean, who preceded me to Palestine as a welfare worker. While there, she was very severely wounded during a terrorist raid on the military camp of Sarafand. Fortunately the Military Hospital was near by and she was operated on without delay and after a few weeks was able to return to England.

I spent most of 1946 in Palestine with 2 Para, engaged with internal security operations necessitated by Jewish terrorism, and returned home at the end of the year in order to attend the Staff College in 1947.

This was not a happy time. Palestine seemed very empty after Jean had gone. We were able to drive to Egypt together where I saw her off in a troopship before going back alone. At that time the 1st Parachute Brigade was presided over by a most unpleasant man, which did nothing to alleviate the unpleasantness of our dealings with Jewish malpractices in an atmosphere of virulent hatred.

However, I managed to visit Baghdad to stay with the Grahams. Alastair was serving with the British Military Mission to the Iraq Army. Baghdad was, as ever in those days, enormous fun and from there I went to Habbaniya where I saw all my old friends in the Levies and the hounds in the Royal Exodus Kennels. In company with my batman, Ebbons, and driver Thomas, we jeeped across the Syrian desert taking several hours for each leg of the journey, sleeping beside the vehicle, getting absolutely filthy and sore-assed withal.

In November, after fond farewells from all of 2 Para, with which battalion I had been fully involved since September, 1941, Pat Hayward, the CO of another para battalion and I moved down to Ismailia for a staff attachment to HQ British Troops in Egypt. Afterwards, on the journey home, we both managed to lose all our money on separate occasions. In each case the survivor was able to drive home the lesson that 'He who has the lolly rules the roost'.

CHAPTER VII

STAFF COLLEGE

THE FIRST YEAR-LONG COURSE at the Staff College after the war was not as strenuous as it became later, mainly because the Directing Staff had not been given sufficient time to add to the curriculum in existence for a six-month course. So it was a case of embellishment to the subjects taught and the addition of attractive items like visits to outside establishments and battlefield tours. Many of the students were older in age and more senior in rank than the normal run, for it would be positively the last chance that many of us would have to qualify for staff appointments unless we did so then.

Many of us had been more accustomed to fighting battles than carrying out meticulous staff work and we might have had more experience of the former than many of those who were now going to teach us. We were a motley collection, which included several brigadiers and a few others who had had promising careers halted through capture. All were anxious to be indoctrinated into the magic world of the General Staff, for without the much coveted symbol 'psc' behind one's name in the Army List, there was scant chance of promotion to higher things.

Our Directing Staff, now headed by Dick Hull, who later became Chief of the Defence Staff and a Field-Marshal, were a specially select body of officers who were dedicated to their profession and determined to teach us to be likewise. Most of the work was done within syndicates of ten officers and each subject began with the issue of précis, then a lecture and demonstrations, discussions by means of questionnaires, the preparation of written work and finally an exercise, during which the students had to act out the roles of staff officers in the battle. At some stage there would be

82

what was known as a TEWT, or Tactical Exercise Without Troops, held out in the country. Anyway it will be seen that the subject, for example the Attack or the Withdrawal, would be very thoroughly covered. Included also were all the administrative minutiae such as the supply of ammunition and the care of casualties.

Much depended upon the skill and patience of the individual instructors for many of us were unaccustomed to long hours of work indoors. On the whole, they succeeded in keeping our attention from wilting but sometimes a guest lecturer might be less skilful and then the walls of the Rawlinson Hall, where the evening talks were given, could reverberate with the snores of the inattentive. One member of the Army Council, having bored his audience stiff and then invited questions, was asked if he attended many conferences.

'What do you mean, boy?' he shouted. 'Do you mean do I do any work?'

Sir Watkin Williams-Wynn who had engaged to give a talk on radar decided to treat us to a diatribe on boffins instead. At the end he asked for questions with an obviously expectant air, but there were none. Not even after a prompting prod from the Commandant.

Addresses from people like Monty, Alanbrooke, Gerald Templer and 'Jorrocks' – Brian Horrocks – were in the sublimity class and I think that they always felt so much at home at the Staff College that they could speak entirely without notes. They must have been very conscious of the degree of admiration and respect that they had earned.

Syndicate instructors changed over every four weeks or so, which enabled several of them to report on several students. Their methods varied quite considerably. One of them, Willie Pike of the Grenadier Guards, prided himself on saying as little as possible. On coming in he would say, 'Good morning, gentlemen. James, will you speak first.' Thereafter he would conduct the discussion by means of facial and manual gestures only and at the end would rise to say, 'I think all the points have been covered,' then depart.

Jack Masters, a Gurkha and later famous author, would harangue us to such an extent that it was difficult ever to get a word in. One day when he had sat down, we all knelt down and chanted, 'Oh

Masters, who should be in heaven so hallowed is thy word, have mercy upon thy students, whose thoughts are never heard.'

Heavy snow storms came soon after our arrival and the snow lay thick and firm for several weeks. The whole country was still in the grip of wartime privation so the heating was limited and so were the rations. The rather splendid living rooms were kept fairly warm but our bedrooms were icy. It was nice to be able to escape at weekends. There were many old friends on the course and one quickly made new ones.

There was plenty of time to discuss other types of warfare with those who had taken part. Among these were David Lloyd-Owen who had been one of the leaders of the Long Range Desert Group during all the North African campaigning. Also Mike Calvert, one of the Chindit Brigade Commanders in Burma, who was prepared to argue about almost everything. Tag Prichard had led the very first parachute operation of the war when his party had tried to blow up an important aqueduct in the south of Italy. Unfortunately their escape route was jeopardized and they were rounded up. There were many others with remarkable experiences behind them, including two most distinguished Indian Officers, Harry Badwar and Drag Dagalkar, who had both been taken by the Japanese in the early part of the Malayan campaign and had been grossly maltreated.

There were some fine pictures on display in the downstairs rooms, some of distinguished old soldiers, but there was no picture of the monarch. Some of us got a subscription list towards the cost of trying to arrange to have one painted but the amount we raised went nowhere towards the sum currently being asked by all the well-known artists. As it happened I had an old friend called Denis Fildes, the son of Sir Luke Fildes, an ex-President of the Royal Academy, who had recently left the Navy to take up portrait painting. He had in fact tried out his skill on me and I asked him if he knew of anyone prepared to take a smaller fee. He then suggested himself, for if it could be fixed he would gladly do it for nothing. At that time, General 'Boy' Browning was Personal Secretary to the King and he undertook to ask. The King agreed, provided that the sittings could be kept to the very minimum. Denis had been working on a technique whereby he took a lot of photographs of his subject and did most of the work from these. So it all came off. The Royal Family were delighted with the result and many of them subsequently went to Denis, and many of the London clubs display his royal portraits today.

It was decided to restart the Staff College Drag Hunt and a most intrepid Dragoon in the shape of Mick Lindsay undertook to do this. How on earth any student was able to find the time to collect hounds and set up the whole business, yet pass the course, defies credence. Yet it was done and before the end of the year they were hunting fox when cubbing started and running draglines which had been thoroughly prepared.

An old friend from Iraq Levy days kept a horse and he very kindly mounted me on occasion. Not only was the real business of the day under way but all the social trappings too, for it was decided to have a hunt ball. For that night the Staff College was properly 'en fête' and the whole building rang with the sounds of dancing, the popping of corks and the inevitable twang of a horn.

As we got into the swing of things, the whole course became a great pleasure. We were thoroughly interested in what we were doing and, as each problem was presented, we took much pride in trying to solve it. The tennis and squash courts available and impeccably maintained could provide all the exercise we needed to fit ourselves for the strain of our brains. Perhaps these were not under sufficient duress because it was decided to organize a Staff College dinner to which we would invite a number of distinguished speakers to pronounce on the problems of the day. Unfortunately we invited far too many, for in the event all wanted to speak, plus many of the students, who were paying for it after all.

For some reason I had been asked to chair the proceedings. I did not start the evening very well for I had hacked several miles to ride a dragline and came back rather weary. It seemed to me that 'Uncle Alcohol' would see me through, specially as everyone else was in like mind. Among the guests was Captain Basil Liddell Hart, the very well-known military commentator, and after I had called on him to speak, he would not stop. By now my judgment was not exactly gentle and after banging and banging with my gavel, I finally threw it towards him and went off to bed.

He graciously accepted my letter of apology and later we corresponded about another subject and became friends, but, even if others have, I have never forgiven myself.

Throughout the course I had been walking out with the Jean whom I had met just after resuming command of 2 Para on Salisbury Plain in the autumn of 1946. She had been living with her parents either in West Sussex or at a flat in London. We managed to meet nearly every weekend and sometimes she came down to Camberley to stay with friends there. We were both resolved to marry but circumstances dictated that the only possible date was the 31st of December.

At the end of the course we were told what our appointments would be. I was to go to the 52nd Lowland/District Headquarters in Glasgow as the GSO 2. Not exactly exciting but it meant that I would be back in my own regimental area working among friends and with many people I knew. There was not going to be much time to tie up all the arrangements for the wedding, have a honeymoon and move up to settle in Scotland by the end of January when I had to report. We made a flying visit to Glasgow before this and very luckily found a flat through the auspices of the taxi driver who picked us up from the Central Station.

The landlady was horrified when he drove us to her house because all accommodation was so scarce that anyone with a vacancy was apt to be snowed under with applicants of all types. However, once she had seen us she was glad to accept us but was worried about our ability to pay. 'It's an awful lot of money,' she said, 'Five pounds a week.'

We were married in the Grosvenor Chapel. Alastair Graham was best man. I had acted for him in that capacity during the war. The reception was in Jean's parents' flat in Berkeley Square. Nearly everyone we wanted to come came and, like most people on these occasions, we much enjoyed the whole thing. Drama was not to be denied because, during all the kerfuffle, my ankle wound played up and so the day after our first night of married life saw me in the Military Hospital at Millbank having yet another operation to try to extract a piece of shrapnel embedded within since the Arnhem battle. The hospital authorities said that I had created a record by being the only recorded case of a patient having been discharged

6 Ranworth, the house at Oxshott in Surrey which we bought in 1958 when I assumed command of the 44th Parachute Brigade, TA (see p. 128).

7 On Royal Favour, my favourite polo pony, in 1958. I kept my ponies with Billie Walsh whose stables were just outside the Richmond Park gates (p. 138).

8 *Above*: Waiting to parachute into Wroxham Broad, Norfolk, 1959.

9 *Right*: On the way down.

10 *Below*: Taking part in the falling plate competition at a Rifle Meeting, while GOC, 52nd Lowland Division (see Ch. XIII).

on the same day after a war wound operation. Anyway we were back in Berkeley Square that night and off on our honeymoon the next day.

Financial restrictions then in force meant that we had to stay in the UK, but the Imperial Hotel in Torquay provided all that one could possibly want. Poor Jean had to dress my ankle every day, for it was by no means healed. Otherwise there were no complaints.

CHAPTER VIII

THE LOWLANDS

THE FLAT WAS AT 60 Clevedon Drive in the Kelvinside district of Glasgow. It was not really a flat, for we shared the ground floor with another family and the first floor with Miss Linton, our landlady, and her sister, Miss Annie. There was a woman reporter in the basement too. It was bare of all furniture and utensils so we had to look sharp at getting bedded in. I took a day or two off before reporting for duty and we had great fun buying our few first pieces of furniture, some of which we still use with pride. The old Victorian house was in a most attractive position well off the main Western Avenue and as an edifice was as solid as the proverbial rock.

The Headquarters was in Park Terrace and overlooked the Kelvin Park. Although the buildings were nondescript for their role as an HQ, the site was ideal for a Glasgow office.

The Army in Scotland then consisted of two Territorial Infantry Divisions and the Yeomanry Armoured Brigade. Both TA Divisions had made great names for themselves in two world wars. The 51st Highland Division had been isolated and captured during the aftermath of the Dunkirk fiasco, but had been reformed to take part in the North African campaign. The 52nd Lowland Division, after a fleeting experience of the war in France after Dunkirk, had been trained as a mountain division throughout the war, presumably to take a leading part in the conquest of Norway. Instead they had been fully committed to the clearing of the River Scheldt on terrain which was at or below sea level. Both divisions still contained numbers of experienced old soldiers who belonged to some of the most famous regiments of all time.

In peacetime territorials had always been part-time soldiers who paraded on perhaps one night a week at a local drill hall for rudimentary training, administration and comradeship and attended several weekend exercises during which they could practice their military skills and requirements; but, most importantly, underwent a full fortnight's training annually in camp, when the whole unit came together to function as a unit.

Territorials had originally been formed for home defence and could not be given wartime roles overseas without special Acts of Parliament. But now they were scheduled to receive large numbers of ex-National Servicemen, when they went to their annual camps, which would bring them up to full strength and, on paper, make them very formidable indeed. Unfortunately, the TA was not really geared to this kind of thing. Highly trained regular army reservists could hardly be expected to take kindly to being commanded by those with noticeably lower standards and it was obviously going to take a considerable time before they were fully assimilated. Before the 1914 War not very much was expected of the TA, indeed it was decided to give higher priority to the formation of completely new army divisions before some of the TA divisions were sent to France.

In contrast, shortly before the outbreak of the Hitler war, the TA was doubled and though this did nothing to help its efficiency, some of the divisions were sent overseas within a month or two of the regular ones. Within the division the efficiency of the units varied very considerably. I had twice attended the annual camps of the Cameronian TA Brigade as Signals Officer. Whereas one of the signal sections was almost up to regular army standards, such was the enthusiasm of the members, the others were obviously going to take months to reach a reasonable proficiency. In the long run it was almost impossible to differentiate between the regular and TA divisions. It was probably best when the brigades consisted of one regular and two TA units.

When it was decided to have a home army of part-time volunteers, instead of vesting the responsibility firmly on the shoulders of the regular army, who would have known precisely what sort of back-up they needed and would have been ready to make provision, if not actual sacrifices, for the production and maintenance of such a force, a large part of the responsibility was vested in county Associations of local men of distinction, usually headed by the Lord Lieutenant.

It was thought that these Associations would be able to encourage recruiting, press employers to let the volunteers take the necessary time off and generally provide support and backing with land to train on, et cetera. However, it was inevitable that such organizations would diversify the authority of the regular army chain of command, which had to keep them fully informed, attend their meetings and conform over the use of the accommodation which was entirely in the Associations' hands.

Despite the valuable work done pre-war in peacetime by these devoted bodies, they could play little part after mobilization in time of war. They had continuing responsibility for all cadet units which provided a useful introduction to military training for male juveniles.

Now, in the aftermath of the war, the Associations had resumed their responsibilities, which in some ways meant forming another tier of command, for their chairmen thought it proper to visit units on exercises and when in camp, which was of course the direct responsibility of the regular chain of command. It is seldom that advantage can be gained by division of responsiblity in any sphere of human activity.

In addition to the TA, there were two regular major units within the command and training depots for all the Scottish infantry regiments, plus a number of administrative establishments far flung throughout the countryside.

The Lowland Division/District was commanded by Major-General 'Hake' Hakewill Smith, a Royal Scots Fusilier. He had led the Division with distinction during the war and was a most experienced old soldier.

Jock Maxwell, the GSO1, who was my immediate superior, worked in an office next to the one which I shared with two others. These offices were at the rear of the building and looked out over a mass of ugly rooftops. All our telephones rang continually as we tried to find answers to the seemingly unfathomable questions that poured in. The training and everything connected with it was my main responsibility, so it soon became obvious that I would have to spend much time travelling about the district to look at the training areas and the ranges. Some of the TA units were spread over considerable distances.

Within the territorial units, there were many experienced and notable officers and men who had fought right through the war and who were capable of producing excellent results. Sometimes perhaps more effort than was necessary went into the ceremonial aspects, for the Scottish infantry have considerable advantages in this respect. Indeed it is reported that one CO was heard to say, 'Thank God this bloody war is over. Now we can get back to proper soldiering.'

It was seldom that any of the expertise I learnt at the Staff College could be brought into play, but a divisional indoor exercise was held each year and it would be my responsibility to write it. I had to set it using maps which were readily available, so the venue was somewhere within the Lowlands. The exercise would be attended by over one hundred officers who had to be accommodated, so we booked one of the big hotels for this. When I had hatched out the general idea, I would go to General Hake for his approval. He never wanted to be tied down to divisional problems but liked to dabble in higher things and was always merging into the Corps Commander's aspect. He would rattle off material concerning this at a tremendous rate and would then want to see what I had written. I had to confess, 'You can't see this, sir. I cannot read it myself.' Anyway, we always succeeded in producing an imaginary battle which would have everyone who came arguing vociferously throughout the weekend and they would go off happily convinced that, while they were budding Montys, everyone else was a bloody fool.

Jean and I managed to make ourselves very comfortable in our higgledy-piggledy flat, gave dinner parties, and even had people to stay. Jean, who had never cooked in her life before, soon became expert. The main trouble was the rationing still in force since the war. I normally lunched in the Mess but even so, when a meat ration for two people for one week consists of the equivalent of only two chops, there are problems. During the winter months, we managed a certain amount of shooting, but here again petrol was severely rationed so we had to be very circumspect with our travelling arrangements. We were using Jean's small eight-horsepower car and when I went anywhere on duty, we were given a ration card to cover the journey, so as often as possible we combined duty with pleasure. We made several trips down to the Solway and, if we were lucky, roast goose would appear on our menu. There was reasonable mixed shooting on the army training area at Stobs near the border.

Fred Wallis, an old friend, owned two adjoining deer forests in Perthshire, so venison too quite often eased the pangs of hunger. We could not drive there, as it was outside our parish, so the business of bringing haunches by train had to be overcome.

Despite the petrol rationing, we somehow managed to get to the South of France for a three-week holiday. At this time we were allowed to take only £35 each out of the country and the French were very generous with petrol vouchers for visitors. Our drive very nearly came to a premature end when a man drove into us on the Route Nationale from an almost indescribable farm track. However, we got to Le Lavandou, which was then a lovely little fishing village, without further incident and found an old farmhouse newly turned into an hotel. Two delightful old ladies ran this so economically well that we were able to have a night in Paris on the way home. It all made up for the honeymoon abroad that we had not been able to have.

Back in Glasgow, we played tennis at a local club and I could get to one of the golf courses from time to time. The army owned a 'swordfish' dinghy which was moored on the Gareloch and we occasionally made rather hair-raising sorties in this. Somehow the time passed pleasantly enough until Jean began to feel pretty wretched. It was always on the cards that the very severe tummy wound she had sustained while in Palestine might cause trouble and now it did. Unfortunately, for a time we accepted the assurances of some medical advisers in Glasgow to the effect that it was only a minor setback, but in fact she now required the services of a 'maestro' and so a major operation had to be undergone in London. This meant that the rest of our time was 'sotto voce', for she had to be careful for a considerable time.

Major-General 'Roy' Urquhart took over from Hake during my second year, but soon there were rumours about a posting for me and then came the news that I was to be an instructor at the Senior Officers' School near Devizes in Wiltshire.

I had, perhaps rather vainly, hoped to be welcomed back into the Cameronian scheme of things with open arms. One never forgets one's first regiment. It is almost as though one has been born into something. Perhaps I was unduly sensitive. All the time I was with the Parachute Regiment, I felt that I was representing my old regiment and, as I had not done too badly, would have liked a pat on the back. But now, when I talked with the older members, it was implied that airborne troops were quickly in and out, that we creamed off the best of the infantry and that we got far more publicity than we deserved. Few of them had even heard of the part played by the 1st Parachute Brigade in Tunisia, or of how much the 6th Airborne Division had achieved in the infantry role.

However, I was very much drawn back to things airborne. I became a trustee of the Airborne Security Fund, which must be one of the most effective service charities ever, and also a member of the Parachute Regiment Association Committee which now had to establish every detail of the background of what had become and would remain the greatest regiment in the army.

Meanwhile there were rumblings about the future of the infantry in the Lowlands. The Ministry wanted to amalgamate the Royal Scots Fusiliers, Hake's Regiment, with the Highland Light Infantry, which was Roy Urquhart's. Independent observers were saying that it would be more logical to merge the HLI with the Cameronians. The Scots Fusiliers were an Ayrshire Regiment. Quite reasonably and properly both colonels strove hard to keep their regiments separate and for so doing were castigated by Monty, the CIGS, who said, 'They ought to have their heads knocked together.'

However, in the event they were forced to amalgamate and are now known as the Royal Highland Fusiliers. They have Princess Margaret as their Colonel-in-Chief, they wear the kilt and they are one of the strongest regiments in the Army. The Cameronian (Scottish Rifles) were to have a very different fate.

Just before we were due to go, the Chief Constable of Glasgow said he would like to show me something that would interest me, so Jean and I boarded a police launch at Gourock and came in it up the Clyde to Glasgow. It seemed as if the whole of the south bank was one continuous derelict shipyard. Only a small handful were now working. As the Chief Constable said, 'A living monument to trades unionism.'

We said goodbye to Miss Linton and 60 Clevedon Drive with many regrets. It had been our first home and at that particular time it had been fun to share the house with others. The other family were called Prosser and he ran a well-established motor business. They were very sociable with a large circle of friends, many of whom popped in to have a drink in the evenings. Drink was scarce. There was a great shortage of all types of alcohol and cigarettes, so people who were prepared to share whatever they had been able to collect were very popular and we often found ourselves drawn into their parties and made many new friends. Glasgow people were warm-hearted and thoroughly interested in everyone else, which was quite a nice change from the attitude one was accustomed to in the south of England. All the shopkeepers actually want to know who their customers are and each time you re-appear your welcome becomes warmer. But still there were long hard winters up and along the Clyde and it would be wrong to say that we turned the car south tearfully.

Once again it was a cabby who suggested the possibility of available accommodation. On a preliminary recce to the Senior Officers' School, we left the train at West Lavington and asked to be taken to Devizes, as we had been told that this was the only possible place. However, our driver said that he had heard that some people called Hunt-Grubbe might have a sort of flat in their country house. So indeed they had. The whole of the second floor was available, plus a garage and a part of the garden. It was about five miles from the School, so was ideal in many ways. We were to spend more than two very happy years there.

CHAPTER IX

SENIOR OFFICERS SCHOOL

THE SENIOR OFFICERS SCHOOL was mainly housed in a large
Georgian mansion called Erlestoke Park, tucked in under the
Salisbury Plain escarpment and facing firmly north. Brick huts
for the students had been erected in the grounds which included a
large lake and extensive gardens. Cheverell was the nearest village
and Devizes the nearest town. The country to the north was mostly
grassland farming and in direct contrast to the open plains of the
military training area to the south.

The School had been in existence for many years, having been
moved from Shorncliffe some time after the 1914 War. Its role was
to refresh and direct officers who were about to take command of
major units and the curriculum, though mainly tactical, included
the main aspects of administration. The students had all already
been selected for command, so the reports they obtained from the
School did not really affect their subsequent careers. Nevertheless
much could be learnt about their capabilities. The opinions of the
directing staff which emerged during the course were seldom far
wrong and were usually confirmed by the attitudes of the other
students.

The Directing Staff were not of the same calibre as those selected
to teach at the Staff College at Camberley, but obviously had to
be high enough for them to earn respect from all those who
were about to be given command. All of us were qualified staff
officers, headed by a fine old war-horse in the shape of Brigadier
Pat Scott of the Irish Fusiliers. The method of instruction was
much the same as at the Staff College but probably more time
was spent doing TEWTs and much less on paperwork. As DS,
we were younger than and junior in service to the students, but

were given the local rank of lieutenant-colonel to help us on our way.

I had been a student for a short time during the war in 1942 until I was wafted away to go overseas with 2 Para. At that time the troops for the North African landings were being assembled and many others were similarly plucked. I happened to be on weekend leave when the summons came, which resulted in my arriving at West Lavington Station on a Saturday evening. The FANY driver who had to pick me up was not at all amused.

'Have you been naughty or something?' she asked.

In those days the FANYs (First Aid Nursing Yeomanry), a hangover from the First World War, were, though a part of the ATS, still rather special. They drove all the transport for the SOS including the 15cwt trucks which carried the students around the country for our TEWTs. As at the Staff College, all the work was done in syndicate, and each syndicate travelled separately, in a truck, while trying to solve the tactical problems they had been set.

Wrestling with these problems often coincided with the lunch-time hour and then we would all repair to different pubs to jot down an agreed solution in comfort. We obviously had to invite the driver to join us and they usually did. One day the girl, who was listening to our deliberations, suddenly said, 'But that is nonsense.'

'Really,' we said. 'How do you mean?'

'The position you have chosen gives you no depth. They are all on the forward slope. Your weapons have no defilade. Asking for trouble.'

It transpired that she was engaged to one of the DS and often had to drive him around the country while he was making up the TEWTs. Sometimes during the course of these recces he had said, 'Oh God, I don't know what the answer is.'

With nothing much else to occupy her mind at that time, she had got really interested in minor tactical problems. Thereafter there was great competition to get into her truck.

Anyway I now found it a most satisfying challenge to have to convince the members of my syndicate that our official solution was probably the right one and that there were flaws in the alternatives that they had suggested. It was important not to be dogmatic but to stick to the principles; always to be ready to listen and, if you could, illustrate your own arguments with examples from previous actions in war. One rather fascinating aspect of this was that quite often the DS could not agree a solution. Arguments would go on far after official working hours. This is very right and proper, for tactics can never be a very exact science. One particular ploy that may be feasible with some troops can be quite suicidal with others.

Among the DS were some notable characters. Chief among them were Humphrey Weld of the Bays and Peter Marsham of the Grenadiers. The latter was the organizer of our shoot. It was never much good, for all our coverts faced north.

There were always a number of foreign students who came from all over the world and we went out of our way to make them feel welcome. The one I remember best was Kassim, who later became the dictator of Iraq, having bumped off all the opposition. He was a rather wild-looking chap who worked much harder than most. He came to a party in our flat during which he took a number of photographs, copies of which he later sent to us from Baghdad, together with other presents.

At the end of the term he organized a party for the DS at the Bear Hotel in Devizes. This was planned to such an extent that the individual tastes of each of us had already been noted and so on arrival we were greeted with our favourite tipple. At the end Kassim, delighted with the success of the party, went up to the manager to say, 'Double the bill. Double the bill.' It was said that he also approached the manager's wife, saying, 'Madame, I do not care what your price is, but I will pay you double.'

At this time, with the advent of nuclear weapons, the Services, and in particular the Army, were in a quandary as to what our country's defence policy was. Richard Gale was the Director of Training then and he had at least produced a document called 'The Infantry Division in Battle'. He used to visit us each term to insist that we all accept this as the authentic doctrine. We were thankful to have something to work from. 'Jorrocks' used to come and give us his excellent account of the Battle of Alam Halfa, which later became so well known through his television appearances. While talking, he would wind his legs around his pointer to such a degree that we used to wonder if he would ever be able to unwind before he fell over.

Pat Scott made way for John Spurling as our commandant. He was very intense in his attitude to everything and was perhaps not the ideal choice for such an appointment. He had his problems, for during his tenure the main building caught fire and most of it was destroyed. He managed to cope extremely well in keeping things going and in a remarkably short space of time the courses were being run almost normally.

Perhaps the nicest thing about being a teacher is that you have such regular holidays. Although reports have to be written, lessons revised, new exercises and demonstrations planned and rehearsed, during the time in between courses you know that you can plan to go places. We went back to the south of France, if only to note how quickly the crowds were moving in; to Holland, and several times back up to Scotland. We even had time to fly to South Africa for six weeks.

We had one week with a rod on the Wye when there was very little water and no one had a fish for some time. On our last day, fed to the teeth with flogging the water, we persuaded our old ghillie to have a go. Most reluctantly he took my rod. Within minutes he was into a fish, which I gaffed. It was a perfect twenty-eight pound salmon.

Charlie, though at heart delighted, was very scared. 'It's your fish,' he said. 'If it became known that I had done it, I would lose my job for ever. You must say that you killed it. Don't forget that. There's no one about but us. It was your fish.'

We went back to the Green Dragon in Hereford, where we were staying, with it in the back of the car. You cannot easily disguise such things and in no time we were being congratulated and stood drinks by all and sundry. We both had to act our way through the whole evening like professionals of the deepest dye.

It was most interesting to live such a life with the representatives of all the great regiments and corps of the Army. All our students had spent many years becoming imbued with their own slightly different, or in some cases quite different, ways and as we saw them all go by one could draw one's own conclusions. The main one was that practically everything they did was justified in the light of their roles and circumstances. Sappers, Gunners, Cavalry, Guards, Jocks, Rifles, Old County and the services, all had their own ways. It would be terribly wrong for any authority to try to change it.

As an illustration of how the seemingly most favoured looks after his own, I recall mentioning in the Mess one morning, in the hearing of a senior officer of the Household Cavalry, that the son of the house in which we were living had had a father in the Life Guards but he was undecided as to which regiment he would apply to do his National Service. That very afternoon that senior officer went down to Eastwell, with the result that young Hunt-Grubbe was firmly booked to the ultimate advantage of all concerned. That is the way to do it.

Meanwhile I was much involved with things airborne. When it was decided that the King would present colours to the Parachute Regiment at Aldershot in July 1950, Brigadier James Hill, a most distinguished wartime parachutist, and I, with our wives, were asked to show Their Majesties round the newly arranged Regimental Museum there. All went well until the King pointed to the model of an aircraft which was suspended from the ceiling.

'What is the name of that machine?' asked he.

He looked at Field-Marshal Montgomery, who was then the Colonel Commandant of the Regiment. Monty did not know but turned to General 'Boy' Browning, the King's Private Secretary, who did not know either. They then turned to me but neither did I. Then the sergeant in charge of the Museum informed us that it was a G.A.L. Freighter.

'Well, what a lot of clots all you chaps are,' said the King.

One day at about that time, a luncheon was arranged by the Parachute Regiment in Aldershot for a representative gathering of the Commandos, which included Admiral Dickie Mountbatten. This was quite an occasion, which was to be commemorated by a photograph. After the lunch we had all been arranged for this, when Monty asked the photographer, a brash untidy-looking lad, 'Well, how do you think we look?'

'Speaking frankly,' replied the boy, 'really pretty 'orrible.'

Monty leapt to his feet and turning towards us asked with a grin, 'Do you think he means all of us, or just me?'

Unfortunately the SOS was closed down a few years later. I

would have thought that it had well proved its value and in the years to come I never met a dissatisfied customer. The Joint Services Staff College was started up at about the same time as the demise of the SOS. Perhaps this has proved to be well worthwhile, though I would have thought that once one was a qualified staff officer, the 'jointing' part was commonsensical.

My next appointment was proving slightly difficult to arrange. It was considered that I ought to have a turn on the administrative side of the staff as a Lieutenant-Colonel, but in a fairly active theatre and it was my turn to go overseas. Such postings were fairly few and far between, but then the chance of going to Malaya as A/Q of the South Malaya District suddenly appeared. At that time the Malayan emergency had erupted with increased intensity after the assassination of the British High Commissioner. General Sir Gerald Templer was to go out in his place, with increased powers and resources. I thought that I was very lucky to get the job.

CHAPTER X

MALAYA

GORDON FOTHERINGHAM OF THE REGIMENT and now on the staff at GHQ Farelf in Singapore met me off the aircraft and took me back to his quarter for the night. I was fairly weary after the flight and the atmosphere was hot and sticky, especially as I was dressed for take-off in the UK. He gave me the low down as he saw it, but people in Singapore lived a different life from the soldiers and planters up country. I was on a train next day for Seremban where HQ South Malaya was, but when I got to Segamat where the 1st Battalion of the Cameronians were based, I was persuaded off the train to spend a night with them. I had not seen many of the presently serving members of my regiment since before the war, so it was quite an event for me. Bill Henning was commanding and Duncan Carter-Campbell the Second in Command. He was a very old friend and there were many holes to fill in.

Segamat was a lively place in terms of the emergency, with an active local banditry, but I thought it was a horrid little place with no distractions of any kind, yet the battalion was happy and contented with their lot. The rifle companies were spread around the area several miles apart, each on a different rubber plantation. Much of their time would be spent patrolling the jungle area bordering the plantations. At that time the communist rebels' main aim was to disrupt the production of rubber by terrorizing the native tappers at their work and by destroying the simple equipment used to collect the liquid latex from which the rubber was made. Most of the tappers were Tamil labourers who lived in coolie lines on the estate and these were vulnerable to the single-minded Chinese who were working for Red revolution and the end of British control.

It was quite impossible to police and protect all who needed guarding but of course the more active the police and soldiers were, the less chance the enemy had. Much depended on the Police Special Branch, who had to have means of collecting information as to the whereabouts and intentions of the rebels, who had to get their food from Chinese settlements. These were spread about the country and so there was considerable movement to and fro in this respect, which gave the Special Branch opportunities. The opposition became quite adept at growing their own provisions, for it was a very fertile country. But cultivation could give the show away, for it was fairly easy to spot from the air.

The bandits lived in the jungle and only emerged to carry out their terrorist acts or get food, so in the main they had to be hunted, found and destroyed in the jungle. Thus the hunters had to be trained to understand, move about and exist in an environment that was totally alien to them. So here were the Jocks from the mining towns of Lanarkshire and the great built-up areas of Glasgow learning to hack and claw their way through swampy, foetid, clinging, dripping, noisome undergrowth in pursuit of a most elusive quarry.

The battalion's tally of enemy killed was one of the best in the country and they were justly proud of this. It was great to be back with them. That night, while dining, I saw again some of the old pieces of silver and the pictures that I had appreciated as a newcomer many years before. The great regiments go on for ever, or so I thought.

Next morning I arrived at Seremban to meet Brigadier George Collingwood, also a Cameronian, who had assumed command of the District from Major-General Headley, a Gurkha, who had been invalided home. George had very kindly arranged to put me up for the time being. The GOC's house was a fine building in the midst of the residential part of the town. Seremban was an attractive mixture of a place. The central or shopping area was predominantly Chinese, with all the shop signs and advertisements in that picturesque language. There were also Indian stores with English nomenclature. Government buildings were a little apart and all around were Malay houses, though most Malays preferred to live outside the towns in their own settlements, known as kampongs. Low tree-covered hills surrounded the town and the barracks were well outside. The HQ was at Rasah camp, the buildings of a temporary nature made from local materials.

Within South Malaya District were three Gurkha Infantry Brigades, an armoured-car regiment in the shape of the 13/18th Hussars, and a number of administrative units, including the Malay Regiment Depot. It was planned that the District should now become 17 Gurkha Division, which did not really make any difference to anything but might be good for morale. The brigades consisted of two Gurkha battalions and one British battalion, but they were all firmly fixed to their locations, fully committed to operations against the bandits.

In the northern half of the country was North Malay District which comprised two Infantry brigades with an armoured-car regiment.

The whole were commanded from Kuala Lumpur by Major-General Roy Urquhart of Arnhem fame. However, unfortunately for him, the control of operations was vested in a retired and re-employed Lieutenant-General, Sir Harold Briggs, who had his own headquarters. This was a typical British nonsense, for if you do not have operational control of your soldiers no commander is really in command at all. General Briggs, the Director of Operations, worked through a number of State War Executive Committees, Malaya being divided into a number of states, which each had a Malay Prime Minister and Council with a British Adviser. The SWECs were chaired by the British Advisers, who had the local army brigadier and the local chief of police, together with other officials, to plan and organize operations ostensibly at the behest of the Director of Operations.

These arrangements were not proving to be effective. General Briggs, a most experienced and able officer, saw clearly that the solution was the control of supplies to the bandits in the jungle. He therefore planned to concentrate the Chinese settlers, who normally supplied the bandits, into defended villages from which they could no longer do so. However, he had not sufficient authority to enforce his plan and it was not being carried out. The supreme head of the country was the British High Commissioner who, though kept fully informed, was perhaps aloof from the Direction of Operations.

The assassination of Sir Henry Gurney in October, 1951, in

broad daylight, on his way to take a short holiday in the hill station at Frazer's Hill, caused quite a furore. The Prime Minister, Winston Churchill, before dispatching General Sir Gerald Templer to take over, said to him, 'You will have absolute power, but use it sparingly.'

It is said that the General said, *sotto voce*, 'Like hell I will.'

General Templer brought out his own nominee to command the troops, in the shape of Hughie Stockwell, in place of Roy Urquhart, who left to take over the command in Austria. The new General would still not really have operational responsibilities for his soldiers but would work hand in glove with the High Commissioner, who would also be Director of Operations. As before, operations would be run by the SWEC, but from now on a real sense of emergency would be breathed upon all and sundry, and woe betide the laggards.

Gerald Templer was not the average person's idea of a likeable, lovable man. Soon after his arrival he was sweeping through the whole country like the wrath of God. Surrounded with an escort of armoured cars, he travelled at speed and other road users must haste to make way. His destinations were kept highly secret and only those who really needed to know knew his plans, but after he had been anywhere, few forgot his visit. His aim was to win the hearts and minds of the people – all the people – Chinese, Malays, Indians and British. But first he had to be respected and admired. He was right to make everyone fear him a little, too. There was no way that the Emergency could be overcome by half-measures. He himself worked about eighteen hours a day and it was said that the lights at King's House, where he lived in Kuala Lumpur, never went out. His subordinates had to do likewise and put away their golf clubs, etc. for the duration.

'Bandits don't play golf,' was reported to be one of his witticisms. This remark evinced a cartoon in the *Straits Times* depicting a bandit teeing up in a clearing in the jungle, equipped with home-made clubs, giggling, 'Little does he know.'

I believe this was Sir Gerald's favourite cartoon, the original of which he had framed.

Major-General Lancelot Perowne arrived to take over from George Collingwood. He was a sapper who had fought with the Chindits in Burma and was unorthodox in many ways. He had a most delightful German wife called Trudy. He was also to be the Major-General Brigade of Gurkhas, which might prove to be a difficult business because he would be the first non-Gurkha to be so appointed, and wanted to become imbued with all things Gurkha. Colonel 'Guinea' Graham was his adviser as Colonel of the Brigade.

Meanwhile, I had problems over getting Jean out to join me. Married quarters were scarce and any other sort of accommodation almost impossible. Unless one could have a guarantee of somewhere for her to live, the Services would not provide transit. At last Jean managed to book a passage on a small P & O cargo boat which brought her safely and comfortably to Penang, where I was able to meet her and drive her down. George Collingwood most kindly looked after us both for a few days and then the local bank manager housed us until we were able to move into a newly built quarter, which was one of six in a minor housing estate called Ridgeway.

Even while we were moving in, news came that my mother was mortally ill at home. I was flown straight back, arriving in time to talk to her before she died. As was the case with many Army families, we had been apart more often than together, especially during my formative years when she had been in India with my father, while my sister and I had been left to the care of relatives. This must have been a terrible quandary for so many parents similarly placed, when the quickest possible journey between India and the UK was three weeks. Nevertheless, my mother had managed to do everything possible for us, so that we had a most happy childhood, spending holidays with large families, presided over by devoted nannies of the old school.

However, having buried Mama, it was proving difficult to get back to my wife and the job in Malaya. Although I had been flown out three months before at highest priority, and back again even more urgently, I would now have to take my turn. The Movement people could not understand why I should want to get back again so quickly. 'Don't you want to be in England?' they asked, and could not believe my responding, 'No.'

In the end, I was put aboard a York, a terribly noisy, uncomfortable RAF machine, which made three night stops, Malta, Bombay and Calcutta. I was never more thankful for anything in my life than to arrive back in Seremban to find Jeannie in good health and full of the joys of spring.

In the meantime, she had got herself a job typing for the Executive Secretary of the SWEC in Negri Sembilan, which she much enjoyed.

I arrived back to find the headquarters in turmoil. It had been decided that the General, with the whole of G branch, would move south to Johore to conduct operations in that state, which was now the worst in the whole country. I, myself, the A/Q, with the rest of the headquarters would stay at Seremban, some two hundred miles away. It was obvious that this was going to be difficult, for many of the problems which would need the General's decision could not be discussed on the telephone, while letters would take too long and signals be too complex. This meant that I would have to go down to Johore at least once a week. I could drive, go by train, fly Malayan Airways from Kuala Lumpur to Singapore, which meant an extra hour of travelling at each end, or fly in light aircraft more or less from door to door. Sometimes the weather made the latter a trifle hazardous, but I could drop in to visit other units on the way, so it had many advantages. There was a high-powered meeting at Kuala Lumpur once a month which I always had to attend, and Templer himself nearly always spoke to us all about the situation.

At all the headquarters up and down the land the morning's work invariably began with what were known as 'morning prayers' in the operations room, which held vast maps of the terrain. Here details were given of the activities of the enemy and our own troops, right down to the most minor operation and patrol, so at least everyone knew what was going on.

Although we were virtually fighting a war, peacetime accounting and procedures were enforced. All the nuts and bolts had to be entered on some sort of document and woe betide the unit which allowed their equipment or vehicles to deteriorate just because they were on active service. Some units understood this and some did not and the one that didn't caused much extra work for the administrative staff. Courts of Inquiry had to sit in all cases where the blame for loss or damage could not readily be ascribed. Courts-martial had to pronounce on most cases of indiscipline.

Confidential reports were required for all, and in addition to the very high level of operational efficiency obviously required, the Army was called upon to play a full part in ceremonial parades when asked to do so.

Like the Cameronians, all the infantry battalions were deployed in company camps throughout the country. Some of these were of necessity fairly primitive, but as they often had to be occupied for several months or even years, they had to have all the essentials of life. Fortunately, there were no cold weather periods, so that the same conditons applied throughout the year. When the upper hand was gained over the bandits in an area, the troops there would be moved to more unsettled places. It was my job to see that, when necessary, a new camp was built and that everything needed was supplied. A most interesting and fascinating assignment.

At that time we still had a conscript army and practically none of the young National Servicemen was married. A few families belonging to the more senior regular element were kept concentrated in family quarters in places like Kuala Lumpur and Singapore, the husbands being able to visit them quite frequently. This meant that the British battalions could be moved fairly easily, as opposed to the Gurkha battalions, who had their families with them at the main battalion headquarter location. Nowadays, British regular battalions have collected great numbers of families and if these were to accompany the husbands for a three-year overseas posting, there would be problems and great expense involved. However, it seems unlikely that a Malay-type situation will ever arise again.

The National Serviceman is seldom given the credit due for the standards he achieved, but many of them were superior to the regulars living alongside. Among them were the best as well as the not so good and it will often be found that men tend to follow the example of the best rather than the worst. Here, in Malaya, in the most arduous conditions, some of the British conscript battalions could outscore the long-service, highly professional Gurkha Battalions against most elusive targets. Indeed, in our time, the Suffolk Regiment were way out ahead. To be successful, a unit had to be able to obtain the vital information, then to assimilate it, to act on it with the utmost possible speed, to adopt the most adroit measures required and finally to be able to shoot straight. Not all units were good at all these things.

In addition to the emergency, 17 Gurkha Division had a contingency role in the north, should an enemy advance southwards from Thailand. This seemed to be most unlikely, but in this matter we had to agree plans made by the Ministry of Defence in the UK, filtered through HQ Farelf, then Malaya Command, and finally down to us. Unfortunately, we found it impossible to agree with most of the aspects. So now the arguments had to be shuttled to and fro and a lot of unnecessary work was involved. I could never understand why detailed plans for such things had to be made in London at all. It would seem so much more logical, if it was decided that 17 Gurkha Division were the people who would have to do something, to tell them what it was and make them plan it with the resources available. They could then say if they thought it was feasible, or if not why not. London could always tell them to do it notwithstanding.

I always liked the story of the Duke of Wellington, who, when asked to nominate someone to capture Rangoon, named a general of whom he was known to have a poor opinion, but when questioned, he said, 'So he is a fool, and a damned fool, but he is the man to take Rangoon.'

Our off-duty hours were spent pleasantly enough. Our quarter was nicely sited, looking out over a river and a plain. All the windows opened but had shutters, and we relied on fans to keep the air circulating. At first we had a Chinese cook and amah, later, one period with an Indian and his consort. He was superb in his own way and his curries were memorable. But the Chinese couples were hard to beat. For them nothing was too much trouble, and it never mattered how many extra came to dine at the last moment or how many dropped in for drinks.

The Sungei Ujong Club attracted people from all over the countryside. Like all such places, the bar was the centrepiece and rubber planters would drop in from the outback and park their weapons on the counter before giving an order. Saturday nights would see a distinct change, with all the members in evening dress dancing to a proper band. The tennis courts were kept to a high standard and people like Neil Fraser, an Australian ex-champion, sometimes played on them.

It was apt to rain quite often just as evenings were approaching, but the courts drained in a trice and the sudden showers left the atmosphere cool and cleansed.

A six-hole golf course was built while we were there and this made a good alternative to the tennis. It was patronized by all four races, like all the other games in Malaya. In the last foursome I played before leaving, I partnered a local State Malay Prime Minister against a Chinese businessman and a bearded Sikh doctor.

Port Dickson, a seaside resort, was less than a hour's drive from Seremban and we spent nearly every Sunday there. The conditions were almost the same on Christmas Day as they were at mid-summer. There was a sailing club which provided dinghies of the Australian 'Idle Along' class and there were races and regattas on most weekends. I became the Vice Commodore, for the lack of anyone more accomplished, and when people asked me what I did in Malaya, I was tempted to say, 'I am the Vice Commodore of the Port Dickson Yacht Club'.

Apart from the occasional storm, the sea was calm and balmy and very warm. There was a very pleasant little social club where we drank after sailing; the only problem being how and when to break away from those who continued drinking until their lunch merged into their dinner.

In very little time Jean had a garden growing round our house in Seremban, in which the blooms soon attracted butterflies. I had been a keen schoolboy collector and now I began again. There were places in the country where they were prolific. When travelling by road, I took a net with me and when I had a Gurkha orderly, I had nets for him and the Malay driver as well. Whenever I saw a prized specimen on the roadside, I would shout stop, and out we would all jump to try to catch the insect.

There was excellent snipe shooting on all the old tin tailings, which were often waterlogged. The birds would fly off at various angles as we approached but come whizzing back at different heights when they thought that we had gone. Baba, my Malay driver, had a sixth sense at retrieving and before long Prem Bahadur, my Gurkha orderly, was almost as good. One day when we were about to start beside a Malay village, Baba beckoned me over to see something and there was a huge python lying up, I suppose in the hope of bagging a pig. We watched it fascinated for a little while, then perhaps it sensed us, for the muscles in the great back tensed and it was away. Not a pleasant customer to blunder into but quite magnificent to see.

In February, 1953, Jean and I were granted an indulgence passage for a fortnight's leave in Ceylon. The voyage was quite a pleasant change but we found Ceylon disappointing. The Galle Face Hotel at Mount Lavinia was overrated. I was stung by a very poisonous something on the beach and was in agony for a few hours. Up in Nuwara Eriya, at the Hill Club, we found everyone a trifle unfriendly until we were about to leave, when they said that they had thought that we were a honeymoon couple who would want to be left to ourselves. It was nice to get back to the rough hurly-burly of the emergency in Malaya.

Now considerable effort was going to be diverted to celebrating the Coronation of our Queen in London. As the Garrison Commander in Seremban, I had to arrange and command a monster parade at which the salute would be taken by the Sultan of Negri Sembilan, our local state. We decided to stage a *feu de joie* as part of the ceremony and as the troops involved would include British, Malays and Gurkhas and also a contingent of police, this was going to need considerable practice. On the right of the line, instead of Royal Artillery pieces, we disposed six-pounder anti-tank guns to be fired by REME, who had to manufacture the blank ammunition. This latter ploy failed to amuse Brigadier Rupert Brazier-Creagh, the Chief of Staff at Malaya Command, he being a dyed-in-the-wool gunner officer himself.

Anyway, when came the day, it was a great success. The end of the parade coincided with news of the conquest of Mount Everest by the British team, which added considerably to the general euphoria. The British Adviser, Mervyn Sheppard, had arranged a pageant for that evening and Jean played the part of Queen Elizabeth to everyone's satisfaction.

On 7 December our daughter Caroline was born in the Military Hospital in Singapore. We had some good friends in the headquarters there, which made things easier, but there were problems facing us back in Seremban, where the amah made off and Gomez the Indian cook gave notice. Fortunately, Jean managed to find an excellent Chinese cook called Ah Lim with a Eurasian wife called Joan and these two stayed with us to the end of our tour. After some weeks, a very capable Dutch girl called Willie Ruggaveen arrived as a nanny and from then on we enjoyed domestic bliss.

Meanwhile, under the dynamic leadership of Gerald Templer, the much stricter measures were having considerable effect and it became possible to declare certain areas as 'white' or free of danger. For some time, the bandits had been rechristened 'Communist Terrorists' and now they were being driven deeper into the jungles.

The 13/18th Hussars were relieved by the 11th, the famous 'Cherrypickers', and a battalion of the Fiji Regiment came to Johore. They soon distinguished themselves on the rugger field, scoring prodigious victories and actually running down a terrorist or two on foot. They also had a wonderful choir. Their great deep male voices in harmony made unforgettable contributions to many almost impromptu concerts.

'Honker' Henniker was one of our brigadiers. He had been one of the original members of the 1st Airborne Division and now he devoted all his latent ingenuity to trying to think up ways of winning our war. Alas, most of them came to naught. There was no short cut to stopping the supplies of food. Charles Howard and Billie Burke were the other two brigade commanders. Malaya was not much of a stamping ground for senior officers. All the really successful actions were initiated and carried out at platoon or perhaps company level. Whenever large-scale sweeps were arranged at the behest of higher authority, they nearly always proved to be a waste of time.

During 1954 the Templers left Malaya for home. Lady Templer had worked with might and main and had done much to help her husband to win the hearts and minds of the people. The emergency was by no means over when they left, but he had reversed a downward trend, giving everyone a thorough shake-up and finally pointed them all in the right direction and made certain that they took it.

The farewell of the Templer family from Malaya was a quite unforgettable experience. General Geoffrey Bourne had already arrived to take over as Director of Operations and as GOC Malaya, so he was able to command personally the Guard of Honour assembled. All the Sultans from all the States, all the Chinese and Indian notables, and absolutely everyone from the British community were lined up to see them go. As the great man and his great lady walked slowly down, shaking hands with them all, there were tears and nods rather than words. There was no more to be said. They boarded the aircraft while the band played. One last salute from him and then they were off. We all felt that something quite splendid had gone.

General Sir Geoffrey Bourne was no ordinary person. He had lost an arm in a motor accident before the war but had managed to play a full part in everyday life. Despite his disability, he could play tennis and golf and shoot very straight. He was a most reelaxed and cosy character with a ready smile and an apposite quip to put people at ease. As a headquarters, 17 Gurkha Division's relationships with headquarters Malaya had not been easy. Hughie Stockwell and my General Lance Perowne never saw eye to eye and when that sort of thing happens, the underlings on the staffs tend to take their cue from their masters.

Now, with the advent of a new man as our immediate superior, I hoped that all our relationships could take a turn for the better, and so they did for a little while. But before long vituperative letters began to flow. I did my best and even tore up some that Lance Perowne had meant to send but, in the circumstances in which we lived, people are always apt to be on tenterhooks. Aspersions are seen where none are meant and now and again snarls begin to take over from smiles.

I had been doing my best to make the HQ proud of itself. I thought it appropriate that, being a Gurkha establishment in which all the major infantry had their pipe bands, when we had a guest night in the Officers' Mess, pipers should play, as they did in the battalion's messes. I managed to get this custom established with some difficulty, because many of the officers hated the idea of any guest nights at all. I commissioned Katherine Sim, a local artist, to paint pictures of all the different types of soldiers we had in the division. There were contrasting British Infantry, Cavalry, Gurkhas, Malays, Fijians and Iban trackers from Borneo, so it was quite a motley collection. Having discovered that the local sanitary squad could make tennis courts from laterite just as easily as they could kill the mosquitoes in their breeding places, I arranged that they should build four excellent courts in the gardens outside the Mess, which I had also designed. In the end, the whole Mess complex looked rather nice.

Meanwhile, the Police Special Branch were becoming more skilful and, with each success, they gained further sources of information and did better than ever. The helicopter squadron manned by the Royal Navy became more adept at getting troops into deeper jungle and 22 SAS were beginning to pay dividends. They developed a technique of parachuting deliberately into the jungle trees and subsequently lowering themselves to the ground. On the face of it a most hazardous undertaking, but surprisingly few casualties resulted. Later the SAS, under Tony Deane-Drummond, became really expert at living in the jungle and were able to bring the terrorists under constant pressure. I believe that finally their score of successes made them the champion unit of the whole emergency.

Staff officers had to travel about on visits unescorted. It was best to use a civilian car and discard uniforms as far as possible, though often this had to be put on to gain entry to the military establishments. The main central road had a bad reputation during the height of the troubles and there was one particular place known as 'Windy Corner'. Once, when approaching this with Lester Allan, the D/Q Quartering, I felt my hackles rise and said, 'Step on it', but nothing untoward happened and we arrived safely at Segamat. Ten minutes later news came that the ration lorry convoy had been ambushed at Windy Corner. The enemy must have been there as we drove past.

The most unpleasant drive I ever had was after I had stopped to pick up a very badly injured Indian. It was a public holiday and unless I took him with me there was no way of getting him to hospital. I had him put in the back of the staff car, telling my driver Baba to hold him. The poor chap was in agony with his ribs stove in and kept asking me to knock him out. Baba didn't help much by laughing. The duty nurse wasn't pleased to have another emergency case: a man with half his bottom bitten off by a crocodile had just come in. I went round the next day to see how the Indian was, to be told by the same nurse, 'Oh, he died.'

Towards the end of our tour, in 1955, we had two bits of good news. One that I had been given a brevet lieutenant-colonelcy and the other that I had been appointed to be Commandant of the Support Weapons Wing of the School of Infantry as a full colonel. Unfortunately, we could not all go home together, as the family had to sail in a troopship and I had to wait to hand over to my successer and follow by air. We arrived back to the full vigour of the English winter.

CHAPTER XI

NETHERAVON

WE WERE TO HAVE SEVERAL MONTHS' LEAVE as my next job at Netheravon did not start till the autumn. Luckily my parents-in-law had a most beautiful large house near Liphook and we were able to settle down to enjoy this. The gardens and grounds were quite lovely with tennis court and swimming pool in perfect settings. I worked hard at my golf, playing on the Liphook course practically every day.

Jean and I flew to Tunisia in the spring where that country was in something of a turmoil. The then French Government intended to grant self-rule which was bitterly opposed by most of the French farmers and settlers. The French Army were busy, but very successfully keeping the peace.

We were able to revisit all my old battlefields of 1942–3 and find some of the people who had been kind to us, including a family who had given us eggs and bacon with champagne when the Battalion were hard pressed at five o'clock in the morning.

The whole country looked lovely and was quite unspoiled then. I think that there were no other British tourists but us. The only people we met socially were the Archdeacon and the Consul-General. Finding that the memorial that had been erected in the Tamera Valley to commemorate the 1st Parachute Brigade was being vandalized, we made arrangements to have it moved into the Anglican Church in Tunis. We photographed much of the ground the 2nd Battalion had fought over but most of the hills were too much for me now and at other places the trees had grown to disguise what had been familiar before.

We returned to continue living a most comfortable life at Waterside until it was time to start soldiering again in the autumn of 1955.

Then, most sadly, Philip Lyle, my father-in-law, became very ill and died. He had been quite wonderful to both of us. A kindly, loving, gentle person. Not very long before he became ill he had said, 'I have got everything just as I want it now.' One had so hoped that he would have been able to continue enjoying it for many years to come.

So we went to Netheravon. Our quarter, though unfortunately backing on to a main road, faced almost due south overlooking the Avon Valley. It was largish but not really solid and would obviously be difficult to keep warm. However, it could not have been more convenient from its proximity to my work. While we were moving in with all the kerfuffle involved, Jean developed jaundice. She could not bear to be elsewhere at a time like this, so had to sit about miserably among the packing cases directing the placing of our furniture as best she could.

We arrived as winter approached in 1955 to take over the Support Weapons Wing of the School of Infantry from Colonel Hal Deane. I had been highly delighted on being told of this posting. I had always been interested in the fire effect of weapons and now Hal Deane assured me that being Commandant at Netheravon was one of the most pleasant jobs that the Army could provide. However, it was not likely to last very long because it had been decided that the Infantry was to be streamlined so that it became a much simpler and much less expensive arm, equipped on a rifle and light automatic basis.

The role of the infantry 3-inch mortar would be taken over by the gunners, their guns being quite capable of providing all the overhead and indirect fire support required. The anti-tank responsibility would devolve on to the Royal Armoured Corps, whose tanks were far more effective at destroying enemy tanks than the infantry anti-tank guns. Medium machine guns would remain as long as General Sir Richard Gale, that great lover of the Vickers, was in the Army. However, as soon as he went, so would the famous old man-killer weapon.

I was horrified to hear this. I had been serving in Malaya during the past three years, well away from current Army gossip. I now learnt that there were few in high places who really believed that one could afford to strip the infantry of their own intimate close support, but needs must when financial savings are called for by the politicians. Economies there had to be and the surrender of so many weapons looked good on paper. Careers must not be jeopardized, come what might.

I had been an airborne soldier throughout most of the war and had often been left to suffer dearly as a result of the lack of close support. I knew that whatever assurances were made, support from other arms was often lacking at the crucial time and place and all the lessons and every experience had shown how vital it was for the infantry to be as self-contained as possible. Moreover it was accepted by all experienced infantrymen that they themselves suffered and inflicted more casualties with mortars than with any other weapons. As for anti-tank, there had been many occasions when small numbers of infantry anti-tank guns had seen off greater numbers of German tanks, while our own tanks had been defeated time and time again by the enemy's SPs and 'eighty-eights'.

I determined to do all I could to defend the infantry's weapons. My first priority was anti-tank. It was the most endangered. The current armament was the BAT, the letters standing for Battalion Anti-Tank. It was a clumsy-looking thing with a heavy shield of steel attached to protect the crew from small arms fire and splinters. One's first thought was to do away with this in order to reduce the weight and make it easier to handle. At the time, the Chief Instructor Anti-Tank was Major Philip Salusbury-Trelawny and the officer in charge of research and development was Lieutenant-Colonel Alan Lane. These two could see no reason why the shield should not be stripped from one of the guns – so we did this and immediately seemed to have a much more lively weapon with all-round traverse. Moreover, we had obviated the requirement for the heavy generator needed to traverse the bat at all.

We had been lent one of the latest American anti-tank guns. This was very much smaller, being 106 millimetre calibre, as opposed to the bat's 120 millimetres. Both were recoilless with the breach open to the rear. As much of the force of the explosion came out backwards, there was no recoil and so the heavy recuperators needed on the normal artillery piece, to counteract recoil, could be dispensed with. Of course there was a penalty to be paid. This lay in the weight of a round of ammunition which needed a sufficient charge not only to propel the shell forwards but also to discharge backwards against the atmosphere to balance the propulsive effort needed for the main task. Thus the weight of the bat round was 80 pounds and the handling of any number of these created problems.

The warhead was normally of High Explosive Squash Head (hesh). The missile, when it hit a tank, squashed itself against the armour, developing a terrific explosive force that made metal scabs come off the inside of the armour which whirled about inside the tank to the detriment of the crew and any equipment inside. Moreover the crump was likely to upset the setting of the radio and damage the armament, so any armoured vehicle hit by a round of hesh would not be very effective thereafter, quite apart from the near certainty that any such vehicle would be set on fire.

The American gun had a coaxially mounted .5 inch machine gun which fired a special explosive round matched to the trajectory of the main armament. This simple device enabled the gunner to establish the range to the target without disclosing the position of the gun. As soon as a hit was obtained, the gunner fired the 106mm and a hit was virtually assured. (This principle will now be familiar to many who have seen the ranging gun on Chieftain.) We were unable to get a .5 machine gun for our weapon but, as luck would have it, we found that the trajectory of the Bren was almost identical to that of the 120mm. Although we had no explosive 'spotting' ammunition, we also discovered that ordinary tracer served pretty well.

So we seemed to be in business.

We christened it the mobat. The idea behind this was that it was much more mobile than the bat. It could be towed more easily and manhandled into position much more easily. We got no thanks or encouragement from any quarter. Infantry anti-tank was on the way out, they all said; moreover, the flash from the rear of the gun would be even more pronounced without the shield. We tested this and were able to prove that as the gun would, or should, always be sited in an enfilade position, the attachment or otherwise of the shield had no effect. But, compared to the conventional anti-tank guns, ie the 6-pounders and the 17-pounders, or the German 88 millimetre, the flash was much reduced and it would be much more difficult for the enemy tank crews to locate our gun than had been the case with these earlier weapons. We took coloured films and photographs to prove our point but nearly all our pleading fell on deaf ears.

However, two bright young officers at Fort Halstead got in touch and said that they were most interested in what we had been doing and would like to see if they could design a gun of much lighter materials but with the same calibre as ours, and they did. In a remarkably short time they produced a prototype. This could be fitted with either the Bren or the .5 and the results were most impressive. Gradually we were wearing down the opposition. 1st British Corps in Germany, who were faced with the actual problem of dealing with large numbers of Russian tanks if the Warsaw Pact advanced, took a much more realistic view of the infantry anti-tank problem than the Military or the theorists at home. Even Lieutenant-General Pyman, a dedicated tank man, commanding the Corps, was interested and invited us to demonstrate.

General acceptance soon followed and approval was given for the conversion of all bats to mobats. We were to teach the mobat and an issue of .5 machine guns, to take the place of the Brens, followed later.

It just went to show that, if you believed, all doors could be opened unto you. We were still not popular with our immediate superiors. One day Philip Trelawny told me that we must now think of a name for the new gun from Fort Halstead. I remember saying: 'Something that conjures up more mobility than the mobat. Even more mobile. Let me see now, more, more, worm, wormbat, wombat. There you are, what about wombat?' Philip was delighted and that is how the weapon actually came to be named.

I have since then seen an article in which it said that the name derived from the amount of magnesium that was put into the metal from which the gun was made. So it was Weapon of Magnesium and thus wombat. Not as far as I am concerned, it wasn't. I do not know how much magnesium was involved but, whatever it was, it was not nearly so important as the weapon's relative lightness and therefore mobility through ease of handling and so on.

The effect of the big hesh round on concrete or any other form of defensive work was 'smashing'. There could be no doubt that as an assault gun for the infantry we had a winner – once again most unpopular, as assault guns were not in the book. Recently, during the Falklands campaign, 2 Para used the current anti-tank weapon, the wire-guided missile, or Milan, against Argentine prepared positions with devastating effect, thereby saving the lives of many of their own men who would have fallen if the orthodox assault techniques had been used. The snag to the wire-guided weapon is that it is almost impossible to control at night. Provided that the battlefield can be illuminated, the wombat can perform.

The 120mm round could be hesh, conventional high explosive, or canister, the old-fashioned grapeshot, which is devastating against large numbers of enemy infantry at short range. By fitting a machine-gun dial sight on to the wombat, we had excellent results at targets up to 4,000 metres away when firing indirect with the gun well hidden from view. This made us very unpopular with the School of Artillery for we were here impinging on their role. Nevertheless we felt it right and proper to get the utmost possible use out of what the taxpayer had provided.

Needless to say, we tried out, proved and then advocated the mounting of the gun to a carrier as an alternative means of bringing it into battle, but firm approval for this was not forthcoming either.

It seemed ridiculous to even have to consider the case for the retention of the infantry mortars. They were and are such a simple means of damaging an enemy without having to incur danger and, during lulls in more active events, an ideal means of keeping the foe aware of one's hostile intentions. The only problem is and always has been the supply of relatively heavy ammunition. When this has to be carried up hills and down dales, the bearers are apt to curse their loads and feel that there must be easier ways of killing than this.

All who have been at the receiving end of the enemy mortars well know how vicious, unpredictable and casualty-making they can be. Except at night there is very little flash from the weapon and no smoke. The sound of the firing is more of a dull hollow thud than a gun blast and even when their positions can be located they are relatively easy to move to alternative positions where they can be dug in and concealed again. Apart from the skills of a very small number of the crew, the duties are simplicity itself and replacements can be trained in the field with scant delay.

The currently supplied British 3-inch weapon was clumsy and

inaccurate compared to the American 81 millimetre, which also had a greater range. Our 3-inches could be replaced at a minimal cost and, with this rearrangement, our infantry would become much more formidable. We worked out a drill of easing the work of those who had to dig the mortar pits by blowing a small charge of the requisite proportion before the work began, and we designed an umbrella-type camouflage apparatus which could easily and speedily be used to protect the weapon from view, and incidentally the weather.

Apart from the lethal effectiveness of the mortar, its ability to lay a smoke screen at almost immediate notice is a most important factor in helping infantry to cross open spaces in the face of the enemy. I suppose if gas ever came to be used again, the mortar might well be one of the most effective means of introducing it. I never met a soldier who fought through the war who would willingly denude his formation of its services.

All detailed accounts of the fighting in the Falklands campaign confirm all the claims made on the weapon's behalf and its one limiting factor, namely the supply of the ammunition, should be greatly alleviated, if not overcome, by the increasing availability of helicopters in the years to come.

Which brings me to the last of the threatened weapons – the medium machine gun which had dominated the First World War on the Western front and in German hands had practically stultified movement across open country in daylight. In those days they had had to be water-cooled, which added weight to their portage, but by the outbreak of the Second World War the Germans were achieving similar results with an air-cooled successor. We had to go through the whole war before we developed a gun that could withstand the rates of fire needed.

Anyway, when I arrived, the old 1914 Vickers water-cooled weapon was still very much in our armoury and there could be no doubt that in the hands of the well-trained it was still a most formidable man-killer. But, the gun numbers had to be skilled. When I had been with the Iraq Levies, we were armed with them and so were the RAF Armoured Car Squadron. At the annual rifle meeting, which included an event for the Vickers, the performance of the airmen was almost a cause for despair, while that of the Levies was superb. It was a difficult piece.

We in the Levies had the time available to master it – the RAF had not.

As a part of official War Office policy, efforts were made to disparage the gun by noising it abroad that its claimed ability to deliver indirect fire from concealed positions at a distance was untrue. So, to disprove this, I set up a group of four guns 4,000 yards from a target area which could be easily observed by interested spectators and invited them to watch while the guns engaged. You could hardly hear the guns from the distance but suddenly, as from thin air, the hail of bullets arrived, bang on target and no one could say exactly where from. It was most convincing but there were doubters still. While we were doing this, General Sir Richard Gale, the C-in-C Rhine Army, himself a most distinguished machine gunner, laid on a much bigger demonstration. Unfortunately, one of the spectators was killed and even today we can only surmise that his death was caused by the collision of two bullets in the air. However, the accident did nothing to minimize the lethal reputation of the famous old gun.

In all the major phases of war, the advance, the attack, the defence and the withdrawal – although one hopes that one's campaign will not progress in that sequence – the recognition and elimination of targets which are highly dangerous to one's own troops requires the utmost effort accurately and skilfully applied as quickly as possible. This means that one should be able to apply the effect of all possible weapons for the purpose at all times. A major mistake is to think that this means that the weapons themselves must be kept concentrated to do the job, but this is to invite recognition by the enemy with subsequent elimination of their potential.

Modern communications should always allow of the weapons being dispersed, relatively undetected and therefore secure, while their fire effect can be brought to bear at the crucial time and place.

I had been able to prove this contention in one particular battle in Tunisia when my battalion had been attacked by two enemy battalions, while we were holding a very extended front. Our medium machine guns and mortars, though widely dispersed, were controlled by the Support Company Commander sitting beside me at Battalion HQ. In fact, we virtually won the whole battle. Only the most forward sections of the rifle companies had to use their weapons to push the enemy into the areas where they could be punished by our supporting ones and, after that, all we had to do was to lay on an infantry right hook in the dark to round up the remnants. Admittedly the opposition were not top class but the results were two hundred casualties to them, as against two to us. At that time we were supported by French artillery who had no communications at all, so we had to leave them out of our calculations.

I became convinced that it was reprehensible not to take every possible measure to be able to concentrate the effect of the supporting fire available and we therefore designed a battalion fire control centre, which could be sited alongside the battalion HQ, and from which the commanding officer, or anyone else, could direct the fire of the MMGs, the mortars, the anti-tank guns, the supporting artillery, the supporting tanks and the air forces, if any.

I tried this out and found that it was perfectly feasible to switch all or part of what was on offer, depending on the type of enemy needing attention. The targets were called for by observers with the forward companies, as is normally done, the difference being that they could now be engaged by many more and more suitable weapons than is the case if all they could call upon was their own allotted section of particular weapons. One criticism was that the system would be vulnerable to any successful enemy strike upon the centre. This is valid, but it was never envisaged that the weapons would be completely tied and if the course of the battle were to be such that control was slipping, then all concerned would quite clearly be free to do the next best thing. In other words, engage the enemy wherever he was to be seen.

I discussed this centralized fire control with many others. The Americans and the Germans entirely agreed at that time. Most adamant were the Israelis. I propounded my ideas at the Infantry Conference at Warminster and the brightest among the brigadiers were keen to try it. Funnily enough, it was the artillery who were most against it. They were afraid of losing their special position as advisers to the infantry commander. They could not see that they could use the system as much to their own advantage, by being able to concentrate their fire on what was most suitable.

My own boss was Brigadier Geoffrey Musson, who, even though I got him to work our system successfully in practice, said, 'I still do not believe in it.' But by then the dictat had gone forth and he was not going to kick against the pricks.

When the 1st Parachute Brigade went to war in Tunisia, we had had our support weapons decentralized out to the rifle companies and we quickly brought them together in the light of experience.

Now there was one particular GSO2 in the Infantry Directorate at the Ministry at this time who was quite determined that the right answer was to have company groups of infantry each with their own support weapons. Although he had no experience, superior logic or reasoning to back his argument, he won the day and for a time a firm decision was taken to have the weapons decentralized to the rifle companies.

Despite all the controversy about our weapons, the courses continued to be run and we continued to qualify instructors for the rest of the Army. Our own instructors were members of the Small Arms School Corps, a body of most carefully selected non-commissioned officers from the infantry. They were all literally outstanding as teachers, who could make the most mundane subject of vital interest and inspire the most backward student to greater efforts. Nearly all the work was practical. Parts of the weapons being taught, or the complete weapons, were always available and had to be handled. Thus even the shortest verbal instruction would be followed by the order, 'Now do that,' and it had to be done to the satisfaction of the instructor by all the members of the squad. The next order would be, 'Now teach me to do it.'

The rest of the squad would then be invited to criticize the performance of the squad teacher. By this means, and relentless repetition, all concerned were forced to get to know their subjects backwards. Anyone failing to come up to scratch during the working hours would be most strongly advised to spend his leisure hours punching up and there were few who failed to take that advice.

The ranges for the various weapons were adjacent to the School, so little time was wasted in travelling and students had plenty of opportunities of firing the weapons they would subsequently have to teach. The School had always had a reputation for extracting high standards from its customers and we did all we could to maintain this.

★

The main part of the School of Infantry was at Warminster, a few miles away. When I arrived, the Commandant was Cosmo Nevill. He was a most charming and amusing Royal Fusilier, who never seemed to take anything very seriously. At any rate he always delightfully pooh-poohed all the talk about the abolition of our support weapons. The GOC Southern Command was Lieutenant-General Sir Eric Down, who was also a staunch supporter. He had commanded the 1st Airborne Division for a time in Italy and in the UK and had rightly earned a reputation for integrity 'par excellence'. He gave me every encouragement.

Our School at Netheravon was very much part of the village and had been for a great many years. Soon after I arrived, the local vicar came to see me with a plea for support. His congregation on his advent only a few weeks before had slipped to a mere handful and practically nobody from the School ever attended. Would I now please set an example and read the lessons on Sundays as often as possible? I could hardly say no, and very soon regular attendance became a habit and indeed a pleasurable one. Roger Irwin, the incumbent, was a most willing, amusing and attractive man, ably supported by a like-minded cheerful wife, and once they had got started, the congregation soon multiplied. Before very long, many more people both in the School and the village took an interest, so that the weekly service followed by local drink parties was a focal event for bringing people together.

The lovely old Georgian mansion which served as our Officers' Mess was a bonus, as were the gardens, which included some well-kept grass tennis courts. In the grounds stood one of the biggest dovecotes ever built and I got myself into considerable trouble with some authorities for bringing it back into its proper use. The River Avon ran through the lands with the fishing lovingly tended by Sawyer, a most famous riparian, so much so that the rods were much sought after. There was also a well-established shoot. Pheasants were put into what coverts there were, but as there was no full-time keeper available, they never came to very much. However, there was an abundance of wild partridges which required no tending at all. The main difficulty was to get them to fly over the guns, for most of the shooting was over the ranges, which were without hedges or barriers of any kind. The speeds and aerobatic skills achieved by the coveys were often more than a match for many of the inexperienced guns, so that there was always a very healthy stock to carry on for the next day or season.

When soldiers from the Brigade of Gurkhas began to attend courses, many of them gladly volunteered to come out as beaters. This was a great advantage for they dearly loved the game. In fact they welcomed any activity that brought them into touch with other people. Being determined to succeed in everything they undertook, they were always keen to better their use of English. They were all given three months with a family in England before the courses began so that they could learn enough to take in the instruction. To polish up their linguistic ability, they soon learnt to play darts in the local, where they could pick up all the jargon too.

I bought a horse to hunt with the Royal Artillery Hounds on the plain but found that I had lost my enthusiasm of pre-war days and now the Tidworth Polo Club restarted playing in the summer months. A gunner, Lieutenant-Colonel John Pallot, was the first chairman, ably supported by Brigadier Jack Cardale, a Sapper. In the offing were two great players, in the shape of Gerald Balding of international fame and John Morrison, who later became Lord Margadale. There were about a dozen keen members and I soon managed to buy two reasonable ponies. I sequestered the stables at Syrencote House, which was almost within my domain. The Parachute Regiment very kindly lent me a groom and so I was in business.

We exercised the ponies before working hours every day. One of the local farmers let me make a 'stick and ball' ground on one of his grass fields and Smith, my groom, would hack the ponies across the ranges to Tidworth on polo days. Just beyond Tidworth were all-weather grounds at Perham Down and at first there was only one ground in action at Tidworth in front of the old Tattoo stands. The really lovely Fisher ground was still being grazed and therefore earning money, so it was quite a job to get it back for the polo club. When finally the argument was won, I brought over the mowing machines from Netheravon to cut the grass down to a playable level. I only had to do it once; thereafter Tidworth Garrison felt constrained.

Everything gradually fell into place. Brigadier Dick Hobson, a 12th Lancer, was in charge of administration at Southern Command, so he was a tower of strength, as also was Major-General

Peter Gregson, who was the District Commander. He had been a Horse Gunner for much of his service and now the 3rd Regiment Royal Horse Artillery arrived on station with a string of Arab ponies that they had been playing in Libya. Although the ponies were relatively slow, they soon won a tournament or two through superior teamwork. Among their players was Paul Withers, who later won international fame.

Though relatively inexperienced and unskilled, my enthusiasm landed me with the chairmanship for the latter part of my time at Netheravon. We were given help by George Bathurst, who was then running the Cirencester Club and accepted visiting teams from us and, when we staged our own tournament, Windsor, Cowdray and other well-known clubs entered teams. Although the Tidworth Polo Club of those days could hardly claim to be one of the best, I think that we could suggest that it was perhaps the happiest.

Towards the end of our time, we heard that I was to command 44 Parachute Brigade TA. The HQ was in the Duke of York's HQ in Chelsea. There was no quarter available, so we would have to find a house.

CHAPTER XII

44 BRIGADE

THE BUSINESS OF HOUSE-HUNTING now took up much of my time. We had to leave the Grange at Netheravon when my job finished as the new Commandant had to be able to come in. Unless we could find a suitable house by that time, our furniture would have to be stored with all the resulting kerfuffle. After looking at dozens of houses, which were limited to the south-east of London because of the location of the HQ, I finally arrived outside a house called Ranworth in Oxshott which was owned by Guy Salmon, the well-known luxury car man. The agent, who was with me, said, 'He has just spent a lot of money doing this house up but by now he will be bored with it. We might just strike lucky.'

It was Saturday morning, after I had been to a regimental dinner in London. Guy Salmon answered the door himself. He was not pleased at the agent's inquiry as to whether the house was for sale.

'What on earth made you think that?' he said. 'We have only just made it habitable. Well anyway, it will do no harm for you to have a look around.'

So we did. I loved it, although I knew that Jean would not like all that Guy Salmon had done. It was a lovely Lutyens-style house, facing towards the sun with nice big rooms surrounded with well-designed gardens, with a swimming pool and woodlands reaching down to a stream; completely private for such a relatively built-up part of the world and all a bit bigger than we needed, but still.

Guy Salmon said, 'Well it is not really for sale, but if you could make up your mind straight away, I might sell.'

I went back to Netheravon to tell Jean and we returned together on the Monday. She liked it. So we bought it and never regretted our rather hasty decision. Anyway we now had somewhere to go to on leaving Netheravon and I arranged that Billie Walsh, of the Ham Polo Club at Richmond, would take the ponies, of which the string of two had by now risen to four.

Once again there was to be a nice long gap between my two jobs, but this time I was caught by being detailed to take part in a war game at the Army Operations Research Establishment, as it was then called, at West Byfleet. I could do this while staying at Ranworth.

Like most army officers, I had never heard of this place and I knew little about War Games, except that the German and Japanese General Staffs had set great store by studying the outcome of the artificial conflicts that were arranged to represent the conditions that would apply in any military adventure they happened to be contemplating. It would take too long for me to attempt to explain just how the whole battle is set up. Infinite trouble is taken over every detail and the war begins when the two adversaries have assumed their commands. In this case I was in command of forty enemy divisions modelled on those belonging to the Warsaw Pact and my opponent disposed of the four divisions comprising the 1st British Corps.

I cannot remember the exact conditions, but each commander had to make a decision every so often, which in game time might be a day or two, but in real war would be an hour or two, so that the actual few weeks that I and my opponent had to do as much as possible harm to each other's armies would have covered some twenty-four hours of battle. Each commander had a team of assistants as his staff. These were skilled Civil Servants in real life. All the procedures were strictly governed in terms of the weapon performance as far as was known.

I was fascinated and to this day cannot think that there is any better way of studying any possible campaign that could ever be envisaged. I subsequently wrote a paper on how I felt the British Army should be organized, armed and equipped to meet the Warsaw Pact threat. As it was written some thirty years ago, it would probably be considered laughable by those who now face the problem. In those days, armour provided considerable protection from nuclear weapons but I gather that this is no longer the case.

Nevertheless, I still contend that it is the ability to concentrate fire-power that will win the battle, as opposed to the gullible's insistence on concentrating weapons and formations.

Gerald Lathbury, Lieutenant-General as he then was and about to become the Director General of Military Training, visited the ORG Establishment while I was there and went off with a copy of my paper, and I was told that it helped him to produce what was known as the 'plum-coloured pamphlet', which was the first of its kind relating to nuclear warfare in the field.

Meanwhile we were settling in at Ranworth. After living in army quarters for several years, we had become accustomed to being able to phone the Quartermaster when anything went wrong or needed attention, and he, or one of his minions, would be around in next to no time. Now we were on our own and finding that it takes quite some time for newcomers in any area to get to know those who will bring effective help or services in reasonable time and at reasonable cost when things go wrong. Luckily for us the Salmons had put everything in the house into good shape, but there were bound to be teething troubles and these could take much telephoning and cajolery to overcome.

The Army had also provided or paid for staff but in those days were ungenerous towards families who lived in their own houses, even though no alternative was offered. As Ranworth included seven acres with the gardens and seven bedrooms in the house, there was much to look after. After some weeks of discomfort, we managed to find a suitable married couple who agreed to live in the house until we could build a cottage for them in the grounds. Thereby hangs a tale, for one neighbour took great exception and managed to delay the project for many months. This involved us in a lawsuit, which fortunately we won, and trouble with the Crown Agents, which fortunately we overcame, but we were rather breathless when it was all over. Anne and Lewis Appleton from Yorkshire were the couple who were to look after us and Ranworth for many years to come.

I took over 44 Independent Parachute Brigade Group (TA) from Peter Young, a very old friend and a member of the famous old 43rd Light Infantry. My first appearance was at Brigade Indoor Exercise where they were studying mobilization and so nearly all the officers were present. Alastair Pearson, an old contemporary of the Tunisian campaign, was the Deputy Commander and there were three other full colonels who had had considerable experience, Peter Foster, George Aris and David Maude. The Brigade was well and truly spread across the kingdom. One infantry battalion covered London and the South, one the Midlands, one the Newcastle area and one Scotland. There was a gunner regiment with an HQ in London and also an engineer regiment and a signals squadron.

Most of the units were very nearly up to strength, but the turnover was rather uncomfortably high because many of those who willingly and enthusiastically joined subsequently found that it was too much for them, or their civilian commitments did not allow them to maintain the standards required. Nevertheless, the brigade group was always able to muster some 75 per cent of its paper strength, which, considering the type of man involved, made it an outstanding bonus to the nation's hard-pressed defence resources.

All the members had to qualify as parachutists under the same conditions as those applicable to the regular soldiers in airborne forces. While these had had the benefits of several weeks' training at the Aldershot Depot, the TA had had only a few weekends, based on their drill halls, and while they were living at home. Despite this great disparity in the preparation available for the two different classes of soldier, the actual results achieved sometimes made it difficult to differentiate between the two. Indeed, when one visited the RAF Training Organization at Abingdon, it was almost impossible to tell the TA and the Regular squads apart.

Such was the enthusiasm within the brigade that it was sometimes difficult to remember that one's soldiers were not comfortably tucked up in barracks and readily available for action. Yet the very real dedication of all concerned was such that they could feel disillusioned if they were not treated just as their regular counterparts and many among them were annoyed if the best possible standards were not expected.

The Headquarters was in a building called Turk's Row at the Duke of York's Headquarters. It was a scruffy old place with all the windows facing north and stone-floored passageways connecting the various offices. However, there was everything that we needed. The Brigade Major was Roger May, initially of the Hampshire

Regiment. He was an enthusiast who was also a gifted athlete. John Roberts of the Welsh Guards was the DAA and QMG, a rather outstanding character who later commanded the 2nd Parachute Battalion. Norrie Giles was the Staff Captain, a bright and unfailingly cheerful officer who would have a go at anything, and, absolutely essentially, there was an RAF Officer, Squadron Leader Gerry Brierley, who had to spend literally hours every day beseeching his superiors for an allotment of the aircraft we always so badly needed.

We were a very expensive nuisance to the Royal Air Force. Nearly all our training had to be done at weekends when they would have preferred to be uncommitted. Moreover, our activities meant that airfields had to be kept open at weekends and many of these depended on civilian labour, so there was an overtime bill. There were not many RAF Officers who were interested in what happened to the parachutists they delivered after the drop, so it was perhaps expecting quite a lot to ask them to enthuse about our aims. I tried visiting the squadron which were going to drop our soldiers before a particular exercise, but I made absolutely no impression on the young pilots and in the end could claim to have a friendly relationship with the local station commander only.

Soon after the end of the war, when we still had a complete TA Airborne Division, the RAF said that they could no longer provide aircraft at all. Claude Rome, the GOC at the time, approached the United States Air Force, who agreed to step in. This produced a change of heart by the RAF and the Division was retained for a time. Perhaps it was in fact a rather luxurious offensive adjunct to an army that was beamed almost entirely towards the defensive and few voices were raised in protest when the Division was reduced to a Brigade Group, which I had now inherited.

At this particular time, 1958, we still had a home army of several TA Divisions and many garrisons abroad to safeguard places considered of strategic value, but the nub of our defence policy was the Army in Germany, alongside our NATO partners, backed by tactical nuclear weapons. It was a trifle difficult, for even the most enthusiastic para, to envisage an airborne role for the TA Brigade in this setting. However, if one looked at the flanks of our European defence problem, it did seem that the availability of a brigade group such as 44 might be of immense value to somewhere like Norway. But whatever happened, our splendid units, provided they could be mobilized quickly, would be a tremendous asset in any role to the inevitably hard-pressed British Army of the Rhine.

It seemed to me that I had to establish a wartime role for the Brigade and demonstrate that our territorial soldiers could be available for operations as quickly as the regular soldiers in an emergency. Failing this, the airborne aspect of our way of life might gradually fade and with it everything else that made us what we were.

One of my first duties was to command the brigade at the Royal Review of the TA in Hyde Park in 1958. This should have been quite a splendid occasion but the weather intervened. It rained continuously from the time the troops formed up to the time they dismissed and so the crowds were absent. Most of the soldiers were camped in the Park, having come from all over the kingdom. There was no possibility of a postponement and we all just had to get wet. I had to have my tunic rebuilt.

There now followed three years of seemingly relentless travelling all over the UK. All the units had several sub-units in different locations, often several miles apart. They only worked in the evenings or at weekends, so if one wanted to visit each sub-unit – and this inevitably had to be done for their annual inspection – a lot of detailed planning was called for so that the visits could be dovetailed in. The spread was from Aberdeen in the north to Southsea in the south, with many of the drill halls in heavily built-up areas in the Midlands and the environs of London. Weekend exercises would be arranged in any of the Army training areas, some of which were not easy to reach. Sometimes travelling at weekends is preferable to travelling during the weekdays and sometimes not, but for me there was no option.

I nearly always used British Airways to reach Scotland, although on some occasions the night train could be more convenient; Newcastle and Durham likewise. I usually drove to anywhere in the Midlands because I could make calls on the way. Sometimes I was driven in the staff car provided and sometimes it was more convenient to drive oneself. For part of the time I owned a VW Caravanette, in which I could sleep near an Officers' Mess, if that happened to be appropriate. In this, I could carry and make changes of clothing, so it was perhaps the most convenient of all. At other times I could use a light aircraft, which would pick me up at Wisley nearby and fly right over the London airport complex without interference.

But best of all was the occasional helicopter. On the first occasion I had been given an open bit of ground on Oxshott Common, adjacent to the railway station, as the rendezvous, and after the machine had arrived and I was about to get in, a harridan came to curse. I said, 'Madam. If you read the notices pertaining to restrictions on the uses of Oxshott Common, you will see that there are many things you must not do, for instance, light fires, deposit rubbish, ride motorbikes or make music and many other things, but nowhere does it forbid helicopters.' With which I got in and flew away.

The next time when I had arranged to meet the machine at the same place, I was horrified to find the site teeming with Brownies. I explained the predicament to the woman in charge, who said, 'Do you mean to tell me that you are about to bring in a helicopter, get in and go off?'

'Yes Ma'am,' said I.

'What absolute bliss,' said she and blew a whistle, which alerted the Brownies to move aside. In I got and off I went but not before hearing the screams of approval from the Brownie pack.

On one other occasion, we landed on the lawn at Ranworth, but the effect of the downdraught on the flowers and the spillage of fuel on the lawn made me eschew this most marvellous means of transport into one's own front garden from then on.

I found that, if I held a conference every Monday morning, which everyone on the staff had to attend, much of the work to be done during the week could be properly planned and all the decisions made. We would warn the adjutants of our widely flung units to be available near the phone at that time so questions could be put and even answered immediately. At any rate, those concerned could be alerted and this system let me off the hook of having to spend hours in the office during the week.

The TA really comes to life at the annual fortnight's camp. 44 Brigade parachute battalions always went to camp together during my time. Sometimes it was better for the supporting units and services to go on their own but during my first year we nearly all gathered at Thetford in Norfolk.

We had a reasonable allotment of aircraft from the RAF but a great bonus in the shape of the Joint Service Helicopter Squadron manned by the Royal Navy. Nothing was too much trouble and they laboured night and day to keep the machines flying, so much so that almost always eleven out of the total strength of twelve could be serviceable. One would see the arc lights on well into the hours after midnight to achieve this almost incredible result.

The Hon Hugh Fraser, at that time the Secretary of State for Air, spent a day with us. He seemed to be taking particular interest and when I tackled him about the possibility of the brigade being given a worthwhile wartime role, although he could make no promises, he gave me to understand that I need have no worries in that respect.

Field-Marshal Lord 'Tiny' Ironside, the CIGS during the early stages of the Hitler War, whom I had met in very different circumstances twice before, came to lunch. He was a most amusing guest.

44 Brigade were partly responsible for 23 SAS, which was a TA Unit under the command of David Sutherland. I knew nothing about their operational role or training but was responsible for their administrative backing and welfare. I visited them only to find their camp practically deserted. However, they invited me to their end-of-camp party and I then discovered that they had spent the entire period doing their own thing without using any of the accommodation or usual facilities available. I did not want to pry into their affairs but asked David what they had been doing. He said, 'Observing without being observed.'

We left it at that, but the fact that they, the civilian territorial soldiers, were able and willing to live in this way was something I would put to future reference as regarding our brigade.

The weather was kind during that particular camp so we managed to get a lot of work done. Nearly everyone was out on the excellent training areas all day long and maximum use was made of the air lift available. All the senior, more elderly members of the brigade staff did a water jump into Wroxham Broad. Although the yachting fraternity had been asked to keep their craft at their moorings while the parachuting took place, many of them couldn't bear not to take a closer look and moved out to do this. The thought of becoming impaled on a mast was distressing; however, everyone entered the water unhindered and was picked up without incident.

There was a quiet period after the annual camp when it was possible to get away abroad for leave, although the build-up for the camp could be so hectic that there was little time to think about or plan this. The winter months would be much taken up with the annual general inspections and the travelling involved. There was also a hefty social life to contend with. Drinks parties, dinners, dances, indeed balls, were all a part of every unit's activities and attendance at these gave opportunities of meeting people which could not be missed. Initiating, or supporting, the confidential reports of all the field officers within the brigade was quite an ordeal. One had nothing like the same time or opportunities of getting to know people as did one's regular counterparts, yet the reports were in much the same form as for regular soldiers, so just as much trouble had to be taken.

The 1959 Brigade Annual Camp was held at Castle Martin in Pembrokeshire. This was a difficult place to get to to reconnoitre the areas to set the exercises beforehand. It was mainly a tank range so the tank tracks had churned up most of the land, which tended to make it unpleasant for infantry following later. By now the RAF had taken over the Joint Service Helicopter Squadron from the Navy and instead of 95 per cent availability of their aircraft, we had to make do with 30 per cent. There was now no question of midnight oil being burnt to keep the machines serviceable, until this became sheer necessity to enable them to get away at the end. At this particular camp we were not too unlucky with the weather, as it only rained for half the time.

One of the daily papers offered a prize for any team that could win a race to bring a bottle of that year's vintage of Beaujolais from Paris to London. We entered a team, not that we thought there was any chance of winning, but to show that we could do the job quite quickly by motorcycling to the aircraft from Paris, parachuting out at Hornchurch and motorcycling into London from there. We were unlucky in that a parachutist landed on the roof of a hangar at Hornchurch and had difficulty in getting down, but our time was not unreasonable. There were several entries, including a team from BEA who travelled by the normal means.

We certainly tried to make the maximum possible use of any aircraft allotment we were given at weekends. For instance, one party would emplane in Oxfordshire early on the Saturday morning, fly up to the north of England and drop there. The aircraft would then pick up another party there to drop in Scotland on the Saturday and Sunday; then a party there to drop in the North of England on their way back; and finally the aircraft would bring home all those belonging to the south. On one of these weekends I did my last ever jump at Otterburn in Northumberland. I had what was known as a thrown line, which means a much quicker descent. However, I landed on a rabbit burrow which crumpled to meet my landing and I walked away unhurt but vowing never to do it again.

We had been allotted the Otterburn Ranges and training areas for the brigade camp in 1960. I was determined to show that our soldiers were as capable as regulars of going straight into battle from their civilian occupations, indeed in many ways more simply, as they had nothing in the way of military responsibility to hand over. So we arranged that the units would go into an exercise immediately after arrival and that the exercise would be continuous until the end of the camping period. There were some raised eyebrows from some of the 'old and bold' when this was made known, for the TA Camp had once upon a time been looked upon as a holiday. Prophets of doom predicted that the brigade would lose half its strength as a result of this sort of treatment and worse still if it rained.

We took much trouble over the setting of the exercise. The 17th Battalion, based at Newcastle under Graham Mills, would be enemy to the rest of the brigade. In order that they should look different, they were forbidden to shave for the duration and wore cap comforters in place of berets. They would be the first to drop.

Michael Walsh took over from Roger May as Brigade Major beforehand and he proved to be a tower of strength. Early on the Monday morning, he brought me the news that Jeannie had borne us a son at 27 Welbeck Street. By the courtesy and kindness of the RAF, I was able to get there by lunchtime and, as all was well, I returned the same day. High-powered medical advisers had told Jeannie that as a result of her wounding in Palestine and subsequent operations, it would be most unlikely that she would ever be able to conceive; so she could be justly proud of producing twice.

Each of the other battalions was taken out of the battle to emplane and drop in again as part of the exercise. Although there were difficulties over controlling events through insufficient communications, things had gone very much as I had hoped up to the weekend. But it had in fact rained every single day and night and all the troops were soaked, so much so that some were beginning to look a little pea-green.

So we called a break for the weekend, opened the camp sufficiently for everyone to have a bath and arranged transport to take people to Newcastle. The exercise would recommence on the Monday where it had left off. The doomsters reckoned that there would be many absentees. In fact there were two, each of whom had a valid reason. The battle finished before the weekend and all went home, most of us feeling that our case was proven.

I had made a real nuisance of myself to those who had been the GOCs-in-C at Eastern Command during my time, generals who had included Jim Cassels and Gerald Lathbury. How much they did to help I really do not know, but Pat Weston, who was the Director of Land/Air Warfare at the War Office, did everything he could. Although the brigade group was dissolved some years later, three of the TA Parachute battalions survive to the present day, and they all have their wartime roles.

I could now spend more time on other things. The polo ponies, which Billie Walsh of the Ham Club had taken into his care when we left Netheravon, had been moved to stables I had found within easier reach of Ranworth, with three small paddocks nearby. The Army always very kindly let me have a groom and I soon found that there were many girls around who would muck out or clean tack if they could exercise the ponies. This meant that every weekend the girls could do most of the work and make things easier for us all.

For the first part of my time with 44 Brigade, I played quite a lot with the Household Brigade Polo Club at Windsor. I had bought a cattle truck which took four ponies comfortably and in those days Windsor were not over-subscribed with players who could mount themselves. So much so that on one occasion Claude Pert, Manager at Windsor, phoned me when I was in Edinburgh to ask me to be there on the Sunday afternoon.

That state of affairs did not last for long and then Aldershot tried hard to start up. They had the benefit of a splendid ground, but there were no soldiers in the garrison who played. Despite prodigious efforts on the part of some local enthusiasts, it faded away. Meanwhile, the Ham Club, in and out of Richmond Park, welcomed a heterogeneous number of members, which included Colonel Billy Whitbread, Jimmy Edwards, Harold Bamberg, Peter Buckenham and a tycoon or two more, under the complete dominion of the redoubtable Billy Walsh himself. He, in fact, had done as much as anyone to get polo going again after the war. The Club's very proximity to London could have been made more use of than it was by anyone who was keen to play but, by its very nature, it lacked some of the amenities considered essential by those who could afford to mount themselves.

Comedian Jimmy Edwards was a well-known enthusiast and he invited me to play with his team, which he called 'Whacko', named after a television programme in which he played the star part. He entered a team in most of the low goal tournaments with considerable success. He was a good, unselfish captain who, from his position at the back, fed his forwards well with opportunities provided by his not inconsiderable skill as a striker of the ball. I was very happy to be a member of his team, which won the Ruins Cup at Cowdray Park in 1960. The Queen, who seldom watched that class of polo, stayed to watch us defeat John Morrison's much more favoured finalists.

Towards the end of my time with 44 Brigade, I heard that I was to be GOC 52nd Lowland Division/District with the Headquarters in Glasgow where I had been in 1948 and 1949. We would have to find tenants for Ranworth for at least two years.

I now heard that my successor was to be Tony Deane-Drummond, a most distinguished officer who had made two successful escapes from being a prisoner of war and was the British gliding champion. He was wanted as a victim for the *This is Your Life* programme on television and I contracted to deliver him to the studios. This was an awful business of subterfuge, which involved downright lying, and when I finally handed him over to Eamonn Andrews, he turned on me with well-merited imprecations. However, it was great fun, which I think he and his family enjoyed as much as we did.

Ranworth, with its lovely garden, was a delightful place to live in. The swimming pool was well sheltered and heated up easily. Our woods were home to families of both fox and badger, while pheasants and pigeon fluttered about. Most precious were kingfishers which darted up and down the stream. If we had had more time, it would have been worthwhile to dam this up. We played a lot of tennis on our grass court. I had entrée to several golf courses, and so with polo several days a week I was able to fill very profitably the few months between giving up 44 Brigade and going up to Scotland.

I decided to keep two of the ponies and take them up to Scotland with me, playing at clubs in Cheshire and Yorkshire on the way. I pensioned one old pony off and sold another to Pamela Bishop, who had been helping me for a long time. This was an animal we called Sabeo, which had been schooled by the famous player, Johnnie Traill. He had never been out of action during the five years I had owned him. He was lazy but had a great turn of speed. He was a bit of a 'card' and one winter when he was out to grass in a field which had a public footpath running through it, he would sneak up behind people in the gloaming and put his great head over their shoulders. He was delighted if this caused a panic, as was the farmer, who did not want the walkers anyway.

By this time I had a Cameronian groom, Lance-Corporal Adams, and he was to take the horses up in the box. I would go ahead of the family by three months so as to fit in with schooling arrangements.

Before going, there were to be some great farewell parties within the brigade. The three years had been full of effort and struggle, through which I had been supported up to the hilt. As well as my deputy commander, Alastair Pearson, and the other colonels, all the commanding officers were men of great ability. With all the calls made on their time, it seemed amazing that any Territorial officer could accept the responsibility and carry out their duties so well. Jimmie Graham of the 15th Scottish and Gordon Pollard of the Midlands Battalion were never at a loss. Regulars Graham Mills and Dickie Morton commanded the 17th, which was in the midst of the DLI fraternity. This was the only part of the brigade where there was inclined to be a clash between the old and the new, but both officers coped exceedingly well. Glyn Gilbert commanded the 10th Battalion based on London for most of my time. He was an outstanding officer, who could persuade his territorials to do things that had not been done before. The only trouble between us was that when we were on the phone I could never get a word in edgeways, and when he reckoned that he had made all his points he was apt to say, 'Well, sir, I suppose that will be all?'

Ian Wellstead commanded 131 Parachute Engineer Regiment with quite amazing aplomb. I do not believe that anyone could have been more inventive and dedicated. It was largely through his hard work and initiative that the many members of the brigade were able to visit the Sicilian and Arnhem battlefields. Ben Parker had the supporting Royal Regiment of Artillery. On their big days, they would deploy both the Master Gunner and Admiral of the Fleet the Earl Mountbatten of Burma no less; the standards had to be kept high.

Perhaps a culminating point was a return to Bruneval, most of us aboard two naval frigates, the rest parachuting in when the wind speed was over the odds. Everyone there knew that the drop should have been cancelled but there was too much at stake. Down came our weekend soldiers, buffeted and swirled by the wild gusting winds. One broke the roof of an ambulance, two brought down the telephone lines, but nary a one was hurt. At the lunch afterwards, Richard Gale made his best ever speech, which was, 'Vive la France'. But perhaps the most apposite remark was from a young naval officer, 'We shall have to adjust our ideas about pongos after this.'

CHAPTER XIII

BACK TO LOWLANDS

WHEN I HAD BEEN TOLD that I was to be the GOC of 52 Lowland Division district with the HQ in Glasgow, I had had mixed feelings. Having initially been almost frog-marched into the Cameronians by my father, which was his choice rather than mine, for I had already opted for the Cheshires, which was his old regiment, I had never fully embraced 'MacJockery' and I knew that in the eyes of many real Scottish soldiers I would always be a Sassenach. There had always been many Englishmen in the Scottish regiments and they were usually fully accepted within them. Moreover I think that we went out of our way to become one of them and were glad and proud to do so. But there was always a little 'if' about it.

Although I had gone so far as to get myself transferred from a comfortable wartime employment abroad back to my regiment in 1941, I had never been in action with them and had spent the whole war as a parachutist, so I had none of the 'binding' that comes with having served in combat. Now I was going back to my own regimental area, having joined there in 1932, and been a staff officer there from 1949 to 1950, yet feeling that there would always be reservations.

Frankie Festing, the Chief of the General Staff, sent for me before I went up to say, in so many words, 'There are going to be reductions in the infantry in the future. You should do all you can to persuade the Lowlanders to become one regiment.'

Soon after I was apprised, I had visited John Macdonald, who was commanding the Lowlands. The GOC's house was called Ardarden in the village of Cardross on the banks of the Clyde some three-quarters of an hour's drive from Glasgow, and outside the Lowland area altogether. It was a lovely, big, old-fashioned mansion with large rooms and spacious grounds, a walled garden and lots of outhouses including excellent stabling. The view south towards the northern banks across the Clyde was lovely, ever changing as the tide came in and out, with a multitude of small seabirds swooping in to feed. The drive up to the main road was about a quarter of a mile, and from then on the land rose to heather-clad moorland with an outlook far beyond into real highland country at its best.

A few miles westward was the township of Helensburgh with all the shops one would need and the yacht club at Rhu on the Gareloch where Jean and I had ventured when we had been here before. Cardross was a nice little village, boasting most of what was needed but, above all, an excellent eighteen-hole golf course.

I arrived driving myself in a car packed to the eyebrows and spent the first night at the Headquarters Mess in Park Terrace, which I already knew so well.

In the morning I went into the quite lovely big General's office with its glorious view over the Kelvin Park and across the Clyde; such a contrast to the horrid little office at the back where I had worked as a GSO 2 and which the present incumbent still occupied. I met all the staff and, having had a good look round, drove on out to Ardarden to begin settling in. There was a household staff consisting of a cook and a batman, dailies came in to clean and there was a general factotum who looked after the gardens. Mr Strachan was a great standby over all other matters as he and his wife had lived in one of the cottages for several years.

I was now joined by my first ADC, George Stephen, another Cameronian. Although I might have had reservations about coming up to the Lowlands, I had none about becoming a General. I had served three and had been commanded by many more and one thing I had realized was how important it was to have a good ADC. The General is the Army's maid of all work. There is no such thing as time off. When all the rest of the staff go home, the General starts all over again. He is answerable to not only the Army, but to the other Services for all the other social activities, such as the drinks parties, the dinners, the dances, the prize-givings, the weddings and all the finals of the sporting events. Moreover the schools, the hospitals, the factories, the cadet organizations, the charities, even the churches are apt to say, 'Let's ask the General'.

So I well knew that when one became a General, one had to adopt a completely new way of life but at least one could say that most of the time one was being helpful to someone.

However, the dovetailing of everything, which includes a tremendous amount of travelling, and the activities of one's own spouse, plus the entertaining, which is a must without which much offence can be caused, means that the ADC has to have very particular talents, with a memory like a notebook and a skin like a rhino to help him through. Soon after I arrived, I was asked by someone at a drinks party what I did for a living and I replied, 'I am in the General business.' Later I saw him roaring with laughter as the penny dropped.

Willo Turner was the C-in-C Scottish Command with his headquarters in Edinburgh and Derek Lang as his Chief of Staff. They were very kind and helpful throughout my tour of duty. In the Division were one artillery and two infantry brigades, a sapper regiment, a yeomanry armoured-car regiment and all the normal services that went with a division in those days; also various non-divisional administrative units, including the depots of the four Lowland infantry regiments. There were training areas and ranges for which one was responsible, plus all the cadet units which included the combined cadet forces of the public schools, of which there were quite a number in Glasgow and Edinburgh.

So, once again one had to be on the move a great deal of the time. Everywhere in the Lowlands could be reached by car, but, with the GOC's house positioned where it was, it meant that one had to go through the great City of Glasgow before being able to reach anywhere. This meant that a tremendous amount of dead mileage had to be covered during the year and there was then no way of overcoming it. In the winter months icy road conditions often caused delays and hazards, so that extra time always had to be allowed.

In addition to visiting the units, there were meetings of the territorial and cadet associations which one was expected to attend from time to time. These committees of very public spirited people provided the backing for territorial and cadet units within each county. Sometimes they would be chaired by the Lord-Lieutenant, no less, but most of the members were men of substance, many of whom had served with the units concerned.

I had happily managed to command the Territorial 44 Parachute Brigade for three years without ever attending a single meeting of any of these associations, but I now found that umbrage resulted from avoidance of the meetings. I had always felt that these associations were an anachronism dating back to the days when the monarch required his Lords-Lieutenant to produce soldiery to protect the realm. When discussing this business with my peers in the army, they all said, 'Play along with the associations. They will not like it if you don't and they often have a lot of influence.'

However, I could never accept that they were necessary, but, as they cost very little, there was never likely to be much support for their abolition. Their chairmen and some of the members were assiduous in wanting to visit units during annual training camps, as did the colonels of regiments, honorary colonels and other well-wishers. They could not seem to realize that a lot of time and effort had to be put into making arrangements for their reception and entertainment for these visits and, later, when I tried to insist that the main object of the annual camps should be for training rather than receptions, I was not popular. On my next appointment on Malta, I was to find three territorial units under command. There were no associations there. They were not missed in any way and life was very much easier for my staff and myself without them.

During the summer camping season, training in England was popular as it made more of a change and gave a chance of better weather, so there were many flying visits to be paid to such places as Brecon, Salisbury Plain, Dorset, Kent and Norfolk. Fortunately the RAF could quite often provide transport and, failing that, my Jaguar could eat up the motorway, for there was no speed limit at that time.

After experiencing the enthusiasm evinced by almost everyone in 44 Parachute Brigade, I was naive to expect the same thing in the Lowlands, yet it was difficult not to strive for it. I laid on exercises which made use of the local naval support and the quite glorious countryside, but these never seemed to click. I attended shooting on the ranges on Sundays and even drill nights during weekdays, only to be met with 'Never seen a General here before'.

The Duncan-Sandys-accepted policy of subordinating our defence to nuclear weapons, with a consequent overall reduction in conventional formations and the abolition of conscription, meant that the concept of the TA divisions being required to fight in Europe alongside the British Army of the Rhine to help repel huge numbers of Warsaw Pact was dead and buried. Moreover, because nuclear weapons would be used at the very start of a conflict, it was considered most unlikely that the TA would have to 'repel boarders', so even the conventional home defence role was doubtful. However, a nuclear exchange would obviously bring the need for massive assistance to the civil population and probably support to the police to maintain law and order. So, it was Civil Defence that now loomed most largely as the TA's wartime role and it was not going to be easy to inculcate much enthusiasm for that or other things.

Meanwhile, the yeomanry had their armoured cars, the gunners had their guns, the sappers the wherewithal to carry out engineering tasks, so they could all do their own thing. The services could all continue to supply, transport and recover things and repair them. The medical would have a future whatever role emerged, the police would have to police and the signals send messages. It was more difficult to arrange worthwhile things for the infantry to do. However, nearly all the battalions had their military and pipe bands and they could always be relied on to lay on a good ceremonial parade. The presentation of colours or the visit of Royalty could involve a whole year of training time and perhaps it would have been best to leave it so. I found it difficult to accept.

Derek Lang, who had been Chief of Staff at Scottish Command when I arrived, had now gone to command the 51st Highland Division/District and he wanted to turn the whole local army into a project-achieving force. I was so averse to this concept that I never fully understood his ideas. He later became GOC Scottish Command but by that time the divisions had been abolished anyway.

I had become frustrated at having the headquarters in Glasgow, which would in any case have been a likely target in a nuclear war and was on the western extremity of the divisional area, but worse still at having the GOC's house so far away in the wrong direction.

It was planned that in the near future all the infantry depots should be combined at Glencorse near Edinburgh and this would leave the excellent modern barracks at Lanark, which was currently the Cameronians' depot, redundant. I therefore suggested that the headquarters should move there from Glasgow, for Lanark was almost equidistant from Edinburgh and Glasgow and much nearer to all our responsibilities in the lowlands. A suitable house for the GOC would have to be found nearby. This would have been quite possible if the command secretariat had been able to agree to pay a reasonable price for what was on offer, but their margin was always so much below the current market price that in the end my unfortunate successor had to continue living at Ardarden, although the headquarters moved to Lanark.

If it had been known that the TA divisions were going to be abolished, no one would have even contemplated moving, with all the consequent disruption. On the face of it, it was the right idea, for it would have saved much from so many points of view.

In the meantime, we were all being pressed to do everything we could think of to encourage recruiting for the regular Army. The public image of the Army had to be thrust forwards by all possible means and the local General must play a full part. One should try to become a public figure, accept every invitation, miss no opportunity of making a speech and flaunt oneself gracefully around the district. In fact, it was difficult not to do this. There were countless invitations and on the whole life was the reverse of peaceful.

For the frustrations there were many compensations. The Army was much more revered in Scotland than below the border. There were the great occasions at Holyrood for the garden parties and the dinners. At the former the Queen's Bodyguard of Archers were a reminder of the real loyalty and the ever-present pride in their nationhood that is not conveyed in the same way down south. It was quite an experience to be asked to speak at some of the big dinners in Glasgow and to attend the balls that were so well laid on in the Lowlands. Taking the salute at the Edinburgh Tattoo was an unforgettable experience.

I had always been a keen shot and though I did not get many

147

invitations to good shoots, I was able to be a member of several small syndicates where I had enormous fun, added to the occasional big day. I organized a little shoot of my own at Glen Luss on Loch Lomondside, on land belonging to Ivar Colquhoun. We put down a number of pheasants under the care of a marvellous old keeper called Duncan Macbeth. There were red deer on the hill above and I had permission to shoot hinds when in season. The whole environment was so lovely that even a most mediocre day could be a great pleasure. I bought a well-trained yellow labrador bitch, who added greatly to my enjoyment of all the days I had.

Soon after my arrival at Lowland, I had played in a golf match versus the Highland Division at Gleneagles and we had been thrashed. I vowed to avenge this humiliating defeat and managed to play a lot of golf on many courses all over the country, always taking my clubs with me wherever I went. We improved, and though we only drew with the Highlanders on the next occasion, I am glad to say that we trounced them before I left. I even managed to keep my hand in at polo for in the spring of 1962 I played my way down via Catterick, Toulston and Cheshire to Ham, where I finally sold my last two ponies for as much as I had paid for them seven years before.

Robin Buchanan-Dunlop took over as ADC in 1963. He was another Cameronian and I knew his parents well. George Stephen left to get married to a charming girl whom he had been after for some time. My principal staff officers had been unchanged, with Gordon Dinwiddie as the GSO 1 and Brian Carson as the AA & GMG. They had both been towers of strength. There were no weak links all the way down the chain.

David MacConnel had commanded the brigade based in Glasgow during most of my time, to be relieved by James Bowes-Lyon towards the end. I hope that they liked being commanded by me as much as I liked having them under my command. Noble, one of the famous Scottish soldier family, had the Edinburgh-based brigade when I arrived, to be relieved by Jack Monteith, a Black Watch, soon after. Despite a few differences of opinion, I think we coped with each other well. Our gunner brigadier was Pat Cook, who was a most able supporter throughout.

We managed to fit in some periods of leave, which included a foray into the Highlands, from thence to the Orkneys and back via the Isle of Skye. Another included Gibraltar, Tangier and the Marbella Club.

There had been close links between Norway and the 52nd Division throughout the war, as it had been trained in mountain warfare with a view to liberating Norway when the time was ripe. A number of Norwegian officers served with the Division and in September, 1963, I was invited to visit the Norwegian Army and attend some social functions. Needless to say, much trouble was taken to make all this a great pleasure, which went to confirm the high opinion of all things Norwegian I had formed as a result of being there just after the war. I came back via Copenhagen and Amsterdam and while in Holland did a battlefield tour of Arnhem with the 15th Scottish Battalion of the Parachute Regiment.

I had kept close relationships with all things airborne, attending meetings of the Para Regimental Committee and Airborne Security Fund Trustees. When I was at a memorial service to the Suez landings at Aldershot, the preacher, Bishop F. F. Johnston, fell dead while addressing us from a rostrum. The whole sad episode might have been rehearsed, for after his wife had gone to him, put her hand on his heart and shaken her head, four red-sashed staff sergeants took his body away and the service continued with the hymn, 'For all the Saints'.

Liaison with the Royal Navy involved visits to Abbotsinch across the Clyde, from whence I went through the sound barrier in a Sea Vixen. Not a very comfortable experience and worrying, in that I could not fathom how one's knees could fail to be smashed against the bulkhead if one had had to use the ejector seat apparatus. HMS *Maidstone*, depot ship to the submarine flotilla, was in the Gareloch and this was a favourite port of call. Jackie Stewart, who became the famous champion racing driver, used to work in his father's motor-car business not far away. Among other things, he was outstanding with a shot gun and he introduced me to the local clay bird shoot. I never saw him miss anything. To add a polish to his performance, he would always catch the ejected empties with his right hand.

During August of 1963, I was given the glad news that I was to take over from Harry Thurlow as GOC Malta and Libya in the spring of 1964, and that Henry Leask, who was currently in the Ministry of Defence, would relieve me. I did a quick trip to Malta to see the form and very much liked what I saw, so we could go through the winter with the future nicely settled.

I had been able to achieve absolutely nothing regarding the Chief of the General Staff's injunction to persuade the Lowland Regiments to combine. None of the regular battalions was stationed in Scotland, so one could do little more than spread the gospel at the depots, with the territorials and among the retired officers living nearby. Although some younger serving officers were not averse because they could see that their career prospects would be furthered if they were in a bigger regiment, nearly everyone else was hostile to the idea and I gained nothing in popularity for broaching the subject whenever I did.

Meanwhile, Jeannie had welded our household staff into an excellent team and we were able to entertain without qualms. We had coped with General and Mrs Lemnitzer, who were the big white chiefs in Europe at that time, also all the chairmen of the associations within the Lowlands, but perhaps best of all was a party on St Andrew's Night for the members of the Regiment living within reach. The Athol Brose put real heart into the pipers and the dancers to make the whole great house echo to the skirl of the pipes and shake to the thrum of the feet as reel followed reel, till we had all had enough.

I was able to make one really worthwhile contribution before I left, which was to obtain authority and make the initial arrangements for a battlefield tour at Walcheren for the past and present members of the Division. They very kindly invited me to join them for this while I was in Malta. I was unable to accept but I gather that this return visit was an enormous success.

Perhaps unfortunately, we had to leave before our time was up because Harry Thurlow, who had been booked to take over Scottish Command, was taken ill in Malta and I had to go there before the designated time. So it became all a bit of a rush, with scant time to say proper farewells. It was a wrench to leave the Great City with all the warm hearts that beat within and around.

11 *Call Boy*, the Royal Corps of Transport launch which was at my disposal while we were in Malta (see pp. 155–6).

12 "My own quarter, known as GOC's House, was on the waterfront at Tigne" (p. 153).

13 Signing the book for Dr George Borg Olivier, Prime Minister of Malta when the Island gained Independence in 1965.

14 A tussle on the polo ground with my ADC, Geoffrey Kent. "Geoffrey was to go on in later years to play in the top international class" (p. 167).

CHAPTER XIV

MALTA

I ARRIVED AT LUQA AIRPORT to take over command as GOC Troops Malta and Libya at half past two on Friday, 25 February, 1964. I was met by Brigadier Brian Kingzett and several other officers of the HQ and, after a short conference in the VIP lounge, I was driven straight to the Governor's Palace at St Anton. Sir Maurice and Lady Dorman were very professional old hands and the new GOC was to be carefully briefed and methodically introduced to the life of Malta, for Malta was a fortress with a very special hierarchy and the heads of the three services had a unique and elevated status on the Island.

St Anton Palace had housed many notable governors or rulers, including Napoleon for a short period. It was a delightfully gracious old sprawling building surrounded with a secluded garden which included a beautifully designed Roman-type swimming pool. The house was suitably staffed by a most experienced team of Maltese who well knew how to look after the stream of visitors who came and went throughout the year.

I was particularly grateful to them for having me because of my predecessor's early departure and my hurried briefing in London. I had been seen by the Chief of the Defence Staff, Admiral of the Fleet Lord Mountbatten, Lieutenant-General Sir John Hackett, then the Vice Chief of the General Staff, in the absence of the Chief of Staff, and other senior staff officers. I visited officials from the Foreign and Colonial Offices, the latter not having yet been merged with the Foreign Office. I discovered that I was to have a plethora of bosses which included the CGS, the Naval C-in-C Mediterranean, the UK Commissioner in Malta, the British Ambassador in Libya and the Governor of Malta. To all of these I would owe allegiance and for all of whom I would carry out certain duties. Perhaps one may be forgiven for not having pleased all of them all of the time.

My army consisted of a Maltese LAA regiment, a Maltese Fortress Squadron RE, two British infantry battalions and all the necessary services on Malta, while in Libya there was a battalion of British infantry and an armoured-car regiment, together with all the services for garrisons in Tripoli and Benghazi. For good measure, there was a company of infantry from Gibraltar in Tobruk and a small unit or two on the airfield at El Adem quite near the Egyptian frontier. Last but by no means least there were three major Maltese TA units on the Island: two of the Royal Malta Artillery armed with 40mm Bofors AA guns, like their regular regiment already mentioned, and the King's Own Malta Regiment of Infantry. I was also responsible in part for the Military Mission to the Libyan Army, which consisted of a specially selected group of officers and NCOs under a colonel. Meanwhile there would a fairly constant stream of units from the British Army of the Rhine coming to use the superb training areas within easy reach of both Tripoli and Benghazi.

I had a splendid HQ and staff to enable me to carry out my duties. It would embarrass them if I were to mention any names but somehow the environment and the conditions in which we lived brought out the best in everyone and I think all those who served there then look back on their time in Malta as one of the happiest in their lives. Our headquarters in the Castille could only be described as magnificent and is now the seat of the Government of Malta. The site dominated the approach into Valletta, the capital city of the Island. All the rooms were spacious, even palatial. My own office was a delightful place in which to work and greet visitors or my staff. The Officers' Mess looked out towards the old harbour and was so comfortable and yet dignified that it was a real pleasure to arrange to entertain people who came to us from everywhere. Pure white was the dominant colour, cool and stately, utterly appropriate for the time. Yet up on the rooftop was an operations centre from which we could have controlled affairs had it been necessary to support the civil power in any eventuality or prevent a political coup which could have interfered with the security of the fortress itself.

I spent the first few days calling on all the people with whom I would be chiefly concerned – the Naval C-in-C, the Air Officer Commanding, the UK Commissioner and, next in importance for me, the Prime Minister, the Archbishop and the Chief Justice. We were a very close-knit community, living cheek by jowl, and the Army had to play a very full part in almost everything that was done.

My own quarter, known as GOC's House, was on the waterfront at Tigne and had been built for a lieutenant-colonel commanding the unit in the barracks there. With the downgrading of all privileges enjoyed by the services pre-war, this was now considered quite adequate for the local General and so it proved. There was certainly room for anyone with a family of not more than two children. A nanny was a must, for the social commitments meant that we would either be out or having people in on an average of five nights a week. Our two spare rooms were often used by visitors from home or within the command. Malta was a popular port of call for all those with responsibilities in the Mediterranean.

For travel on Malta two Austin Princesses were available. Lovely big limousines into which one could slide and from which one could debouch with dignity wearing sword and medals. A glass partition between the back and front allowed confidential talk during journeys and there always seemed to be room for everyone. Both the C-in-C and the ADC had had aircraft allotted to them and I was nearly always able to borrow one or other of these for my flights to Libya. They were well fitted out for VIP travel and so all my visiting was done in comfort. I was delighted at the very high standards I found within all the units. I had inherited a happy, efficient and well-disciplined command which knew exactly what it was about. The only real worry was that it was so much a married army. Nearly all the problems were related to the families. Most of the time, money and effort was geared to administering them and if trouble arose with the local population in Libya, all our resources would be expended in protecting them. Moreover, in Malta, where the battalions might be needed elsewhere at short notice, one could be faced with a problem of abandoned families for quite considerable periods. This was my first experience of the full-time professional army. The last time I had been involved with regulars was in Malaya when we still had National Service and only very few of the soldiers were married.

Anway, I was highly delighted to join the ranks of all the married when my own family arrived on Saturday, 14 March.

Now our social life redoubled in intensity and there seemed to be an almost frantic need to meet everyone as soon as possible. The HQ of the Allied Naval Forces in Southern Europe was situated in Malta and the senior members of this organization were on our list. Moreover, the American Navy's Sixth Fleet were fairly frequent visitors and the captain of every ship that anchored offshore had to call and be called on in return. My ADC, Robin Buchanan-Dunlop, coped with the business very well. He had been with me in the Lowlands of Scotland which was fairly busy in the same respect, but there we had to spend hours travelling between various places all over the UK. Now we had the mixture of acute concentration on Malta with great dispersal in Libya. Anyway a great deal of work was entailed in trying to dovetail it all in. Fortunately there was a very effective ADCs' union which marshalled their protégés from place to place and made certain that we all knew what we had to do. The famous Mabel Strickland was one of our first callers and she was ever near at hand with information and advice. She dwelt in a lovely old villa tucked away in a village in the centre of the Island and somehow, no matter how often we went there, we always found it difficult to find it again. We quickly got to know several Maltese families with whom we have been friends ever since.

I soon found myself back on the polo ground. I had always been an enthusiastic but indifferent player, my polo career having begun in Iraq before the war. On Malta, the polo season lasted throughout the year with a short pause mid-summer when the temperature neared the hundreds and ponies and grooms needed a break. In other seasons heavy rain could quickly turn our normally dry-earth ground into a mud bath but then the sun soon put matters to rights and it was seldom that a week went by without a game. Most of the ponies came from Libya and were comparatively easy to train – Barbs and Arabs, some with a trace of the English thoroughbred.

The Army, closely followed by the Navy, produced most of the players. It was one of the oldest clubs in Europe and some of the crowned heads had been members. Between the wars, when 'Lord Louis' was stationed there, naval polo was in its heyday. He had brought a string of English ponies with him and the annual match between the Army and the Navy for the Rundle Cup saw some spectacular victories for the Navy. Latterly the record of victories had been evened out and I was highly delighted to captain the team which put the Army ahead during my last year there.

In those days there were some noteworthy Maltese players. Tony Cassar and the two Galea brothers were rated at a handicap of four. Tony was a most experienced player, hard, grizzled and bow-legged, a great man to plough his way through. Salvio Darmanin was a genuine six. He had his own stable for polo and racing and was as good a striker as one would see anywhere. These four made up a team called the Maltese Cats and it was almost impossible to field a British combination to beat them, although when Salvio was having an off day we came near to doing so. When I arrived the polo was in the very capable hands of Brigadier Brian Kingzett. He was a fine horseman whose enthusiasm had maintained the club during his time as Deputy Commander. It had been a tradition that the GOCs played polo and one had actually died at the edge of the ground.

We mounted visiting teams from the Cyprus garrison and the cavalry regiment station at Benghazi, also on two occasions teams from the UK. It was a great fillip to have these matches, for, as in every other form of activity, variety is welcome. During my last year we took a team to Italy to play against the club in Rome. Unfortunately appalling weather very nearly ruled out play altogether but we managed to hold our own in two rather scrappy games.

The polo grounds, the racecourse, a golf course, several tennis courts and a hefty old club house were all part of a complex known as the Marsa. It was then held on trust for the United Services and was situated on low ground liable to flooding after heavy rain. It was a godsend to any games player. The racecourse was an ideal circuit for exercising the polo ponies and on most mornings some of us were up before breakfast to hack, stick and ball or school a pony.

The availability of a sixty-foot RASC motor launch which could be taken out with its crew of three on Sundays and holidays was a great boon. There was room for fifteen people with some children aboard. All round the islands were small bays and coves where one could anchor to picnic and bathe. It was nearly always possible to find calm water and shelter when the winds blew. Mostly the water was clean and clear, reflecting the blue of the sky. Landwards was nearly always interesting with white-walled, red-roofed buildings neatly fitted into villages, hamlets or small towns, the hinterland rising in the distance with hills interrupted with rocky outcrops and patches of green. We usually towed a speedboat for water-skiing at intervals and in places snorkelling could show so many things that one had heard of but never really expected to see.

Meanwhile our lunches were normally of delicious rice dishes that could be eaten with a spoon, washed down with copious draughts of local Maltese white wine. It was always with a sad feeling that at the end of the afternoon we had to say to the coxswain, 'Time to go home.' The three big diesels churned us along at sixteen knots past all the familiar landmarks on the way to our landing steps at Tigne.

A considerable proportion of the Maltese populace celebrated Communion every morning. In such an atmosphere it would have been unseemly for us to have been less than 'Once a weekers', so practically every Sunday found us doing our duty at Matins at the Anglican Cathedral in Valletta or our local garrison church at Tigne. Most of the British civilian population followed this example so that the services in these churches were thoroughly alive and meaningful. The interior of St John's Cathedral in Valletta was quite beautiful in its simplicity and the choir was graced by many of the nurses from the Royal Naval Hospital at Bighi. Except on special occasions, the services were voluntary for serving personnel, but on Trafalgar Day or Remembrance Sunday a Service band would lead the singing. In contrast we sometimes had to attend the traditional High Mass in the Cathedral with the Archbishop of Malta presiding. The elaborate ceremonies and variations kept one guessing right up to the end when after a session lasting for up to two hours, Mrs Borg Olivier, the wife of the Prime Minister, who was usually immediately in front of us, would turn round and wink. Then we knew that the end was nigh. Nevertheless, one was glad to be privileged to share in these great occasions with all that was best in the Island of Malta and it was warming to be accepted as one among them all.

Although our main task on Malta and Libya was the preservation of law and order, generally known as internal security, we also had an external commitment in Libya in that there was a threat there from Egypt. Nasser, the Egyptian dictator, had been casting eyes on the Libyan oilfields and it was thought that he might be adventurous. If the Egyptian army marched westwards we had little to stop them with; if the Libyans asked us we could try to delay them with the armoured-car regiment until either the Libyans or UK-based forces arrived to oppose them. Therefore the security of the airfield at El Adem and possibly the port of Tobruk was our main concern, yet one knew the world would expect us to oppose any incursion on the soil of our ally. In any case, in the event of any such upheaval, I would not be left for long with any responsibility for it. I had no operational headquarters with the necessary signals to conduct operations and it was planned that HQ 3rd Division from the UK with another major-general would take over almost immediately. Moreover this formation was to be supervised and commanded by HQ Southern Command, now nominated as Strategic Command HQ, and this would operate from Malta.

What would happen if there was another upheaval elsewhere was never explained. The most important aspect, which was talking it all over with the Libyans, was a closed book as far as I was concerned and, in this respect, as the local General on the spot, I was the one person who should have been given full responsibility and with it the adequate staff and signals and services able to receive and command or coordinate any operations which were within the capabilities of the forces at my disposal.

It was immediately obvious that availability of the troops currently stationed in Libya would be governed by the internal security situation pertaining at the time. An exercise practice in Tripoli revealed that, once all the places that had to be protected were accounted for, only one platoon was available for operations elsewhere. The presence of the British garrison in Tripoli had a stabilizing influence on people of all races there and helped to build up a sense of confidence within the British and Italian communities. Therefore the British Ambassador was totally opposed to any suggestion that the garrison be withdrawn, but if subversive elements in any such conurbations make things difficult for what may be regarded as an occupying power, unless that power is prepared to be utterly ruthless in their methods of suppression, the position of a garrison, with their families spread all over the area, will soon become untenable.

Anyway, having had a good look round, I felt I ought to recommend that the garrison be reduced to a company group stationed outside the town and that the remainder should come to Malta, with their families, and be available to return to Tripoli if a request came from the Libyan government. At that time there was adequate accommodation on Malta, which was a much more attractive station for families than Tripoli. The addition of another infantry battalion to the Malta garrison would have been beneficial on several counts, not least the availability within the theatre of climatically conditioned troops. Malta was required to send battalions to both Cyprus and Aden during my tenure of command and in each case it was found that these were effective far quicker than troops sent from more temperate climates. Maybe there was not much room to manoeuvre on Malta, but the rifle ranges were superb and the facilities for infantry to scrabble about over rough, rocky country and get hardened up were as good as anywhere else in the world. However, the Army was so heavily stretched that there could be no question of Malta having another battalion and the troops released were quickly slotted in elsewhere.

The rundown and withdrawal of troops from Tripoli took several months and their going left a great gap within the community there. However, their continued presence could never have prevented the takeover of power by Gaddafi, which took place several years later. In the event, when trouble brewed in Benghazi our armoured cars were sent out into town without ammunition or the means to defend themselves. As a result, fine British soldiers were burnt to death. There is nearly always a heavy price to pay for half-measures on such occasions.

The Queen's Birthday Parade was always a red-letter day on Malta or anywhere else in what had been the old Empire. Traditionally ours had always been held on the Floriana Parade Ground in the middle of the town and it was important to make it a popular occasion for all sections of the community. This would be the last such parade before the Island became independent so it was important to get it right, and fortunately we did. The Governor was a great supporter of these occasions and after it was over he spearheaded all the hierarchy, gallantry and beauty of Malta into our mess in the Castille for a celebration the like of which was probably being held all over what was left coloured red on the maps of the world. It is perhaps rather awful to think that being coloured red has a rather different implication now than in the days gone by.

Soon after the parade, Brigadier Lord 'Christy' Grimthorpe arrived to take over from Brian Kingzett. He was the ideal person for the job and entered into every aspect of the life of the garrison and despite owning a massive physical frame was able to cavort on the tennis courts and strike most mightily on the polo ground. His experience on the turf at home made his advice and patronage a great boon for the racing fraternity.

Now Independence loomed ahead. No one quite knew what effect this would have on the Island. Our treaties would guarantee the facilities for a while. Yet the Labour Party under the vociferous and volatile Mr Dom Mintoff was determined to disrupt the carefully laid plans if they possibly could, and equally determined that as little credit as possible would accrue to the Nationalist Party, now in power and led by George Borg Olivier. Prince Philip, Duke of Edinburgh, was to perform the actual ceremony of handing over power, and various potentates would come to Malta at the same time. Very elaborate arrangements had to be made, for apart from the actual handing-over ceremony, there would be a session in the Parliament, services in the churches, a state ball and a banquet. The armed Services would be fully involved and rehearsals took up quite a lot of time.

When the day came, all and sundry were present at the airfield for the arrival of Prince Philip, among them Duncan Sandys who represented the British Government. The Chief of Police, having discovered that Mintoff and his merry men intended to be rude to the motorcade on its way from the airport, arranged to divert this at the last moment. However, Duncan Sandys' car managed not to be diverted so the rest of us had to follow him. The Mintoffians did not know who he was so he got off scot-free, also the Admiral following immediately behind. Jean and I, next in the queue, survived a jeer or two, the Air Vice-Marshal a brick or two, but by the time the Italian Consul General appeared, the crowd was getting nasty. They stopped his car and wrenched the Italian flag off the front of it. The Italian diplomat was not accepting this and, having leapt out of his car, despite the hostile mob, seized back his emblem, cursed everyone in sight, got back into his car and told the driver to drive on.

One other event was marred by the Labour Party supporters, but otherwise the whole programme flowed gracefully to the end when we watched Prince Philip fly himself away. At that time the granting of Independence made no difference to the attitude of the Maltese to any of us and, though officially we, the heads of the Services, were no longer entitled to the very privileged positions we held in the Island's hierarchy, these were not altered in my time.

The three territorial Malta units now became the Malta Land Force under the now independent government of Malta. The Prime Minsiter invited me to continue to command them with the title of Commander, Malta Land Force. I was to have a staff of one Maltese major and one clerk, but we would be able to lean fairly heavily on the existing British headquarters. There had always been a Maltese full colonel as the head of all Maltese units in the British Army. In addition to the units on the Island, there was the Maltese Royal Artillery Regiment with BAOR in Germany acting in a transport role. The Royal Malta Artillery were very much a part of the British Army and had played a major part in fighting off the German and Italian attacks during the war. Colonel 'Tabby' Tabona was, though Maltese, a British Army officer. We were already great friends. Anyway there were to be no difficulties in that direction and he continued as before, though trying not to interfere with the now Maltese Land Force.

My first duty, which was to call on the Prime Minister and sign his book as his subordinate commander, very nearly went wrong. Immediately prior to this engagement I was in Libya watching an exercise, during the course of which two of the light aircraft I was flying in had engine failure one after the other and had to force-land. Fortunately, on each occasion friendly forces were close at hand so I was not much delayed. After that, while over the sea in a twin-engined RAF Anson, one engine packed up and we were forced back to Idris airfield near Tripoli, shadowed by a huge American air sea rescue machine. Fortunately, I was able to clamber aboard an RAF Canberra bomber and, with the RAF's help, was able to keep my appointment on time.

George Borg Olivier was a charming person to work with and for and always did what he could to help. However, things were not so easy when it became known that the whole future of the Royal Malta Artillery within the British Army was under consideration. Soon after Independence, the British Government apprised the Maltese through the British Commissioner that there would be a bill to pay for all the equipment, vehicles and weapons that the Malta Land Force were in possession of on Independence Day. This was a very considerable sum, even though the values had been well written down.

When I was being briefed by 'Lord Louis' at the Ministry of Defence before coming out, he had said, 'Don't get emotionally involved.' Just as I was going out through the door, he said, 'But you will, you know.'

'What?' I replied.

'Get emotionally involved,' he said with a smile. And off I went.

But get emotionally involved I did for sure, and now the future of the RMA and the equipment of the Malta Land Force became matters of vital importance in my mind. In my capacity as GOC Troops Malta and Libya, I began to get rather unpleasant messages from the Ministry suggesting that if the Maltese Government refused to pay what they considered was due for their equipment, et cetera, I would have to sequester it all. A quite impossible thing to do but nevertheless I felt bound to press the Prime Minister when I saw him at our monthly meetings, which I went to with the UK High Commissioner.

Eventually the PM promised me that before our next meeting he would have a special Cabinet discussion about our problem and that after that he would be able to tell me what his government had decided. So as our next meeting began, I said, 'Now sir, I do so hope that I can have a firm decision and be able to tell the Ministry at home.'

'Well, General, I am glad to be able to tell you that we have decided.' I leant forward with an eager expression.

'Yes, we have decided not to make a decision.'

All three of us roared with laughter and from then we argued about other things at our meetings, the main one being whether it would be proper for us to play our British National Anthem on the Queen's Birthday Parade when there was a perfectly good Maltese National Anthem available. Sadly, this disagreement ended in our having to have two separate parades and I had to take part in both.

After Independence all the foreign consulates were upgraded to become embassies, which meant more and more entertaining. This came to such a pitch that at one time my wife and I had to dine out on seventeen days in succession. Robin Buchanan-Dunlop had handed over as my ADC to Tim Holderness-Roddam of the 14/20th Hussars just before the changes took place. Tim became an expert ADC, being able to gauge timings to near-perfection and with an ability to remember names that I have never seen equalled. Wherever we went we tried to have a photographer in attendance and when his pictures were available, Tim would write the names of the subjects below. We could then study these when next we went to see the unit and could make a brave attempt at showing that we could recall all the nicknames, Christian names and other things about all and sundry.

Malta was an ideal centre for travelling in the Mediterranean. We visited Cyprus, Italy, Sicily, Sardina, Tunisia and of course Libya many times. I also had to return often to the UK on duty to visit the Ministry or attend the CIGS's exercises. So there was no question of feeling isolated. The Italians were very kind and helpful, allowing us to use a training area in Sardinia and arrange battlefield tours in Sicily and on the mainland. They were not popular with the Maltese who at that time still had sharp memories of wartime bombing. Indeed on one occasion when part of the Italian navy paid a visit, there were riots and the visitors had to leave hurriedly.

However, it was the proximity of Libya with its nigh perfect training areas that made Malta such an excellent military station. Many units from Germany and the UK came for two or three weeks at a time. Not only could one manoeuvre over vast areas but there were many places where firing was almost unrestricted. The local population were mostly Bedouin tribes on the move on a seasonal basis, so there was little inconvenience caused to them. When comparing locally based units with visiting ones, the advantages of acclimatization were most noticeable. During the daytime, the strangers would saddle themselves with two water bottles each but we, the locals, might not even have to resort to one. Of course very few men were on their own feet for any length of time.

The differences in approach to their training periods by the different units were considerable, even between the regiments of foot guards. One might spend every available minute working thoroughly at those things that could not be done so well elsewhere; another might erect a massive canvas cantonment in which to waste time and bring 20,000 cartridges to shoot non-existent duck. We met one officer from one such unit at the airfield at El Adem, where he had spent hours trying to get a bet on a horse in a race at home.

Newly arrived infantry battalions to Malta would express a wish to be allowed to settle down and arrange training cadres, concentrate on their administration and practice their foot drill for some great regimental occasion in the offing. However, there was always a chance that, even just after their immediate arrival, they might be called to active service. So I said something like this:

'We have arranged for the whole battalion to move into the desert in Libya next week. There you will dig a complete defensive position as per the book with proper camouflage arrangements, but barbed wire and minefields need to be represented only. There will be a live enemy so you need to have a screen by day and patrols by night. You must expect a full-scale attack within ten days. After that we shall see. There should be plenty of time in between whiles to carry out weapon training.'

Howls of protest were brushed off. No tentage was allowed and conditions were made to be as near to real active service as possible. Anyway, we found that in a remarkably short space of time the battalion was down to it. With everyone having to do exactly what he would have to do in war, they soon began to be proficient and all soon learnt to live with the limited resources and even enjoy them. In the event, I tried to direct the subsequent manoeuvres which included defensive battle, a hasty withdrawal and a counter-attack. Then, after the defences had been filled in, it was back to Malta and the fleshpots. Thereafter I found that all concerned were truly thankful for having been able to practise in peace exactly what they would have to do in war and they were able to go about their other business with a considerable degree of confidence. There could be no doubt that when units went from Malta to Cyprus or Aden at very short notice, they were well able to meet all the demands made on them.

An organized tour of at least one of the great desert battles was a must and I was fortunate in having a most capable lot of officers in our branch of the Army Education Corps who did all the devilling and made out the programme. We were unable to welcome any of the generals who took part but did manage to get a few commanding officers, plus two German Afrika Korps and a Frenchman from Bir Hakeim.

We decided to concentrate on the Gazala Battle, for here were all the possibilities of victory which were thrown away by a series of mistakes, miscalculations and repudiations of the principles of war. So it was full of interest and thought of what might have been. Regrettably the calibre of leadership on the German side was so obviously superior to our own, for it was this that forged the superiority in the handling of the armour and the anti-tank guns in a way that resulted in the constant protection of their infantry and the frequent jeopardization of our own. The enemy also obviously had an advantage in the intrinsic value of their weapons, so all our sympathy could be for our soldiers who always had to fight when outgunned and less well mounted. Back on Málta we stripped a three-ton truck and rearranged the seating so that the troops being carried would face outwards and could debus in a twink. We found this to be a far better way of mounting lorried infantry than in the orthodox vehicles. Such a cheap and simple expedient might have been an advantage in the war. We tried to discover why greater efforts were not made to use some of the 3.4 AA guns available in the anti-tank role, this gun being similar to the German 88 millimetre guns which were so devastating to our tanks. Only specious answers could be obtained.

All those attending the tour were accommodated in the RAF

Base at El Adem which was commanded by a Group Captain who was also called Frost. In no time the wags were referring to us as Air Frost and Ground Frost. We hit it off together very well and during the proceedings he suggested that we might arrange to visit His Majesty the King of Libya on the morning of our last day, and this we did. King Idris was a delightful person. He had been quite a warrior in his time, for he was head of the Senussi tribe, based in the hilly area of Cyrenaica. They were a far superior type of people to those inhabiting the rest of Libya. The King himself had been known to cover more than eighty miles a day on a camel. Anyway I think he enjoyed our visit as much as we enjoyed him.

I thought no more about it till I met the British Ambassador in Tripoli on our way home. He was furious. He had been listening to the BBC World News when he heard about Air Frost and Ground Frost having an audience with the King.

'It takes months to get an appointment like that,' he said. 'Heaven knows when I will have another chance now.'

I had never meant to disadvantage our Ambassador and did my best to mollify him, but I do not think that I was every really forgiven.

The following year we studied the Battle of Cassino in Italy. Of all the really unpleasant battles of the last war to have to fight, I think that this must take pride of place. We clambered over some of the slopes in fine spring sunshine, unburdened and fresh. To have to do likewise heavily encumbered, under unceasing shot and shell, under severe wintry conditions, faced by one of the most skilful and relentless enemies that emerged on either side would make some other battles seem like a picnic. At one stage, the whole outcome of the thing depended on one company of the Royal Sussex Regiment. They did not fail.

The contentious business of the bombing of the monastery (which has now been completely rebuilt) was still very much in the mind of the present abbot and we were not received enthusiastically. Who could blame him? The Italian Bersaglieri who accompanied us throughout did all they could to ease our journeying and we were left with nothing but admiration for them.

In the meantime, we continued to have streams of visitors, many of whom we much enjoyed. We had to see that they met everyone they should, from HE The Governor-General downwards. Among them was Field-Marshal Dick Hull, who was an old friend of the Tunisian campaign, also Lieutenant-General John Hackett, the VCGS, who unfortunately came out with a hatchet. At that time our political masters were bent on making economies and it must have been difficult for him and many members of the Army Council who brought bad tidings. The Army teaches you to look after your own like a tigress her cubs and it is difficult to be able to acquiesce when the axeman cometh.

We also had bishops who were very easy guests and easier to please than some of the generals. It was interesting to hear them preach after having them to stay. I have never forgotten one sermon which ended, 'Try to let God work through you.' When you come to think on it you could not get a better tip, but the same bishop came again a year later and when I reminded him of what he had said, he came up with, 'Did I really say that?'

We had two visits from Lord Louis, one as a farewell visit on giving up being Chief of the Defence Staff and the other to make the Malta sequence of the television progamme *The Life and Times of Lord Mountbatten*. He had spent much of his service on Malta but I was mainly concerned with his polo activities. We had great fun making film for this and most dangerously mounted a camera on a Land-Rover to photograph during a chukka. Anyway no harm was done. I played during part of the film and if you ever see that film again of the polo in Malta and you hear a shout, 'Get off the bloody ball!', that was me.

When he was about to leave after his last visit he said, 'You have, you know.'

'What sir?' said I.

'Become emotionally involved.'

The polo was enormous fun all the time we were there. We invited the Ham Club to bring out a team in the autumn of 1965. Billie Walsh was organizer and with him were Peter Buckenham, George Bathurst and Jimmy Edwards. The latter flew in his own aircraft with Valerie his wife on board. It was all huge fun. The Maltese population did not care much about polo but they did know about Jimmy Edwards and quite a crowd turned up to watch him play. The parties were as fast and furious as the polo which was a little bit diminuendo because of a bad break in the weather. However, it all went very well until the time for leaving, when Jimmy Edwards could not take off because of the weather and when he did eventually go, he soon came back for the same reason. To make up for his extended stay, he borrowed two of the regimental bands for a couple of days, at the end of which he conducted a band concert which brought the house down. Practically every instrumentalist played a brief solo turn and I think that they enjoyed the episode as much as the audience.

Our children went to school on Malta, Caroline to the convent and Hugo to the Army children's school. We had to have nannies for them because we were out and away so much. We chose girls whose parents we knew and they were able to play a full part in the social life. Indeed HQ Southern Command came out for an exercise while Jean was back in England. General Ken Darling stayed with me, and Bridget Duke, as she then was, had to do all the honours, which she did and with a flourish. She was followed in our household by Sarah Curtis and after that Caroline Sloan. It is nice to know that all three are very happily and successfully married since. During the long summer months the bathing was superb for the children. There were two beaches within easy reach, one in fact just outside the house, and these provided everything needed. There were some very pleasant places for picnics too.

I discovered an old 9-inch gun emplacement which had a wonderful view of the south coast of the Island and also the Island of Gozo. It had been empty for many years and we turned it into a retreat. It was quite a way from anywhere else and surrounded by unspoilt country. Moreover there was an almost unknown path down to a minute beach which made a change from the usual populated places. When the launch was available on a weekday, some of the more popular places, normally crowded, could be described as idyllic.

For our last year Geoffrey Kent of the 5th Inniskilling Dragoon Guards took over from Tim Holderness-Roddam as ADC. His regiment had succeeded the 14th/20th in Libya. My own regiment could provide no one and in a way this was fortunate because both the cavalrymen were keen polo players. Geoffrey was to go on in later years to play in the top international class.

Archbishop Gonzi was one of the great characters on Malta. He was in his nineties while we were there and was a great influence for good. Tiny in stature yet lion-hearted in nature, he was traditionally an Honorary Major-General in the British Army and enjoyed visiting us from time to time.

Dom Mintoff, the leader of the Labour Party, was a difficult character from our point of view and the sort of person who could have staged a political coup in circumstances that might result in bloodshed. However, if he became Prime Minister by normal legal means, which seemed much more likely, I would find myself serving him as the commander of the Land Force, so I felt it would be sensible to meet him and get to know him as much as possible.

This was not altogether easy because at that time he did not want his people to know he was meeting the British General. So it was arranged that Jean and I should come together after dark, driving our own civilian car and leaving it two hundred yards away from his house. David Hilpern, our public relations officer, fixed it all and he came with us. In fact the meeting was fun. Mrs Mintoff, an Englishwoman of good family, was present and though Dom Mintoff drank tea, I was well supplied with whisky.

After that he phoned me occasionally to see if I could help him with redundant army accommodation for his youth clubs and when we could, we did. During one of these calls, I said, 'Come to lunch in broad daylight at GOC's House.' And they did. Once again we seemed to get on very well and I taxed him with his unsociability. I suggested that life would be much more pleasant for all concerned if the Leader of the Opposition mingled with Service and other people, even if only occasionally. However, he was adamant that all parties were a gross waste of money. All our energy and time should be devoted to developing socialism. I suggested that such an outlook must be so dull and boring but he maintained that if his ends were achieved it would all have been worth while. Anyway he was relaxed, even cosy while propounding his view and did not leave until well after 3 pm.

I was a little unpopular with some people for having done this and the High Commissioner expressed surprise. I am still sure that it was right.

The interest and welfare of all three Services were all so interwoven on Malta that it was necessary for the three Heads of Services to meet quite often. Some of the meetings were chaired by the High Commissioner who gave us political guidance. Admiral Sir John Hamilton was the Naval C-in-C during the time I was there. He was away a lot, largely because he was also Head of the Allied Naval Forces Southern Europe. There always were a lot of admirals about but very few, if any, British naval ships. We had seen the last Malta-based submarine sail away; also the Admiral's yacht. After that, apart from a flotilla of minesweepers, we had only visiting ships. The American Sixth Fleet was often nearby and it was comforting to see their massive vessels from time to time. The carriers appeared to have aircraft at instant readiness and one did not ask too many questions. Invitations to meals on American ships were not much sought after as they were 'dry' and this deprivation meant that the cuisine could be on the dull side too.

However, they were a fine lot of men. We invited them to various things which they seemed to appreciate, among them a rifle-shooting match; here I am glad to report that the British soldiers were on top.

One of my last assignments was to take over the running of the Marsa Sports Club. Each Service had to take a turn over this, but the Army was by far the biggest user and had much more interest in its continuance. It would have been better if we had had the responsibility earlier, for by various innovations and improvements we soon turned a monthly deficit of several hundred pounds into a profit. We completely refurbished the catering and bar arrangements, redecorated everywhere, invigorated the gardens and started the building of a children's splash-pool so that they could be amused while their parents played tennis, for there were several good courts available. I had asked the sappers to see if they could lay on water to the greens on the golf course, which was not an integral part of the Marsa Club, but was within the complex, and one morning after I had been away for a day or two saw that this had been done but, unfortunately, every tap was in a direct line between each tee and green on every hole. However, this was soon rectified.

Anyway the Club went from strength to strength and is far better than ever now.

Towards the end of our last year I was informed that this was to be my last appointment in the Army. Although I had not thought that I was likely to go much higher, one always lives in hopes and it was a shock to be told that the Army Council could not see their way to employing me further. I had never really thought that I would be much use as a peacetime soldier, but having done not too badly, one would have liked to go on. This news, when it comes, is apt to take the shine off anyone, for obviously stardom is not exactly looming ahead. Service life and Malta was now being upset through a series of strikes, called by the Labour Party as a protest against the proposed rundown of the British Services, which would cause unemployment. This was a quite maddening development for it was the one certain way of making the UK Government do just exactly what the strikers did not want. It did nothing to help our day-to-day relationships with our local employees.

Earlier during our last year I was made a Grand Officer of Merit with Swords of the Sovereign Military Order of Malta and invested by the Archbishop. The members were the direct descendants of the Knights who had fought with such incredible tenacity and fortitude against the Turks, who attempted with all might and main to capture the Island in 1565. They included among their ranks nobles from most of the European nations and were most gallantly supported by the Maltese. The fortresses which they held are still there today as a reminder of one of the most epic defensive battles of all time. I was delighted to be so honoured and when we went to Rome with the polo team, called on the Grand Master who was courteous and charming.

Then began the rounds of farewell visits and parties which seemed to be never-ending. Among these was a lunch for both Jean and me with King Idris. The Ambassador accompanied us and the Queen joined us, so we all ate together. The Queen spoke French which meant that conversation could be more general than it would have been if we had been confined to Arabic through an interpreter, although there was quite a lot of that too and there was a lot to eat.

Our leaving was complicated because the children had to be back in time to start their first terms in schools in England early in the New Year; but Ray Leaky, my successor, could not take over till the end of January, so I had to go home with the family to settle various things and then return to hand over. Rather an anti–climax. However, we had been extremely fortunate during our time. Malta had been calm under the Nationalist Party with George Borg Olivier as PM. Libya had had their King and I had had much support from my superiors, cooperation from my colleagues and splendid service from my staff. It was nice in the end to look back on all that.

CHAPTER XV

ARRIVAL AT NORTHEND FARM

JEANNIE HAD LOYALLY FOLLOWED THE DRUM during our years of married life in the Army but when we discussed life in general and considered what we might prefer to be doing, she always averred that she would like to be a farmer's wife. So when the time came to decide what I should do on leaving the Army, we looked for a farm.

The house we owned at Oxshott, near Esher in Surrey, which we had bought when I was to command the 44th Parachute Brigade TA in 1958, was rather larger than we needed and had seven acres of garden, etc, but at that time was the only place we could find. It certainly did us very well while I was doing that particular job and, moreover, we had no difficulty in letting it to Americans when I went on to other things.

Like most enthusiastic soldiers, I had hoped for further employment and promotion up till reception of the letter from the Military Secretary to say that the Army Board much regretted they could not see a way to find another appointment on the Active List and must therefore carry out my retirement. As GOC British Troops in Malta and Libya, I had most interesting, advantaged and privileged duties to perform and I was happy in my work. The sudden deprivation of all the activities that make up an ultra-attractive way of life, together with the complete loss of all responsibility, were galling, to say the least. Nevertheless, at the age of fifty-four, one ought to feel that plenty lies ahead.

I had always had a penchant to be a Member of Parliament. I thought I had all the attributes. I had always been interested in politics, had been to the House of Commons several times and had friends among the members. So I applied to the Conservative

Central Office. An interview with Geoffrey Johnson-Smith put me off. And I now know I should be thankful, for I would never have had the patience and long suffering required by that most estimable body of men who submit themselves to the votes of their fellows and thereby must serve them for goodness knows how long.

Most of my friends, when similarly placed, got jobs in the City or looked for some charity, which meant commuting. This I would have hated, so back to the land seemed to be the thing, and this we planned.

I attended part of a course at an agricultural college at Worplesdon. The time would have been better spent doing practical work on a farm. We did not want to spend overmuch of our available capital on buying, nor did we want to have to employ a manager. Although I knew next to nothing about husbandry, I had always been involved with keeping horses, so felt that I ought to be able to manage a beef unit myself, given a bit of luck and a good leading hand. This limited our choice to somewhere with two or three hundred acres, not of really high quality land and yet handy to London, for our children would be of the age when they would need much help and support.

On my very first reconnaissance I found Northend Farm. It was 10 April and a filthy day, the worst possible for seeing anything in a good light, yet the moment I drew up in the drive, I felt that this would do. The house was Georgian-fronted and faced south, with matching buildings all around. It lay beside a secondary road, which bisected the land. Deep in a valley with streams, small copses, coverts and one larger piece of woodland, the view was upwards in all directions and suggested shelter, but not forbiddingly so. Such as it was, the village lay about a mile distant, but Milland was really part of a collection of hamlets in a valley.

Jean was thrilled to hear that I had found something feasible in so short a time and we arranged to visit it together as soon as possible. It was owned by a man who had taken to farming late in life, after being a soldier, and he now intended to settle in Western Australia. He had worked like a beaver to make a success of the farm, and so indeed he had, but the call of greater open spaces was too strong.

On 12 April Jean and I looked at the project together, and this left us in no doubt. That evening we did the necessary phoning and the next morning we heard that our offer was accepted. Now for the business of selling Ranworth.

There were not many applicants. There was a bit of a slump at the time so the pressure for accommodation close to London had subsided. Then came a Mr Fok, a Hong Kong Chinese magnate, who, having looked, said he would bring his wife and family next day.

About six of them came in a small Volkswagen and I could not help but think, 'How would someone with such a humble mode of transport afford our price?' Mr Fok took them all round and spoke to the Appletons, our gardener and his wife, who agreed to continue to serve him if they came.

Then, on leaving, he shook hands, saying, 'I agree to everything.' They all piled in the VW and off they went. That was the last time we saw him.

I visited Milland several times to talk to Clive Jewell-Tait, the owner, John Greenway, his foreman, and John Trimmer, who ran the shooting syndicate that had the shooting rights over the land. Northend Farm had been part of the Hollycombe Estate before the war. In those days it had been well-known for the high pheasants plummeting from the escarpment to the north of the valley. However, now, though the estate had been split up, several of the farms were still well keepered and syndicate shoots took place on Wednesdays through the season. I took a gun on fairly advantageous terms, which allowed them to operate over Northend.

In the meantime things were to continue on the farm and by Michaelmas, when we took possession, about three-quarters of the land would be down to cereals or on the way to it. All stock would be clear and I agreed to buy the equipment.

During my visits it became obvious even to such a layman as myself that things were higgledy-piggledy. The buildings, the fencing, the gates, the water supply, the ditches, the drainage, the storage facilities and equipment generally were verging on the primitive. The labour force consisted of John, the foreman, and one part-time man. Clive made up for the sparsity by working full-time himself, something I had no wish to do. But at the time we had no need to worry about profitability and we gaily skated over problems that might be looming ahead.

I spent my time during that summer playing golf and helping in the garden. We had a biggish swimming pool, grass tennis court and delightful surroundings. Living in the cottage at Ranworth, Lewis Appleton, our gardener, kept things tidy, while Ann, his most attractive and lively young wife, did for us in the house. We went up to London when the spirit moved us and down to the sea, and over the Channel too. But we soon grew bored without a role and looked forward to whatever the farm would bring. But I had grown to love Ranworth and before leaving took one last walk through the garden and across the stream in the wood to feel a great pang of regret. It was dark, gloomy and raining when we arrived. The farmhouse and buildings seemed almost decrepit. 'This is the worst thing we could have done,' said I to my poor wife as we entered as owners for the first time. The whole atmosphere was grim. The house, cosy and welcoming when furnished, now appeared tatty and comfortless. After the warm glow of Ranworth, it now seemed to me that we had boobed in a big way.

However, the business of settling in soon dispelled depression. We ate at local pubs and began to assume responsibilities. There was so much to do in so little time that there was none left for gloom. Within that week Hugo started at the village school, our Ranworth couple came to help, we went to a cattle sale, met several reps from all the local firms, were called on by neighbours, surveyed the buildings and went right round the farm in detail, hung all our pictures in the house and attended a duck shoot.

Nevertheless, we certainly had problems to contend with. The first thing forcibly brought to mind was the state of the buildings. We had been so keen to have the place that we were prepared to accept a most cursory survey. Now we could see the dreadful state of much of the roofing, with worm-ridden beams and wafer-thin lathes barely holding up the tiles, between which gaps appeared. The building layout was quite inadequate for modern farming methods, so that harvested corn lay, higgledy-piggledy, in buildings designed for other things, or in butyl silos, where heating up took place with gusto.

Cultivation had to continue, for much of the planned winter cereals had still to be sown. It soon became evident that much of the equipment I had bought had seen better days, so a lot of time was wasted with breakdowns and the subsequent journeys to fetch spare parts. I inherited two men with the farm. John, the foreman, was an experienced, willing and most capable man, but an asthmatic, which fact was not divulged when I took him on. The resulting frequency of his absences through sickness was a great shock, for I had to depend on him utterly. The number two was a part-timer, who could come or go as he wished, but for most of our tentative start he held the bit nobly.

We obviously had to get stock on the place and this I had to do by various ways, buying in bits and pieces. There was a silage pit which I felt had to be used. The loading and feeding of this was a chore that I was quite horrified to find myself involved in almost twice a day. I had not been particularly choosy over the animals brought in and, now, having to feed the indifferent recipients with what I considered horrible muck was not exactly a pleasure.

Some of what we bought went out to graze and immediately found gaps in the wire fences, so that rounding up, sometimes in the dark, became just another thing, like the patchwork mending of the fences we were forced to do. The reluctance of the animals to stay in their designated areas was largely due to the inadequate water supply, which I now found to be primitive in the extreme, and rather desperate remedies were needed to overcome this.

Meanwhile, when and wherever we worked on the land, it was obvious that the state of the drainage was abysmal. Few, if any, of the ditches had been cleared for several years and plans of any drainage system were unavailable. It was said that when the large estate, of which the farm was part, was sold after the war, the agent, annoyed at a paucity of remuneration for past services, had deliberately destroyed the drainage plans, which recorded the elaborate work done in the 1880s by a Peterborough firm. I now decided to buy a modern ditching machine and resuscitate as much as possible of what had been done nearly one hundred years before.

The house needed considerable alterations to make it really habitable. Heating, wiring, plumbing, insulation, rising damp, the kitchen, the roof, guttering and sanitary arrangements all needed urgent attention, which meant that workmen would be our constant companions for many months to come. One part was so decrepit that one man called me to look at a wall of wattle and said, 'Cor Guv, you're living in a mud 'ut, you is!'

Anyway, we battled on trying to live normal lives, dining and wining with our new neighbours, shooting and golfing, going up to London when necessary and supporting the local church, and depositing, fetching and visiting a daughter at a school near Newbury.

Finding a good local farm accountant was a must, for at that time there were considerable subsidies available for developments or improvements and one had to know about such things or lose them.

We were not given much encouragement by some. For instance, one experienced farmer during a call, said, 'I feel so sorry for people like you what take to farming with no knowledge and experience. An almost certain way to bankruptcy, unless you're prepared to lose a great sum of money.' A local farm equipment dealer said, 'You need highly skilful management to succeed on this heavy land.' An old friend, on hearing what we had paid and proposed spending, said, 'You will never see your money back, of course.'

Among the many callers were the neighbouring farmers. All most friendly, helpful and encouraging. All confirmed that many of the problems of working the land in the valley were universal but that there were compensations. I could see that fending off borrowers would be a problem. Ron Liverton began with the statement, 'I always say, "Neither a borrower nor a lender be," but it so happens that I badly need the temporary use of a muckspreader. I see you have just bought a new one.'

I managed to find an excuse on the spur of the moment, but a certain amount of mutual borrowing did seem to be part of the way of life, as was mutal help when moving stock or when emergencies had to be overcome.

D'Arcy Burdett, a vibrant, ginger-haired, ex-submariner farmed five hundred acres further down the valley. He was thoroughly embroiled with the problems of a large milking herd and seemed to work all night and day, yet we managed to tramp the Liphook golf course at least once a week. On the other side was David Palmer, another comparative newcomer to farming, whose father, having succeeded in industry, suddenly decided to take to the land.

North and south of us were the Jenner brothers, who grew corn, mostly to the exclusion of other projects, apart from some fattening of beef.

My predecessor's main activity had been rearing pigs, so sties and fattening houses were prevalent among the farm buildings. The pig was one of the few animals I could not abide, but their buildings were easily convertible for calf rearing. I planned to buy baby calves from my neighbours, and this project soon brought me into contact with other dairy farmers not far away.

Before we could really get going, we had to have more staff, but first of all another full-time hand. This proved to be a difficult thing. There was no doubt that, compared to many other occupations, that of the farmworker could be described as arduous and unrewarding, yet a splendid way of life for those who could appreciate all that is delightful in our country's environment. The wages, though meagre by other standards, provided all the necessary things, plus some luxuries, but above all there was the farm cottage, rent, rate and repair free, plus some fuel and other perks, sited where the work began so that no time and expense for travel to work was not involved.

Yet, somehow, these concrete advantages had been perverted by the media to become a means whereby the farmer could victimize the worker into a state of serfdom. Reluctance to work on a farm, for any except the most unacceptable, became the norm in much of the South of England and though one used all the means of advertisement and pursued all the possible offers, the number of couples that became available to us was most unencouraging. The local employment agency seemed to be doing their best, yet I spent hours driving to out-of-the-way places to see the unsuitable, and just as many waiting for doubtful applicants to arrive, until at last I found a man I liked, but he had a growing family. Our cottages were close to the rest of the farm, so that troublesome children could prove to be a menace, but in desperation, we engaged Toby and hoped for the best.

When, so blithely, I had agreed with Jean to take up farming as something to do on retiring from the Army, I had never really seen myself as an almost full-time worker. I had imagined a daily meeting with a foreman or leading hand, a gentle saunter to oversee activities, plenty of time for shooting, golf, polo and trips to London, some correspondence or accounting in the evenings and pleasant social activities to boot.

Now I found that I was trying to do most of what I had intended, while desperately trying to grasp hold of a very complex little business. All problems had to be solved immediately. Whatever else might seem important, animals have to be watered and fed. Men, machines, vehicles, lighting and power all too soon demonstrate their importance in the achievement of even the simplest aims.

However, with a modicum of planning, it was possible to fit everything in and I soon took pride in being able to work with, and take over from, the hands when it came to my turn. Parts of the farm were quite lovely, with views of the South Downs not far away. Wild creatures lose their fear when man is mounted on a tractor. Pheasant, partridge, rabbits and deer treat one as part of the landscape and, in the evenings, as one began to look foward to the comforts in store, I rejoiced in my surroundings and tuned my song to the steady thrum of the diesel which carried me.

So, on to Christmas time. St Luke's Church at Linch was on the edge of our land. It was a lovely, simple little building, with a bell in a wooden belfry and could seat about one hundred at a pinch. The site is marked on the map in my copy of the Domesday Book as being in use as a church even in those days. This is now in dispute. The Romans had had a staging post nearby during part of their occupation of Southern England and I would have thought that this alone would have attracted Ancient Britons to trade with the visiting soldiery, a habit of all local populations which persists to the present day. So it would not be remarkable if these, our predecessors in the valley, had built their own little church on or near the site of the existing St Luke's.

John Stevenette was the reigning rector, a dedicated and dutiful incumbent, who knew and tended his parishioners in the accepted style. He had a rather powerful voice in church, which inclined to dominate the singing. All very well till he had to switch off for administrative reasons, whereupon there was a slightly embarrassing lull in the output of noise. We were all thankful when he chimed in again.

All the cosy traditional Christmassy things took place. The carol singing, the exchange of presents and the visiting. It was lovely to belong to an English village community at this time. Fortunately, a willing and experienced daily help came to us every weekday and we had also found a gardener, so that the daily household chores did not impinge overmuch.

Foot and mouth disease now raised its ugly head in the area. We spread disinfected straw in our gateways and hoped for the best. Various restrictions were imposed on movement of animals, which did nothing to help our emergent business. Of all the disasters that could strike a livestock man, this plague might be considered as the worst, and the actual destruction by burning and burying of creatures that one had tended left a feeling of despair. Fortunately, we were not to be inflicted but the threat certainly added to our worries, especially as we now planned to stock up with weaned calves, which would go out to graze in the spring. These were always available, but one needed considerable acumen to buy suitable animals at a sensible price. Proper arrangements for storing grain were also essential, for otherwise that which one had grown with much trouble and expense would heat up, deteriorate and became practically worthless.

We chose the Condor System. The grain was tipped into a pit, from whence it was escalated up to descend into a cleaner, which, through its vibrations, shed unwanted elements before it was channelled on finally into one of the bins. There were three of these, with a total capacity of some 120 tons, which total we could stretch by adding wooden extensions to the bins.

The bins were serrated underneath so that air could be blown through for drying purposes, this being supplied by a tractor-driven fan from outside. As it happened, we had a building which was just the right size to take everything.

We noticed that, in days gone by, there must have been a fair-sized stretch of water in what was now a copse some way north of the house. It was fed by a healthy stream. The dam and some of the stonework that used to hold the water was still there. Now alders, twenty feet high, together with dense bramble and scrub covered the area we thought to reclaim and I had the brilliant idea of inviting the Parachute Squadron RE to do it for us. Ideal training for clearing a jungle base, said I. So they came to work with all might and main when they could find the time. However, it turned out to be a far bigger job than any of us had realized and soon contractors with heavier plant had to complete the project.

I had bought a mechanical ditcher, which could be operated from one of the bigger tractors. It was a most effective implement and very soon began to uncover the bottom of some ditches which had been semi-choked and blocked for a long time. I did not want to tie a trained man to this, when there were so many other things to do, so detailed myself as ditcher-in-chief and continued steadily to deal with all the ditches on the farm, while there was a tractor available, until I had done them all. I became quite a dab hand with it, regarding the business end as an extension to myself and controlling it without having to think.

The polo season began in the early spring at Cowdray Park, where I had so looked forward to being able to play again. I played a few slow chukkers on hired ponies but almost immediately my back contracted and I had my doubts. Injuries from the past had always surfaced whenever I began again after an interval, and now the sharp April weather did not help. I had treatment at Forest Mere and went up to London to see Guy Beauchamp. His advice on seeing an X-ray was, 'Stop it. You will always be having trouble now.'

Now we began sending cattle to market at Guildford, most of which, as they say, 'made the grade', so that there was actually some money coming in. There were those who loved the cattle market, and attended every possible sale. I could not help contrasting these sales with the movement of horses to and from sporting events, and even sales, for that matter. The horses so calm, cool, indifferent, the others so noisy, messy and seemingly full of tension.

I was invited to attend a meeting of the Committee of the Parents' Association of the Milland Village School. My son, Hugo, was now attending there and I found myself promptly elected Chairman. This was a lot more difficult than it might seem, for, apart from the vicar, all the rest of the Committee were ladies. I had never had to chair the other sex before. They have different customs. The main one is that you all talk together all the time and pay scant attention to the authority of the chair. If, as chairman, you manage to get a proposal made, seconded and passed, you will have been doing very well. But the fact that the subject has been officially finalized is no reason why the argument should not continue, and indeed it often does right up until the next meeting.

However, despite the apparent confusion, a lot of business gets done. We had been progressing steadily towards the provision of a temporary swimming pool, when it was suggested that the proceeds from some fund-raising event would give a fillip to any public-spirited donors. All the arrangements for a jumble sale were made within some twenty minutes.

Attendance at the local Conservative Party AGM resulted in my being elected to the Committee. At that time our branch embraced two other villages. I was to have to attend several tedious evening meetings among comparative strangers before we were able to establish our own village branch. Really, most of West Sussex is such a predominantly Tory area that no other political party had much of a chance. So there was practically no local conflict and no unpleasant disputes during canvassing. In fact, canvassing was hardly considered necessary.

All my worries centred round my employees. After much searching, I had engaged Toby, a real old-fashioned hand, who was a delightful man to work with and was highly skilled, but his two sons were difficult. They could dodge attending school to lurk on the farm. Wherever work was taking place, they would be in the offing: sitting about, watching, staring, picking things up and putting them down. They were too small to be able to be of any use in any of the normal things that children like to do to help on farms. Indeed, if they came upon a stack of bales, they would prefer to knock it down rather than build it.

We struggled on through the early months of 1969, gradually learning by hard experience. Then in May two events came up, neither of which we could miss. Firstly, there was to be the centenary celebration of the Royal Malta Polo Club, immediately followed by the virtual demise of the Cameronians (Scottish Rifles), the regiment I had joined from Sandhurst.

15 "During our last year I was made a Grand Officer of Merit with Swords of the Sovereign Military Order of Malta and invested by the Archbishop" (p. 170).

16 Northend Farm, the house in Milland, West Sussex, which we bought in September, 1967 (see p. 173).

17 "I loved the power and simplicity of tractors" (p. 186). With the tedder during haymaking in 1968.

18 "Jean and I, with the Burgomaster, walked along [the bridge] past hordes of young poeple bearing lighted torches, who were cheering, clapping and generally shouting hurray" (p. 236). The John Frost Bridge, Arnhem, 1989.

I knew that our successors on Malta would have made strenuous efforts to make the centenary a success so Jean and I, together with a number of old members, flew from London Airport for what we knew would be a most eventful week.

After leaving the centenary parties, we flew straight up to Edinburgh, where a final regimental dinner party had been arranged. The next day we all drove to Douglas in Lanarkshire, where the Cameronians had been officially raised in 1698, now to witness the disbandment. At the end of a most moving parade, the Commanding Officer, Leslie Dow, marched up to the GOC in C Scottish Command to say, 'Sir, we have to go now.'

With the permission of the GOC, the Cameronians marched away out of the order of battle and eventually out of the Army List, but never out of History. When one joins a regiment, one thinks that it is for ever. It seems to be such a highly durable thing – the territorial background, the customs and traditions, the property, the uniforms, the music and the families and, last but not least, the battle honours and the memorials, including the colours which may be laid up. It comes as a very savage shock to learn that a regiment will be no more.

CHAPTER XVI

EARLY DAYS

AFTER OUR BRIEF FORAY to other places, it was quite salutary to be brought back with a jerk to the harsh realities of life on a farm. Toby's children were still causing alarm and despondency and were thoroughly hated by everyone else. Quite a number of our animals developed a nasty foot ailment called lures. Suppuration starts within the cleft of the cloven hoof and quite severe lameness results. It can only be treated with injections, for which the affected animal has to be caught, confined and pricked. As only some are involved, complicated separating manoeuvres are needed. Sometimes it pays to get the whole lot back to a central cattleyard and then release the unaffected, and sometimes it is best to try to cut off and corral the few and then deal with them in the field.

Whichever way you choose, much strenuous marshalling is needed. Calm, careful and thoughtful herding always pays dividends, compared to rumbustious vigour which the very contrariety of the animals seems to invoke and there is always a feeling that a little more voice will persuade, where in fact a gentle movement will suffice. Anyway, we gradually improved in our ways of dealing with the problem.

We had been quite lucky to have endured a mild winter but now, in the summer, the rains came. Our first experience of haymaking was the worst ever. Rain of some sort came daily and only very occasionally was there a brief spell of sunshine. The weather forecasts were less reliable then, but in any case we were near enough to the South Coast and the Downs to be subject to sudden vicissitudes which could ruin all our plans. The secret of haymaking is to cut just a little at a time and always to have some to turn and to ted while other parts are being baled or stacked or carted, so that when the rain stops or the wind blows or, best of all, the sun shines, one can make the best of it.

With a limited labour force and limited equipment, this obviously requires clever management which can only come with experience, of which, of course, I had none. So I was very much in the hands of my employees and there were obviously times when the best interests of profitability were to be subordinated to the state of fatigue of all those doing the work, myself among them. Soon, haymaking began to coincide with the grain harvest, so vital decisions had to be made each day as to what was going to be for the best. I had bought a new combine harvester in exchange for my predecessor's old crock, so that with our limited acreage of corn I did not anticipate many troubles in that direction. However, all new pieces of equipment have their teething troubles and so it proved with our new combine. A particular trouble with farming is that everyone has to do everything at the same time, so all the same type of machinery breaks down at the same time, and all the skilled mechanics who can put matters to rights are worked off their feet at certain times of the year. Thus it behoves all those who work the machines to be able to recognize a fault when it occurs, find the name and number of the delinquent part on a long and detailed list of spare parts, which will be attached to the operating instructions, and finally hope to find someone on the end of a busy telephone line who will promise to despatch the part, or else dash off to the dealer to fetch it. It is perhaps understandable how time-consuming this can be.

Now, added to the business of baling the hay, came the need to bale the straw left behind the combine – not as important as the hay, yet very much a must. If it were allowed to get soaked in the rain, it lost part of its value and became much more difficult to handle, though usually the bales were considerably lighter and less of a worry.

I found myself completely involved with all of this and while it went on there was no other life. In fact, in many ways it was quite like being in action. Except when rain or darkness stopped play, there were pauses for meals only and then we worked in shifts between the three or four of us. There was even quite a spice of danger too, for it was easy to fall off something, get run over, spiked with a prong or caught up in a machine. Stacking bales into a covered barn in the heat of the summer can be one of the most arduous pursuits that I have ever known, even with the most sophisticated equipment available. The sweat would pour off one to such an extent that one could lose five pounds in weight in a day. One could become almost unrecognizable with dust and dirt, so as to be almost denied admittance into the house in the evening.

I loved the power and simplicity of the tractors. We had Massey Fergusons, three of them, and they were all just like really willing horses. They always started and stopped when you gave the right aids. They did a seemingly incredible mileage on a full tank of diesel. Nothing ever went wrong with them and there was a willingness to pull which could never be overtasked. I was for ever mounted on one of them, from the first stages of drawing the mower to cut the grass for hay, to the tedding, to the rowing up (but not to the baling because I hated that machine), and on to the loading, the carting and the stacking.

It was repetitious in many ways and yet every circuit for each purpose was different. There was always an exactly right way of doing everything, and how difficult this was to achieve.

If one made a mistake by turning too soon or too late, the result of one's error could be magnified and become more obvious with each run down the field. It was always best to pace out and then mark the objectives on each side of every field of operations so that there could be little margin of error. Often one would think that one ought to be able to judge with the necessary exactitude but, alas, this was seldom the case.

One could become lulled by the deep thrum of the diesel and if the going was smooth, false security could lead one to make shameful mistakes. I far preferred to be on an open tractor or combine than in the modern, closed cabin. One of the joys of farming was to be in the open air, even if it needed layers of warm and waterproof clothing in winter. Certainly in the summer it was nice to work stripped to the waist, being gradually conditioned by the wind and the sun. Moreover, it was possible to watch the implement being drawn or driven and listen to a change of noise that could betoken trouble in the offing. At the highest part of our farm you could look across the top of some of the South Downs and see what weather was on the way. It was sad that the sun seemed to shine more on others than on us but perhaps this is what everyone else feels.

While wrestling with the hay crop and corn harvest, we had some eighty store cattle to tend. Now, having dealt with the cases of lures, we found ringworm amidst the herd, so once again the sufferers had to be separated and brought back to the yard for treatment.

Ron Liverton, a neighbouring farmer, said, 'Let me come and have a look at 'em.' So he did that, walking very slowly among them and casting an eye over each one. Afterwards, he said, 'I don't know what good your vet's cure will do but I will promise you that the ringworm will have disappeared in three weeks' time.' And indeed so it did. We never had more trouble with that particular complaint for the rest of our time.

However, with the ringworm defeated, along came yet another complaint called husk. This is a cough which, if untreated, can cause grave loss of condition and even death. The germs are endemic on certain ground and to prevent it every animal of a certain age has to be dosed in the spring. I did not know this and was now paying the penalty – so back again to the yard for treament. We were getting quite good at this now.

This horribly wet summer meant that we had to dry some of the hay by blowing air through the bales after they had been stacked in a barn. This was done by means of a tractor-driven fan, which made a fiendish noise just outside the house. Three tractors and the combine were barely enough to suffice all our needs and one was kept at one's wits' end to ensure that they all earned their keep for every hour of the day. Our team consisted of four of us most of the time, plus friends to help bale-carting, together with some soldiers from the local barracks.

Anyway, we survived and by the autumn all was safely gathered in. In the meantime, Toby's children continued to be as obstructive and awful as only really undisciplined children can be. Apart from knocking things over, they would clamber over machinery, try to start up engines, turn on taps, and on one occasion dropped a cat into a grain silo. So Toby had to go that autumn, and then began the hideous business of finding a replacement. I used to get names from the Horsham Agency and would then try to visit the applicant, which often meant driving for miles down country lanes and byways, so often finding most unsuitable familes at the end of each quest. During these months we had had a wonderful old daily woman whom we called Mrs B, and just about now her husband wanted a local job. He was a splendidly experienced and reliable old countryman who could turn his hand to almost anything, and so he came onto the payroll. In addition, I found an old-age pensioner who liked to work part-time from his own caravan, and after much argument with the local councils, I fixed it so that he could park on the farm and work for me.

By this time I had decided to switch my main activity to beef production. I intended to buy baby calves from all available sources during the autumn, wean them and keep them indoors till the spring, whereupon they would go out to grass and there they would stay for two summers, till they came into the yards as two-and-a-half-year-olds to be finished as fat stock. I had been told that girls were the best people to look after baby calves, so if I could find the right one most of my labour troubles would be solved. Single girls were easier to come by than male workers and we soon had a most accomplished farmer's daughter. Not only did she know a lot about all aspects of farming, but also played the organ in her own parish church on alternate Sundays.

All the time we continued to live a fairly full social life. We gave and went to dinner parties and on most weekends there were drinks parties or visitors. My very dearest mother-in-law, 'Mossie', was quite often down from London and she was frequently my victim at backgammon after dinner. A whole host of charming people lived nearby and if one wanted to conjure up a small party, a few minutes on the phone could bring a quorum that very day. Although I could no longer play polo, it was still a great pleasure to drive down to Cowdray Park to watch the experts from time to time. Of all the grounds in England, Cowdray must be the loveliest and there were always many old polo friends to talk to. I also managed to keep going at golf. Liphook was less than five miles from our house and whenever there seemed likely to be a pause in the struggle on the farm, it was not too difficult to find someone to play with.

Much of the harvested grain had been brought in with a fairly high moisture content, so we had to watch it carefully and when there were signs of it heating up we could always pass air through it if necessary. On one occasion we had to empty a complete bin and transfer its contents to another. There seemed to be no end to all the things that could go wrong.

As the winter approached, we began to collect baby calves by various means. We bought as many as we could from neighbouring dairy farms, which meant collecting two or three at a time, which was time-consuming. We towed a trailer behind a Land Rover to pick them up and this in itself could be an adventurous business. One had to back the trailer into several places where trailers did not really want to go. There were also many calves that did not want to go into the trailer and some of these might weigh up to nearly a hundred pounds.

Sometimes we bought a batch from a dealer, which was less trouble, but if there did happen to be an infection among them, this could spead with dire results. I converted all the piggery buildings to take baby calves and on the whole they served very well. The main trouble was mucking out some of the old-fashioned buildings where the roofs were too low to give access to a tractor or even a grab. We weighed each animal on arrival and put an identifying tab in its ear. To start with, we put each one in a separate pen to feed, with a separate bucket of warm, powdered milk. Sometimes it could take quite a while to persuade them to drink from a bucket, and one had to spend much time getting them to lick a finger covered with milk and gradually pushing their noses into the liquid.

Eventually we found that rubber teats put on to a board with tubes let into containers of milk in each of the pens, holding perhaps six animals, worked extremely well. In this system, they took as much as they wanted when they wanted it and as long as one made certain that none were missing out, it was far less trouble than the old method. To effect castration, we used to put rubber bands over the scrotums to isolate the testicles and normally this caused them to disappear. It was vital to ensure that both these important articles were in the right place because an animal left with just one soon developed all the characteristics of a proper bull and this could have unfortunate results later on. Indeed, one young feller sorted two of us out good and proper when we were least expecting it. Once an animal develops his male aggressiveness, even after he has subsequently been castrated, he is inclined to forget his current condition and continue to be uncertain in temper for the rest of his life.

As in all other pursuits, practice makes for improvement and we soon got better. There is a great art and skill about rearing baby calves as they are prone to every kind of infection. The girls we employed soon learned to notice immediately if one of their charges was a trifle off-colour and in the end, with the help of a most capable vet called Mike Teal, we managed to keep sickness and mortality down to very reasonable levels.

Mike was a wonderfully cheerful character. Indeed, he had to be on arriving at a farm when things were going wrong and the foxhound kennelman was becoming a frequent visitor to collect the dead cattle. He was a great man for chocolate cake and, whenever he came, though we always had some at the start, there was never any left when he went.

While the buildings housing the calves were a hive of activity, our store cattle were in the main covered yard and we used to feed these every morning and evening. This meant loading a trailer with bales of hay and bins of barley which we put into the racks and feed troughs, after having marshalled the animals into an inner yard. It was all quite a neat little business. The haystacks were so positioned that a trailer could be drawn alongside and the required number of bales dropped down into it. The corn bins were plastic dustbins and these were filled from a mechanical mixer sited beside the graincrusher, so it was easy to fill the bins from the mixer and cart them on to the trailer with hay bales. Then, having shut the animals into the inner yard, one drove the tractor into the cattle yard, poured the crushed grain into the feed troughs and stuffed the hay into the racks. The driver had to be quite skilful, for if he misjudged the handling of the tractor and trailer, which had to be reversed rather precisely during the process, he could get into a rather difficult impasse.

This daily feeding was a remorseless routine. It had to be done first thing in the morning and last thing at night. It could be done by one man but it was really a two-man job, which meant that there were two of us feeding the stores, quite apart from the person feeding the calves every day of every year, including Christmas and Easter. Anyway, if you own animals, it is nice to feel that you have a permanent responsibility for them and I never grudged the time spent seeing that my charges had what they needed.

During all this time, ploughing and cultivation for the winter corn was going ahead. There was never any let-up as the months went by. As a result of the very wet summer, much of our land was saturated and some of it was extremely difficult to work at all. On one occasion we had three tractors bogged down in one field and Brian Heath, our casual worker, had to bring his lorry with a winch into use and even this got stuck in the process. But, as so often happens in times of dire calamity, it all got straightened out and in due course the field was tilled, seeded, harrowed and fertilized and we moved on to the next problem.

I still had a gun with the local syndicate, which shot over the neighbouring farms and our land. It was a Wednesday shoot as most of the members could afford a Saturday commitment elsewhere as well. I could not feel exactly at home with some of the members and after a conversation with one of them, I felt even less so. Between drives, this man approached and said, 'What do you like to be called?'

'Well I don't much care. I am a retired Major-General and people who do not know us will usually say General.'

'We are not in the Army now, you know. My wife was an officer's daughter and after she married me she had to change her ideas. There are a lot of important people among the members of this shoot. Indeed I have actually met the Queen.'

There was another who liked to tell us how he always managed to get a passage to Cape Town every year in February after the shooting season and to qualify for this you had to be a member of Boodles.

After two seasons with the shoot in the Milland Valley, I withdrew our farm from the syndicate and ran a much smaller shoot of my own. I was luckily able to continue to have help from one of the keepers and our two hundred and fifty acres, which included the duck pond we had made, could provide quite a reasonable day. Getting beaters was as much of a problem as anything else but we had some great fun, with a bag of a hundred pheasant on occasion. Meanwhile, I had guns in other shoots and was sometimes invited to shoot with neighbours or more distant friends. Gradually, I found that my appetite for killing was waning and I was no longer looking forward to a day's shooting.

The Hollycombe Estate, of which our farm had been part, had been a most carefully laid-out shoot. Birds coming off the escarpment at the top of the valley provided a challenge to daunt the most experienced shot and down in the valley the coverts were placed so that the guns could move to their stands with the minimum of clambering in and out of vehicles and the beaters could flow from one drive to the next. So it was a pity to let it all die away but we all change as we grow older and I now have much pleasure in seeing birds around all the time, while the duck have become tame enough to come to feed when called. There will always be vast numbers of pigeon to keep down.

To add to the general difficulties, my father up in Scotland had been sinking fast, which had necessitated flying visits, and now, on 3 December 1968, he died. Having been painfully ill for some time, this was a merciful release. We had been separated for nearly all my life, so his going did not mean very much to me at his age of eighty-eight. He had remarried after my mother had died some twenty years before.

The number of salesmen who beset us all the time was a feature of the early days of the farm. I had quite quickly decided which firms I would deal with for various things and, as each new supplement came, I could honestly say that there was nothing they could do to help. But that did not stop them and the words would pour forth, together with handfuls of advertisements. One could not help feeling sorry for them but they were apt to waste much time. Even when one was working on a tractor in the field, they would wend their weary ways across the plough, in the most unsuitable footgear, to try for the custom that had already been promised. The good firms had most experienced salesmen, who very soon knew exactly what a particular farmer would need, and they could save a lot of trouble.

Practically everything I had bought from my predecessor fell to pieces and, as they were not backed with instruction books or lists of spare parts, it was almost impossible to keep them going. One soon learnt that the spare parts list of any machine is a vital adjunct. If you could not identify a wanted part on a list, you could spend literally hours queuing at the counter of machinery shop stores, in conjunction with a hoard of other slaphappy landsmen who had elected to take a chance with an implement in days gone by.

There is something about life on a farm that leads to a sense of false security as regards the equipment. So often an implement is used right up to the end of the day when the user has little energy left except to get himself fed, cleaned and into bed. Perhaps the implement he was using is not needed the next day, owing to a change in plan or in the weather, so it may be left rather longer than it should without the essential oily rag, oil can and greasegun.

Having been through an appallingly wet summer, we were now to experience a really cold winter. The first ghastliness was the freezing up of all the cattle troughs so that the animals could not drink. This meant going round the farm breaking the ice on the troughs and then trying to unfreeze the pipes leading to them. Hot water was often the only possible way and it was not easy to carry this around the whole farm. Sometimes the water system in the main cattle yard was frozen so solid that we had to lay a hose from the house kitchen to give the animals something to drink. Within the buildings, we were sometimes successful with a hair dryer. On one occasion, even the cold water pipes in the house froze, as we were not so experienced in heating the house in those days. It could be quite a job to start the tractors, which were kept in semi-open sheds. Moreover, diesel fuel can behave very badly in these conditions. Fortunately the calves and the cattle never seemed to mind the cold, indeed it seemed that malignant germs suffered as much as anything, so perhaps we had a bonus here.

We had much difficulty finding reliable farm hands. We badly needed a replacement for Toby. We had tried one couple for a while and had an odd man or two. Most of the applicants were dreadful. Then finally we engaged a couple in the early spring.

All these difficulties caused us furiously to think and ponder as to whether we were doing the right thing. I developed a desire to visit Western Australia. Our predecessors on the farm were there. They had gone into real estate and apparently had done very well in a short time. I did not think that this would have suited me, but I was quite keen to go and have a look. Jean and I had, on the whole, been happier when we were abroad than in the UK and I began to make arrangements for a one-man reconnaissance. However, responsiblities on the farm interfered with making serious plans. Jean was not really enthusiastic, so we decided to build a swimming pool instead. Our garden was well suited for this and one could imagine what heaven it would be to be able to plunge in after working throughout the long summer days, or to meander round it with all our friends during the easier times.

Anyway, once we had got involved with this project, while still being thoroughly involved with the cycle of events on the farm, there was little time left to think about Australia. We engaged a firm called Europools. Not much was known about them so I went to see some of their finished products and the customers seemed to be quite satisfied. Then the fun started. Europools were really only a management committee and all the various stages of the pool building were done by contract. Nearly all the contractors were themselves skeleton organizations, which arrived in succession without all the essentials to fulfil their tasks. Each in turn took over our telephone for the duration of their particular stint and one could not believe that the thing would ever be done.

Europools had one particular executive who knew all about everything, but as he was probably involved with other pools all over the South of England, it was hard to lay him by the heels. Anyway, it was finally done and came the glorious day when we all had our first swim. It was all well worthwhile. I used to pop in before breakfast and after dinner before going to bed, birthday suit being the order of dress, and it gave us, and still does, infinite pleasure.

We had an oil-fired boiler to heat the water, but the whole aspect was sheltered and facing the sun. In the evening the sun held onto the water till it was time for us to come in for a drink. In later years we replaced the oil burner by solar panel heating and this proved to be remarkably successful. At the end of some hot spells the pool temperature rose to over ninety degrees Fahrenheit and throughout the summer it was maintained at over eighty. A bubble cover floating on the surface helped considerably to keep the heat in. This could be wound up by means of a roller fixed at the deep end and this could be operated easily by one person. I soon discovered that the art of poolkeeping is to keep it clean, properly chlorinated and never to allow algae to rear their ugly heads.

While the pool was being made, Anglia Television came to film part of a programme they were making about the Battle of Arnhem. This was a source of much amusement to the workforce, all of whom were very keen to get in on the act. One point that struck forcibly was how seldom was the sky above us free of some aircraft noise. Production often had to be halted while one aircraft or another passed overhead. We lived quite near Gatwick Airport flightpath so some of this was understandable but much of the noise was from light aircraft based nearer.

From the front of the farm, you looked across a road which was busy morning and evening taking people to work, mums with their children to school, and the normal routine traffic of the countryside. But otherwise it was little used and we could move cattle up and down it with scant inconvenience to anyone else. Unfortunately many of the users liked to belt along it at speeds for which it had not been designed, so one had to move on to it warily. However, it did mean that we were very accessible and well placed to go anywhere, which on the whole is better than being isolated.

Also from the front, the view was out across all the southern half of our land, which fell away to a stream some half a mile away and then rose to a gentle ridge, beyond which the ground fell again to another stream. There was a fine oaken copse to the East, a tree-filled runnel to the West and again over the ridge another copse. Behind the farm the ground rose gradually towards the

Hollycombe Ridge and this included another lengthy copse which sheltered a stream pouring down from that ridge. Eastwards of the farm lay a thirty-five acre field stretching up to yet another stream, which fed into an area we had dammed into a pool. Further away still and in the next parish were another eighty acres which also included streams and woods. In the immediate vicinity were three small paddocks, watered by the stream from the dammed-up pond above. So there was much variety, water and shelter, both for our own animals and wildlife.

Roe deer made full use of our woodland and there were wood pigeon galore. Canada geese and all kinds of wild duck visited the pond and while we had the services of Wally Broad, the shoot syndicate keeper, reared pheasants held their own against the massive numbers of vermin that thrive in this type of countryside. With so much cover, it is an uphill struggle to keep all the predators under any semblance of control and as soon as professional keepers are withdrawn, it becomes a losing battle.

Up to the beginning of World War II all the land in our part of the valley and the ridge above us to the North belonged to the owner of Hollycombe Estate. At that time it was a Mr H. C. Hawkshaw and everything was beautifully kept. There were special cottages for the dog kennels, for the laundry, for the stables, for the gardeners, and the village school was also in his gift. All the farms were fully supported, and in particular the drainage system, so important where the land can be light or heavy in different places, was most carefully maintained.

The gardens were quite lovely, with great banks of rhododendrons and azaleas predominating, and lily ponds falling away down into the valley. In fact the gardens are lovely still, especially in the spring.

During some of the pre-war years, my Regiment, which was stationed at Bordon, got to know the Hawkshaw family, and the Adjutant, Jeremy Fisher, married one of the daughters to live happily ever after. After the war, sadly, the estate was sold off and all the farms were separated.

All the farms in the valley are perhaps unique in that the old buildings are similar: the corn stores wooden and built on rat-resistant stone mushrooms, the dungpits circular and roofed to protect the contents from the sun, the cowhouses cosily sited around a rectangular yard, and the farmhouse always next door, with a lovely big hay barn and stables almost alongside.

All such arrangements were perhaps ideal for the days of yore but nearly impracticable for the mechanical age. At this particular time, I felt it incumbent on me to make the farm a financial success. I had always been told that one could offset losses on a farm against other income and they were therefore nothing to worry about, but when you have soldiered with the principle that whatever else you do you must try to improve, you have to continue to try to do just that.

Early in 1970 it was mutually decided that John Greenway, my leading hand cum foreman, almost manager, would have to go. He had been an enormous help in starting us off. He was a most skilful and experienced man in many ways but his health was a constant worry. Perhaps living in a valley was a contributory cause to his problems. His absences would not have mattered so much on a larger farm but with us they were very damaging. I knew that I was going to miss him greatly and so it proved, as, for some time, he was succeeded by others who perhaps only really wanted the use of the cottage that went with the job. With these, we struggled on for a year or two.

Many of the ex-members of my old 2nd Battalion of the Parachute Regiment had kept in touch with each other and now, under the auspices of an ex-corporal, Ron Holt, they had decided to arrange a reunion at Grantham in Lincolnshire, near where the Battalion had been based for a few months before the Battle of Arnhem, which took place in September, 1944. So this September, some forty, which included wives, met for a dinner in a hutted premises near Grantham. The evening was a great success. This was followed the next day with a church service at Stoke, which was the village within which Stoke Rochford Hall was sited. This vast mansion had been our headquarters and also housed the headquarter and support companies, nearly three hundred men altogether.

So much enthusiasm was engendered by this small beginning that the experiment was repeated the following year and now the numbers grew to eighty odd. Moreover, we moved the venue to one of the hotels in Grantham. After the church service that year, Alastair McCorquodale, who had married Rosemary, the daughter of the owner of Stoke Rochford, brought an invitation for Jean and me for lunch.

As a direct result of this, all future activities of the Para 2 Club were based on the great house itself. This has become the headquarters of the National Teachers' Union and was eminently suitable for all that we wanted to do at our annual weekend.

The Para 2 Club grew from strength to strength until the present day, when the numbers attending have reached well over the two hundred mark. A really gracious dinner dance is the mainspring of the weekend, while we have been addressed by no less than two bishops, among other distinguished clergy, at our services in the church. Jean and I always so much enjoy staying, together with the family, at the Dower House at Little Ponton.

The Club has been able to organize and sponsor return trips to nearly all our old battlefields at Bruneval, in Tunisia, in Sicily and Arnhem and has invited some of our much revered ex-enemies from the German Parachute Regiment to join us. Among these was Colonel Rudolf Witzig, a legendary figure in Germany, who had led his impeccable Parachute Engineer Regiment against us in North Africa. Whenever one of our members died, others would travel from all over the country to be at the funeral. The widows and offspring were made members of the Club and many continued to attend the annual reunions. Stoke Rochford was a very special place which had, at one time, been the home of Isaac Newton and, up to the start of the First World War, had needed ten men and thirty women working inside the house to maintain the standards then considered necessary. Goodness knows how many were employed in the pleasure grounds and gardens which surrounded the splendid edifice. Anyway, this environment was ideal for all of us who had had to overcome our natural fears to jump from aircraft to thwart our enemies, to now meet again and reknit the bonds that had welded us together all those years ago. We could remember how, though the whole great building would seem to tremble when all three hundred men came down the stairs together, it stood as firm as ever – almost as though it were to be an example to us all.

CHAPTER XVII

POLITICS

ONE JANUARY MORNING IN 1971, I met my mother-in-law at the Liphook railway station and she said, 'I am lucky to be here at all. On my way here this morning, I got my arm wedged in the door of the bus and was dragged along for quite a few yards before my plight was noticed and I was set free.'

She always took things calmly and I thought little more about it. She was a fairly frequent and very welcome visitor. Whenever she was staying, we used to match our wits and luck at backgammon in the evenings. The badinage and, indeed, recriminations between us became quite a feature of her visits. We had always been very close friends from our first meeting and she had been a great supporter throughout our marriage. That particular weekend, she had seemed to be full of life and relished a small drinks party we had staged, so it was with no feelings of foreboding that we had put her on the train back to London.

However, in the early hours of the morning the phone rang, with Colin, my brother-in-law, on the end, to say, 'Mossy died a little while ago, having had a massive stroke.'

Whether the accident with the bus door had had a delayed reaction, we will never know. However, it all seemed very sudden and unexpected and cast a gloom for many a long day.

These were the years of children at boarding schools, with most weekends taken up with hours and miles of motoring to either visit or bring home for a time. So completely different from one's own school time, when a brief half-term was apt to be the only break. In those days, all the important school matches were played on Saturdays and the rest of the school was required to be there to shout, 'Hooray!' Sundays, apart from the chapel services, were given over to hobbies, for there was little other time available. Perhaps shorter terms with fewer breaks would be better for all concerned. Meanwhile, a firm called Fernden built us a hard tennis court. The remarkable thing about this was that work started and finished on the planned date and they never once had to use our telephone for any requirement whatsoever.

Now, at long last, we found someone who was to stay with us for several years and become a genuine leading hand. His young wife had had one child and there was another on the way, but I felt that their children were never likely to be a problem, and so it proved. Indeed, their progress through life was an added interest, so that when Tom and Carol Smith left us, it was for reasons beyond our mutual control.

It was about now that we paid a return visit to a very happy old stamping ground, The Support Weapons Wing of the School of Infantry at Netheravon, for it was here that we had spent a very interesting two and a half years. Our main purpose now was to present a memento to our old batman, called Linch, who had looked after a succession of commandants for several years. A highlight of his time with us was when we gave a party during the Suez Crisis and invited our guests thus:

> 'Nassernalised are all of we,
> Come dressed as he would have us be.'

People came as Sheiks, Tarbouched Spivs, Afghans, Belly Dancers, Harem Slaves, and many were prepared to act the parts, so, after a rather sticky start, the party went like the proverbial bomb. Our local General, having driven his car slap across our lawn and into a hedge, brought about a measured retreat and at about 2 am there were only ourselves, Linch and our nanny left. When I suggested packing up, Linch said, 'What, go home? Hell, I have just begun to enjoy myself. Come on, Nanny, you and I will keep cracking.'

However, on this particular occasion we were staying with Peter Young, who lived at Upavon, and we much enjoyed matching our skills versus the highly mobile partridges on the local shoot. Afterwards, we all went back to the mess at Netheravon for the final rites, to leave in the dark, and when we arrived back at the Youngs' house, Peter opened the back of his Land Rover to exclaim, 'That's funny, I started with two spaniels and now have three.' The telephone soon put things to rights.

I was now to become thoroughly embroiled with local politics.

The branch of the Conservative party to which I had been elected as a committee member soon after arriving at Milland looked after three villages as well as our own. This was never very satisfactory for the Milland Valley was very much an entity in itself, and so, much encouraged by some of the habitués of our local, The Rising Sun, I convened a meeting in the village hall of all those interested and we decided to form our own branch. There were some six hundred voters on the list so, although we would be one of the smallest branches, we were by no means inconsequential.

It was comparatively easy to coerce sufficient enthusiasts for a committee and find a treasurer, but by no means so easy to find a secretary. Most of those who were efficient enough were already full committed with other organizations. You very soon find in village life that a small nucleus of people are involved in almost everything and the remainder are content to sit back and complain.

We evolved a system wherein each committee member became responsible for about one hundred voters. I then wrote a personalized letter to each constituent which set out Conservative policy, highlighting achievements and asking for contributions towards the funds. After a tactful interval, committee members then visited all those on their lists to give thanks or to persuade and encourage, or even try to convert. By this means at least we knew where everyone stood and when it came to polling day, through the use of tellers outside the booths, we were able to know more or less how the voting had gone and could chase up the laggards at the end of the day.

When it came to collecting subscriptions, I kept the onus of visiting the known wealthy as my own preserve, and by timing my approach to the 'sundowner' period, I often surprised both my victim and myself by the results achieved. Anyway, by this means we became the champion branch in the constituency, both for fund raising and percentage of the voters on the constituency roll.

Our Parliamentary members always spoke at our Annual General Meetings. Peter Hordern was our first one, then Christopher Chataway and finally Anthony Nelson. The County and District Councillors also played a full part. Peter Hordern left us when the constituency boundaries were altered. Christopher Chataway resigned to go into industry and I was among the delegates who chose Anthony Nelson to be his successor. He was finally selected from some three hundred applicants, for Chichester is one of the safest Conservative seats in the Kingdom. He was much the youngest and the most potentially promising of the finalists but I think that it was the presence of his very attractive wife, Caroline, sitting beside him on the platform that clinched the deal. I also had a hand in selecting and electing the County and District Councillors. Again it is true to say that the Party takes considerable trouble to ensure that the right people are brought forward. It might seem that until a general election is taking place there is little for the political party machinery to do, but in fact the work is endless and embraces almost all aspects of our national life.

I found much of this tedious. As a branch chairman I had to attend a monthly conference at Chichester to listen to reports from all and sundry, most of which could have been circulated on paper. The meetings took place in the evening and clashed with dinner time. I always used to insist that our own local meetings were held before the witching hour so that they did not impinge on the even tenor of our ways. When people complained that this interfered with their working hours, I used to suggest that they should alter their working hours on that day if they were keen enough to take part in local politics, and so on the whole they did.

Colonel Freddie Gough, who had commanded the Recce Squadron of the 1st Airborne Division at the Battle of Arnhem and had been with me at the main bridge, was the person who had led me into local politics. He had been the member for the Horsham Constituency for many years and had become an old friend. When we came to live at Milland, I saw quite a lot of him. Another enthusiast was a tiny little woman called Lillian Morris who was a near neighbour. She persuaded me to attend the Conservative Party Conference at Brighton where we acted as stewards and had sumptuous lunches in one of the big hotels. There we saw all the hierarchy and I well remember looking down the line of the shadow cabinet and remarking on the outstanding appearance of Margaret Thatcher. She was so alive and shining brightly.

Labour was in power during most of my time and I met two of their Prime Ministers. When the Dutch Cabinet were visiting, I was asked to lunch at Downing Street by Harold Wilson to help to amuse them. He told me that he had been reading accounts of the Battle of Arnhem and the siege of Ladysmith at the same time. He had been impressed at the way, at Ladysmith, communication from the besieged and the outside world had been maintained by the garrison sending signals in Morse onto the clouds with their searchlights. At Arnhem we had virtually no communication with the outside. 'You have not progressed very far, have you?' he was able to claim.

I also met Mr Callaghan at the Imperial War Museum but I cannot remember anything we said.

After a time I was appointed Vice Chairman of the branches north of the Downs, which meant attending garden fêtes and other jamborees on most weekends during the summer months and meetings during the winter. Milland lies at the very western extremity of the constituency so a lot of motoring was involved. As Chichester was patently such a very safe Conservative stronghold, I began to feel that I could spend my time more usefully doing other things and when the next local elections came up, I opted for the Parish Council and handed over the Chairmanship of the Conservative Branch to another retired Major-General, Jimmie Barnetson. I am glad to say that the branch has continued to flourish. The chairmanship has been passed to two other succeeding Major-Generals and is now in the safe hands of an Air Commodore.

To the very end of my tenure I had difficulty in finding a secretary, and finally I had to conscript my wife who is quite an accomplished typist and who could keep the minutes of the infrequent meetings. However, I found that I had to hand her over as secretary when I handed over the chairmanship and as she was unwilling to extricate herself, for several years I was involved with all the commitments which inevitably involve the spouse. It is always difficult to gauge how much in the way of events one ought to stage to keep up interest. There has to be some fund raising, and well arranged sales or drink parties can provide most of what is needed. We are fortunate in having readily available the house and gardens of Hollycombe, the home of Mr and Mrs John Baldock. He was once the Member of Parliament for Market Harborough. The only trouble here was a peacock in their garden which liked to make raucous comments when any visiting notable was speaking.

The annual Chairman's letter which was sent to all constituents was an excellent means of keeping in touch with everyone and some of the leftwingers would stop me in the village to remonstrate with my views. One year we failed to send them to everyone and our foremost opponent stopped me to say, 'Where is your annual letter, General? I insist on having a copy.'

Every now and then we found that things seemed to be getting too much for us and though, for the moment, our staff problems had eased, there was never an hour of any day in which no fresh problem emerged. Our lives were passing, while we were tied hand and foot to our land and the rewards hardly justified the effort required, so we put the farm up for sale.

This turned out to be a horrendous business. An unending stream of potential buyers seemed to pour in, many of whom had not the slightest intention or capability of buying and the agent was quite unable to differentiate between the genuine and the bogus. Showing people round a farm is a very much more time-consuming business than showing them round a house, but we soon learnt to recognize the non-starters and were then quite good at finding excuses to fend them off. After what seemed like many weeks, three contenders remained. A tycoon, a Jewish gentleman and an Eton housemaster. We liked them all but unfortunately agreed to the agent's suggestion that we should hold a Dutch auction. In this system all those interested submit their bids in writing by a certain time and the agent then, having read the bid, offers the property to the highest bidder.

As it happened in our case, the tycoon had put in the highest bid and so was the first in the field. But this did not satisfy the other two and both came to see us with higher offers. We had to point out that this was now too late. The tycoon was overjoyed and soon began to press for completion but fortunately I had always said there would be no completion until we had found somewhere else to live, and, until we did, there would be no question of our moving. Our agent had been responsible for us doing things the wrong way round and now he was quite unable to find us anything suitable in the area so we went off to look elsewhere. We had a good look at East Anglia, where Jean and I had been stationed during part of the war. We saw several places in Wiltshire which we both knew well and where we had always thought that we might settle, but there was nothing suitable that was available. We even went up to the Solway in the Lowlands and did in fact find a rather lovely riverside house with farm but when we asked the owner, a newly widowed lady, where her nearest friends lived, she said, 'Only sixteen miles away.'

With youngish children at school in the south of England this remark forcibly brought home the impracticability of living anywhere but somewhere near where we already were and after a long drive down to Northend, we decided to cancel the sale. Our tycoon was not amused and we felt very sorry to let him down, but he was not exactly underhoused as it was and we had always said quite firmly what our conditions were.

So we decided to enlarge the house and stay put.

CHAPTER XVIII

HOSPITAL AND JOURNEYS

JUST ABOUT NOW the Gallaghers joined us. Bob was by no means a skilled farm worker, indeed he had started life as a lamplighter in Glasgow. However, he could drive a tractor and was willing. His wife, Joan, was a gem of a daily help, which made all the difference to Jean. Meanwhile, our old age pensioner with the caravan had left us, while Jim Boxall, our other old stalwart, wanted to retire but would always make himself available in an emergency.

We had already simplified our operations and become a predominantly beef unit, only growing barley to feed our own stock. We needed quite a lot of straw for the calves and the larger animals that we fattened for market in the yard during their last winter with us.

The yearlings were outwintered in various parts of the farm. There was shelter near every field and we made corrals by the roadsides, where we had hayracks strategically placed so that we could fill them with hay or straw directly from the trailer. This method saved much time and labour. The corrals became pretty muddy by the end of the winter but we had put loads of chalk in them, which kept them quite solid.

We fixed up the old cowhouses behind the house so that we could pass the more advanced animals into them, which made it much easier for the dealer to make his choice, and it was from these that the animals were finally loaded into cattletrucks and taken away. One got to know some of our cattle quite well and vice versa, so it could be that their going was a traumatic event. Each group seemed to accept a boss boy and usually, if he embarked willingly, they all did but if he had his doubts, getting them aboard could be quite an arduous business.

Added to this, there was often an odd man out who never agreed with his mates and would prefer to demonstrate his jumping capabilities rather than go along. If there was a weak place in the defences, he would find it, gather himself on his hocks and blunder through with a crashing of timber and the curses of all of us.

Growing our own barley meant that we had to keep all the agricultural machinery including the combine. Whereas one can share or borrow many of the items of equipment, everyone needs a combine at the same time. The new machine I had bought soon after we arrived at the farm and so it was in good shape. At the beginning, John Greenaway, my leading hand, was rather loath to let me drive it, thinking that I might do irreparable damage in no time at all. However, as I could rightly say that it belonged to me, I was soon on board and very much enjoyed using it. As with most things in life, practice makes perfect and in the end I think I became a fairly skilful driver.

At the end of one harvest, when I had finished cutting the last field, I moved the combine into a neighbouring field where the stooks of straw were standing. Putting the machine into top gear, I careered around the obstacles at speed, singing happily at the top of my voice. Fortunately, there was no one else about.

Most of our summers had been disappointing weatherwise but 1973 was exceptionally dry and hot. The grass alongside most of the roads withered to a browney waste but here, in the Milland Valley, the heavy clay soil kept the moisture and we were almost like an oasis. Some of the streams seemingly never stop running and much of our pasture remained green. This, as luck would have it, was the year when I was smitten with the 'Old Man's Disease', trouble with the prostate gland. I either could not urinate when I wanted to or could not stop when I did. Awkward moments arose when I was driving along public roads but I soon developed a practical technique of peeing with the lefthand front door open by the roadside and I don't think that I ever gave offence. One friendly policeman told me that, to be strictly within the law, I ought to pee against the nearside rear wheel. However, I thought that this was more likely to incur an accusation of 'flashing' than the method I adopted.

In midsummer, I was operated on in the Military Hospital at Millbank, a quite splendid establishment now, alas, no longer available, as it has been handed over to the Tate Gallery as an extension for their exhibitions of so-called modern art. One of the nicest things about the locality was its convenience for visitors and so many of one's friends were able to come. Now the hospital has been moved to Woolwich, which is a desperate place to get to, either by road or rail. I was told that the change had been largely due to Prime Minister Wilson's direct intervention.

Although the operation was completely successful, I found it difficult to shake off a feeling of immense depression afterwards. There was absolutely no valid reason for this but it just would not go away. I would curse myself and give myself severe lectures but the gloom and doom would not depart. At the beginning of September, we chartered a motor vessel called *Trout*, based at Cannes, and with my son, Hugo, aged thirteen and an old friend, Molly Jennings, we drove down there against the flow of all the returning French holidaymakers. Apart from just one day, we enjoyed quite perfect weather. We cruised along the coast of the Riviera, stopping at a different place each night. They were all attractive and interesting. Perhaps Port Grimaud and the Isles d'Hyères pleased us the most. We dined on board each night, being served by the most adorable girl called Christobel, whose culinary achievements matched the shape of her quite gorgeous figure and other attributes. Sam, our skipper, was great fun but a little hard to place. Although an American citizen, he had served in a British cavalry regiment during the war and seemed to have had other backgrounds. There was room aboard to live quite separately from us, though Christobel served the meals.

We would set off at a comfortable hour each day and cruise till about noon. We would then anchor in some sheltered bay for lunch, bathe and water-ski from the speedboat which was towed behind *Trout*. After a fairly prolonged session, we would move to our next port of call, where we would have a walk to shop and for exercise. I had thought that being tied up alongside other boats for the evenings might be disturbing but it never was. Our last night, we took Sam and Christobel out to dine in Cannes in a restaurant of their choice, where we ate sumptuously at minimal cost. Then homewards over the mountains by La Route Napoleon. It was a memorable holiday.

Unfortunately, there was a price to pay, for in my rather frantic struggles to get back into the boat after water-skiing, I managed to develop a hernia. Once again, the Army was kind and I was dealt with at the Cambridge Hospital in Aldershot, a place I had nearly managed to escape from many years before the war, when I woke up in a ward after having had a bad fall at the Chiddingfold point-to-point. I was just about to leave in a taxi when a nursing sister, accompanied by two orderlies, clamped me onto a stretcher and took me back to the ward. An X-ray the following day revealed a fracture of the skull, so perhaps I was fortunate not to have secured my freedom. There was no question of trying to escape this time. Army hospitals had made great progress since the pre-war days and one could not give too much praise and thanks for the way everything was done.

During one's service as a senior officer, one is inevitably involved in what the various churches provide for their customers, for in times of trouble they become an essential element and are otherwise a steadying and very useful influence for good. So most of us become quite regular attenders at the available services, which habit tends to prevail in retirement. Within five minutes' drive of us at Northend Farm, there was a dear little church in an idyllic setting. Not long before our arrival, the incumbent had been a Vere-Hodge, who, as an artillery observation officer with my battalion during the battle at the Primasole Bridge in Sicily, had managed to bring devastating fire from the guns of a cruiser onto a German Parachute Battalion, which might well otherwise have put paid to us. Apparently, he was as successful talking to his parishioners as he had been to the naval gunners, for he built up an enthusiastic congregation.

His successor, whom we liked very much, was followed by a character who suddenly announced that he did not approve of matins and henceforth there would be communion and family communion services only. New-fangled services were being introduced nearly everywhere but we were fortunate in that, at the top of the hill, to the north of the valley there was another church, manned by an old army padre, who stuck out for the things I knew and so I transferred my allegiance to him. However, Jean stayed on with the church which was, in fact, our parish church.

Before these changes had occurred, I had been rather perturbed at the tone of some of the speakers on Remembrance Sunday.

Indeed, one of them had cast doubt on the need to have a special service at all. I thereupon rashly offered to give the address on the next occasion myself. Although I had often read lessons in various churches, and even a cathedral, I had not talked from the pulpit before and I found it quite an alarming commitment, not so much once I had got started but in the anticipation. Anyway, nobody booed and thereafter I was in some demand at other churches in the locality. Among these was the chapel at my son's prep school. Here, just before I began, a boy pulled his handkerchief out of his pocket and with it out came a ping pong ball, which bounced gaily down the aisle. I decided to wait until it came to rest and say nothing before my peroration. I like to think that it was a genuine mishap.

A famous American military historian, Cornelius Ryan, who had made his name with his book about D Day, had now completed a book about the Battle of Arnhem, which he called *A Bridge Too Far*. Jean and I were invited to attend a most spectacular launching party in Holland, which included staying at Hilton hotels, visits to the battlefields from luxury river craft and entertainment from Queen Juliana at her palace. Among those invited were the American Airborne Generals, and Matt Ridgway and James Gavin, two of the most gifted soldiers of their generation, with whom it was an enormous pleasure to pass the time of day. There was more of this to come.

Some years before the officers of the 2nd Battalion of the Parachute Regiment had commissioned David Shepherd to paint a picture of the Battle at Arnhem Bridge. He had asked me to help, so we had gone to a convenient site overlooking the bridge and then, with the help of surviving photographs and his most innate skill, he had produced a most realistic, yet striking, picture of the battle. This has hung in the Officers' Mess for several years and when Cornelius Ryan was looking for a jacket cover for *A Bridge Too Far*, this picture was the obvious answer. It proved a great success and it was then decided to use some of the royalty money for a portrait of me. Andrew Freeth was asked to undertake this and he came down to the farm.

I should think that undergoing portraiture could be a most tedious process but Andrew Freeth had a fund of amusing stories and played classical music from a tape recorder. Thus, with fairly frequent breaks, the time passed pleasantly enough. The only snag was that he had assumed that I would want to sit down on a chair but a soldier wearing full regimentals is more accustomed to be on his feet and now I found that my sword kept slipping in my grasp, so that it was hard to feel relaxed and natural. When one looks at the portraits in the service clubs in London, all the best are of the subject afoot or mounted. Anyway, despite this we were all very pleased with the result.

Meanwhile, the local French people near Le Havre had been developing a memorial at Bruneval to commemorate our successful raid there of 1942. This venture seems to have appealed much more to the French than to our own people. At the time, for reasons of security, our purpose had never been divulged and many British people could not understand why the radar at Bruneval had not been destroyed by bombing, and it was not until long after the end of the war that the capture of German radar secrets, which resulted in the development of 'Window', was publicized. 'Window' was merely bundles of tinfoil dropped from each aircraft carrying out a raid, which had the effect of creating complete confusion to the enemy radar. Thus no directions could be given to the night fighters or the AA and countless numbers of our bombers were spared from attack. The first use of 'Window' enabled the RAF to produce the fire storms which virtually destroyed several German cities.

Now, in 1975, Admiral of the Fleet the Earl Mountbatten was asked to unveil a new plaque on an existing memorial and it was arranged that I should accompany him. A guard with the colours of the 3rd Battalion were present and it had been hoped that a party from the 3rd would be able to drop on the original DZ but the wind was far too strong. As so often happens on these occasions, the loudspeaker system broke down and while we were waiting Admiral Dickie said, 'I have often thought that a remarkable thing about your raid was that you had no casualties.'

'It was not quite like that,' I said. 'In fact, we had two killed, five wounded and three taken prisoner.'

'Good heavens! I do not know how I could have had such a wrong impression. For all these years I had thought that you had been able to do the job and leave again almost without traces.'

We had quite an interesting talk about the awards which were so scant after our raid. Boy Browning, when telling me to submit recommendations, pointed to his DSO and said, 'I had to work very hard for this thing when I was the patrol officer of the Guards Division, so do not expect a bountiful issue for this one action.'

Nor did we get it. In fact, I was glad to have the MC because I knew that I would never have another chance to earn it, but the other service leaders got DSOs and this caused some comment, leading some to believe that our action had not been as well conducted as it should have been. It was only later, when we saw the length of the honours list for other combined operations, that we wondered if we had not been rather hard done by. Admittedly, these had brought really heavy casualties, with varying degrees of success, but our affair had been a complete success and our lack of heavy casualties should perhaps have been a point in our favour.

Anyway, the French people have always been much more appreciative about the Bruneval Raid than our own people. General de Gaulle turned up at the first post-war affair, while other French ministers had attended all our occasions. I must confess to being disappointed to see that on the rather magnificent plaque now unveiled by the Admiral, there was no mention at all of C Company 2 Para, who had actually been the only ones to do any fighting at all. I resolved to put this right and when it was arranged that both Prince Charles and President Mitterand would come to the fortieth anniversary, I fixed it so that they would jointly unveil a plaque for C Company. This was done with all due ceremony on that occasion.

I have had to go over to Bruneval again on numerous occasions. Perhaps the most satisfactory was on the forty-fifth anniversary, when nearly all the surviving veterans and many other members of the Para 2 Club went there on the actual February date. We were taking a chance because the weather on that bit of coast can be unpleasant and indeed so it was, with visibility down to a hundred yards. This nearly spoilt our walk over the scene of the operation but we could see all the most important things and we were able to do the honours at the memorial near the beach in the appropriate way. The last occasion was in 1989, when the Mayor of Bruneval invited me to unveil a plaque denoting the name of the road leading to the radar site as 'Avenue General J Frost'.

It now transpired that Joe E. Levine, the great American film mogul, was to make a film based on Cornelius Ryan's *A Bridge Too Far*. A paperback edition was also to be launched in New York and so Jean and I were invited to go over to help with the public relations. The centre page in the *New York Times* was the target and this was achieved to such effect that, several years later, President Reagan, when making his farewell address to the Government and people of this country at the Guildhall in 1989, made quite a detailed reference to what had been printed then.

Joe E. Levine threw a party to celebrate his seventieth birthday while we were there. This was quite fantastic and having signed our names in wet concrete at the entrance, our feet hardly seemed to touch the ground. Suffice it to say that no money or pains were spared to make this the greatest party ever. We then paid a short visit to Washington and while there I was honoured to receive a most thoughtful briefing at the Pentagon. It was fascinating to see, on a vast screen, the extent of the US deployment worldwide. It certainly made me realize just how much our allies had now become the civilised world's policemen.

CHAPTER XIX

BOOKS

HAVING SHED MY ACTIVE RESPONSIBILITIES to the Conservative Party, I felt it was time to look at affairs nearer home and got
elected to the Parish Council. I found this rather a slow-moving
affair, for there were endless discussions and very few decisions.
Not that the parish were delegated much authority but there were
certain areas where they ought to have been, and now some of the
parishioners have formed a Conservation Society, which, in fact,
tried to handle some of the matters with which the parish was
much better able to cope. Our Parish Clerk was a Civil Servant in
the employ of the District Council so that his opinions and advice
were apt to superimpose themselves more than they ought.

The women members of the Council behaved exactly as had
the members of the Village School Parents Association. They
talked to each other most of the time, with scant reference to the
chair and even when a resolution had been passed, the argument
would continue. Nevertheless, excellent work was done and on the
whole the Council was a dedicated watchdog and quite determined
that the village should be protected from anyone with untoward
intentions. The only trouble was that this was apt to include anyone
who wanted to do anything. It was much easier to raise objections
to a proposal than to commend it.

An example of this was the application by a local landowner,
who had a fine collection of steam engines which could operate
roundabouts and such like, to open his gardens to the public on
one day during a weekend so that people could bring their children
to enjoy the thrills and also the quite lovely gardens. Many locals
expressed outrage. The noise of the electric organs would quite
spoil the peace of the afternoon; the resulting traffic would clog all

the roads; there would be accidents galore; very unpleasant people would be attracted and the environment would be ruined.

All this resulted in a public enquiry and it was quite unbelievable to listen to many of the objections. Nice, honest and generally decent villagers found themselves able to make statements which they well knew were quite untrue.

One dear lady claimed that if this development were to be allowed, her view of Iron Hill would be completely spoilt from Telegraph Hill, which she climbed occasionally in order to view Iron Hill.

The Inspector asked her how often she did this.

'Well, not very often,' she confessed.

'When did you last go up Telegraph Hill?'

'Well, I really could not put a date on it.'

There was now a considerable pause till the next question, which was, 'Madam, do you ever go up Telegraph Hill?'

There was no reply.

Anyway, the application was granted and although some living nearby were slightly inconvenienced when the wind was in a certain direction, none of the other dire predictions came about. The whole arrangement turned out to be a distinct asset to a large number of local inhabitants and visitors.

1976 saw the beginning of the making of the film *A Bridge Too Far*. Richie Attenborough had given me lunch a couple of times and he had asked me if I would be his military adviser. I was quite keen to accept but, after reflection, I felt that I had been so thoroughly involved in just one part of the battle that I was not the person to advise on the rest of it. In any case, it was proving extremely difficult to get a glance at the film script. Attenborough was evasive about this, as though it was a matter of little importance, but I had been warned that the script was apt to become the film-maker's bible and once this had been printed with the approval of the producer, it was very difficult to get anything changed.

Eventually, I got a copy through the good auspices of Lady Falkender, Private Secretary to Prime Minister Harold Wilson, who approached me after a lunch party at Number 10, to say, 'I understand that you are involved with the Arnhem film. The

PM is most anxious that it should be a success. Is there anything that I could do to help?'

When I told her about my difficulty about the script, she said that she would soon fix that and in two days I had my copy through the post.

I saw at once that there were certain things that I could not agree to and declared my objections immediately. One particular item might not have seemed unacceptable to an American scriptwriter, and was very much desired by the producer, but I could not be a party to it. The scriptwriter and the assistant producer flew over specially from the States to give my wife and me a slap-up dinner in the Dorchester, while they tried to make me change my mind. In the end, we reached a stupid compromise, whereas if they had stuck to what had actually happened, the film would have lost nothing. Joe E. Levine and his immediate family came over shortly before the filming was due to start and we gave them lunch at the Rag. He brought with him a most impressive list of military hardware that he wanted the British Government to provide. I sent this on to the then Minister of Defence, who replied very courteously, saying that other commitments might intrude but that they would do all they could. Joe said that he was going on to see the Queen later that day. He might well have.

It was now decided that Colonel John Waddy would be the film adviser. He had been with the 4th Parachute Brigade during the battle and he was a most experienced Airborne officer, having been Regimental Colonel of the Parachute Regiment for a time. Much of the actual filming was to be done at a place called Deventer, in Holland. Here there was a bridge over the river which was not unlike the main road bridge at Arnhem and it was possible to construct temporary buildings nearby, which would represent the actual buildings from which we had fought. I was invited to be there while they were to film much of the bridge battle, where Anthony Hopkins was to play my part.

I found this quite an alarming experience, for we tended to be incompatible. However, as the days went by we came to like each other and although I found that film-making is the most tedious, repetitive business possible, the sheer resolve and attention to detail of all concerned was an eye-opener. As for the film itself, although there were disappointments, it was certainly a most prodigious effort.

Every summer the vital period turned out to be the haymaking. Before we started farming we had had no inkling of just how crucial this business could be. One found that as soon as there was a fine spell, many people cut as much as they could in the time available, hoping that the fine spell would continue long enough for them to complete all the necessary processes while it lasted. Alas, this was always unpredictable and, more often than not, those who had several acres cut for ripening in the sunshine found that their acres were lying getting soused in the rain. We had found that it was best to cut a small acreage at a time, yet always to have some that could be tedded, some that could be baled, some bales that could be left and some bales that could be loaded and stacked, while fresh acres could be similarly treated, all depending on the weather. We studied the weather forecasts assiduously and became quite expert at reading signs of local changes. Our own weathercock and barograph were of considerable help. In the end, we very seldom were caught out. We started with very limited equipment and all the bale stacking, loading, carting and storage was done by hand. Very hard work it was too. Gradually we came to marshall all the bales left behind the baler with a bale slave so that a foreloader could dump several bales onto a trailer at the same time. One man was needed to sort out the load on the trailer and to offload the bales onto an elevator beside the barn, into which the bales would be finally stacked.

There are considerable degrees of skill in these processes and we learnt much with experience. Trying to do things too quickly could so easily result in a load or part of a load being shed on its way to the barn and the temptation to hasten the necessary drying time could lead to overheating of bales somewhere along the line. In the early days, we barn-dried quite a lot of our hay by blowing air driven through the bales from a tractor-mounted fan. This was quite successful but it meant that one of our tractors was tied up all the time, blowing air through the fan, and in the end we found that it was better to use the wind and the sun to do the same job. Anyway, the whole thing required much skill, judgement and hard work. Nothing could give greater satisfaction than to get the hay crop safely under cover in our own capacious barns in the early summer of each succeeding year.

Several people gave us considerable help. Among them was Beryl Trimmer, a local farmer whose advice was most valuable in our early days. Perhaps the bravest were Sheila and Leslie Tyler, he being a retired and knighted Major-General no less. They sometimes laboured mightily during the bale-carting stages. There were many others too, the farming fraternity always being ready to lend help and equipment.

One evening in February, 1977, I had arranged to dine with Richie Attenborough at his film studios so as to have a preview of the film *A Bridge Too Far*. While I was peering into an apparatus, I heard the great booming voice of Eamonn Andrews behind me and looked up into his widely grinning face, to be told, 'This is Your Life'. I just had time to curse Richie for his duplicity and Eamonn and I were on our way to Shepherd's Bush in a taxi.

Once, on the way up, when the taxi stopped at traffic lights, I made to open the door, saying, 'Well, I think I will be off now.' Poor Eamonn nearly had a fit. However, knowing as I did how much trouble had been taken to collect one's relations and friends, I had no intention of disappointing anyone.

When it all got going it was great fun. Apart from family, it was mostly made up of people from the wartime 2 Para and included my old batman, Wicks, whom I had not seen since the war. He had helped to get me out of the burning building by the Arnhem bridge in 1944 and had then been very seriously wounded himself. I was thrilled to see Colonel Witzig, perhaps the most famous parachutist in the German Army. He had been commanding a Parachute Engineer Regiment in Tunisia in 1943 and if ever there was a crack regiment, this was it.

Thames Television laid on a splendid supper party for all those attending. When the programme has been filmed, there is a pause to see the result, then back to the fleshpots. No trouble was too much. I shall always treasure the red book containing photos of all the participants. The one thing that has always puzzled me is how my wife, family, farm staff and some intimate friends were able to keep the secret. I gather that if the proposed victim gets an inkling, the broadcasters immediately cancel the programme. Jean used to have to meet the producer, clandestinely, in the car park of the Bush Hotel in Liphook. I, in fact, had absolutely no idea of what was going on.

Later that year, we drove up to Scotland visiting friends and relatives, spending a day in each place. This is a most exhausting business. One seems to be packing and re-packing endlessly and gradually the piles of dirty clothes seem to become unmanageable. It was an exercise that we would not want to repeat.

Then one evening after we were back a voice on the phone from Holland said, 'How would you like to have the main bridge at Arnhem renamed the John Frost Bridge?'

This was not an easy question to answer straight away. Years before, the Arnhem authorities had wished to put a memorial plaque on the bridge and I had discussed the proposed wording of this with Freddie Gough, who had been commanding the Divisional Recce Squadron at Arnhem and became an MP. He had then said, 'Unless you have your name put on the plaque, it will not mean anything to anybody and will be ignored and forgotten in no time. It is the same with all memorials.'

However, I was reluctant and in the event the wording referred to the units involved only and thereafter hardly anyone ever paid the slightest notice to that memorial; indeed, when the reigning Burgomaster came to arrange a new plaque to commemorate the re-naming as the John Frost Bridge, he did not know of the existence of the older plaque, which was housed in a quite prominent erection on the bridge.

Anyway, now I said that, providing the British Ambassador approved, I would be more than happy to lend my name to the re-naming of the great bridge, which had become so famous as *A Bridge Too Far*. Jean, my son Hugo and I went back to Arnhem for the ceremony, which was presided over by the Dutch Minister of Transport. We were treated right royally and stayed in the Rhine Pavilion Hotel, which is of course sited on the river and had a magnificent view upstream towards the bridge itself. This has now been somewhat overshadowed by a new crossing, made absolutely necessary by the greatly increased volume of traffic.

A year later, in 1979, during the festivities denoting the 35th anniversary of the battle, I was presented with the Arnhem Gold Medal, which I most proudly display on my writing desk. Moreover, I was further honoured by the composition and presentation of a Military March bearing my name.

Prince Bernhard graciously entertained a number of the pilgrims at his palace and we, the pilgrims, returned some of the hospitality that we had been receiving for so many years by inviting a number of our Dutch friends on a trip along the river in one of the large and comfortable craft berthed at Arnhem. We also had HM Ambassador's wife on board and, as a previous holder of that office had been murdered by the IRA a little while before, impressive security arrangements were in force. While we moved downstream, speedboats encircled us and a helicopter flew overhead. On our way home to the UK, it had been arranged that we met General Harmel and his wife for lunch. He had been the GOC of the 10th SS Panzer Division, which had destroyed the battalion while we were trying to hold on to the north end of the bridge in 1944. We had a most interesting discussion through a Dutch interpreter. Such conversations never seem to be very satisfactory but it whetted my appetite for more.

This year saw the demise of the headquarters of 44 Parachute Brigade of the Territorial Army. Most of the infantry of that quite splendid formation were retained, but bereft of proper direction and support from other arms and services. At about this time, all the brigade headquarters throughout the army were abolished, it being considered that divisional headquarters would be able to command all their units direct. This was, in fact, a totally impracticable arrangement and now, after a period of very dangerous disruption, all the brigade HQs have been reinstated. Alas, at the time of writing, 44 Brigade are still without a proper HQ, although the Parachute Regimental HQ from Aldershot steps in during the summer training period to command the Para Battalions. These battalions have such a high reputation that they are all earmarked for active operations in Germany in event of war. Jean and I were invited to stay with my old battalion, the 2nd, which was stationed in Berlin. We were given a tremendous time, which included venturing into East Berlin, where we went to the opera and dined in a restaurant. Despite seeing only the very best of everything, it was alarming to experience the actual feel of a communist state. The battalion was in quite excellent nick and seemed to very much enjoy their time in Berlin, as, indeed, did Jean and I.

I became Chairman of the Parish Council at a time when we received instructions from the County Council to draw up plans to counteract the effects of the outbreak of nuclear war. The orders emanated from the Government and ought not to be over-looked. Although there was a great deal of unrealistic think-ing, I reckoned that there was much that we, as a community and as individual householders, could do to alleviate the dan-gers and make life sustainable. So we drew up our plan, which envisaged stocking up with essentials and arranging an area in each house where the occupants could best withstand the shock of explosives landing nearby and seal off the encroachment of deadly fallout from nuclear weapons, which had been aimed at targets some distance away. Certain people in each hamlet were earmarked as wardens and others were selected to use the moni-toring equipment which could read the amount of fallout in their area. Such measures might not prove to be very effective but they were certainly better than having none at all. Moreover, we made provision for the reception of refugees and the care of casualties. Important, too, was the need to keep our com-munications open. Every winter brought conditions which made it difficult for would-be commuters to get out of the valley and the obstacles caused by fallen trees would have to be overcome with our own resources. Although, if a nuclear emergency had arisen, the Government intended to instruct populations to stay put in their own homes, it seemed quite likely that irrespon-sible elements from heavily built-up areas would look for shelter, food and safety in rural areas. In certain circumstances, therefore, we had to be prepared to deny entry to our valley, except to those in dire need. Fortunately, most of our menfolk would have been, and even now would be, available to help in this respect.

When it became known that a retired major-general, with airborne antecedents, was in charge of this in Milland, the media swooped. Accusations of private army-ism were soon being bandied about, although there was a certain amount of sympathy towards us as well. The BBC and ITV sent crews to record and report, while even *Private Eye* published a lampoon. None of this did any harm. Indeed, I was soon in demand from other parishes to come and tell them all about it.

About now, an artist called Fairley painted another version of the battle at Arnhem Bridge. A fairly wide distribution was envisaged and I was asked to sign no less than 1,250 copies. I discovered that this is no ordinary chore.

I now began to get fiendish heart pains from time to time which were diagnosed as angina. The worst effects can now be kept at bay with modern drugs but I was warned against lifting heavy weights. This limitation is a considerable disadvantage when one is working on a farm because quite a lot of weight-lifting is the norm. Even though one has accepted the instruction, when something goes wrong with equipment, a fairly hefty heave is often essential if one wants the current operations to continue. At about the same time, my leading hand, Tom Smith, began suffering from arthritis. Much of the trouble emanated from a knee but there was mumbling from a hip as well. He kept going for as long as he could but in any case the old age pension was in the offing and we had to take stock. With my own disability, I could not manage with less than two full-timers so if we were to continue to live on the farm, we had to consider alternative measures.

An obvious one was to reduce our acreage. This was originally two fifty and included land which properly belonged to Linch Parish next door. By selling off eighty acres to people living there, we could much reduce our responsibilities, especially as these acres were quite a long way from all our farm buildings. We had no difficulty in finding willing buyers from our neighbours and so the hideous deed was done. People say that you should never sell land that you have worked and sweated on. I found it agony to drive past our own erstwhile acres for many a moon. Other friends from a little further away, when we told them what we had been paid, were apt to say, 'Oh, why didn't you tell me? It was just what I wanted. I would have given you so much more.'

At about this time, the son of another neighbour, who had just completed a course at Cirencester, suggested that we might become partners over farming activities. Meanwhile, I was still trying to find a replacement for Tom Smith and indeed had found a couple who seemed eminently suitable.

This September saw the launching of my book about my wartime experiences, which I had called *A Drop Too Many*. It was published by Cassells. It had taken me several years to write – indeed I had started it while I was a prisoner of war at Spangenberg in Germany. The launching party was given by them at the RUSI premises in Whitehall. This was great fun and resulted in a spate of reviews, of which I shall always be extremely proud but among the guests, it was Jilly Cooper who left an indelible memory.

Hatchard's, the famous London bookshop in Piccadilly, staged a special display of the book in their front window, which was a great help to boosting sales. There were a number of broadcasting features, but unfortunately Cassells then elected to cease dealing with my type of book and so there was no thorough follow-up.

A visit to the Bahamas was the next item on the curriculum. We went to stay with Duncan and Phyll MacLean. He had been my adjutant of 2 Para during the Arnhem battle and, in the absence of anyone else more suitable, I had given her away at their wedding in London just after the war. They had moved out to the Bahamas soon after and had a very pleasant house well outside the town of Nassau. Having shown us many of the local attractions, they dispatched us to Harbour Island and the house of Mr Solomon, the Deputy Prime Minister, which overlooked the lovely little harbour. We used to move round the island in a golf trolley, for there was no other practical form of transport. The far side of the island boasted an incredible beach of literally pink sand and it was here that we spent most of our time. There were several splendid little restaurants to eat in and our house was managed by an outstanding black daily. When we returned to Nassau, we flew to Freeport in Jack Hayward's private aircraft to see his almost incredible development there. He had masterminded a dreamworld of his own with all the trappings that could appeal to the discerning – golf courses that have to be seen to be believed and a shopping precinct, within which even a no-go shopper like me could browse. Just to fly over the Bahamas in a really comfortable small aircraft, viewing the multitude of lovely little islands, is in itself an unforgettable experience. A fabulous round of golf at Lyford Cay, a dinner with Lady Sassoon, a call on the Governor and several other parties left us thinking how nice it was that some people could live like that.

Meanwhile, work on the farm continued relentlessly. In the spring, all the grass has to be harrowed, rolled and fertilized, corn crops fertilized and treated with weedkiller, fences repaired, gates rehung, ditches cleared and buildings cleaned out; no ordinary chore when they have been housing cattle during the winter.

On 8 December, 1980, I was invited to speak at an end-of-termish lunch party at the Staff College. Quite an occasion and quite an ordeal too, for I had memories of just how critical the audience could be. However, I think that I got by and came away in a fairly joyous mood.

The Iraqi Levies, in which I had served just before and at the beginning of World War II, could boast some distinguished, if not professionally brilliant British officers among their ranks. One of these was Neville Blair of the Black Watch and he, having got in touch with me, now suggested that we should arrange a reunion of all those who had been connected with the Levies, both British and Assyrian. There was a substantial Assyrian community living in London, among them at least two of our Rab Emmas, the equivalent of company commander. Anyway, with great assiduity, the organizers managed to collect a very representative party of some fifty people down at our farm. This turned out to be a huge success. All those who had served together in the Levies had developed great mutual respect and I shall always feel that among all those nations who have served Britain in the past, none produced more highly talented fighting men than the Assyrians. However, we were all growing a bit long in the tooth for such events and so it was mutually agreed that we would not try to stage another.

We twice visited 2 Para while they were stationed at Ballykinla in Northern Ireland and were given a thorough insight into the ways and means of dealing with the emergency. There could be no doubt that all concerned dealt with the problems in the best possible way, considering the political conditions imposed upon them. One could not help being thankful that in the two emergencies in which I had been involved previously, in Palestine and Malaya, we had been sufficiently far away from central government to be able to get on with the job properly. Here, there was no question of withdrawal or victory but rather of continued containment. Anyway, the soldiers did not seem to mind, indeed many of them much preferred the operational commitment to the humdrum life of a garrison town in the UK.

Colin Thomson was commanding the battalion at the time. I will ever remember one of their dinner parties at which Judge Mervyn Dennison and Philip Goodhart, MP for Beckenham and Under-Secretary of State for Northern Ireland, were their guests. My most vivid memory of Mervyn was meeting him in Sicily, where he was busy destroying all the enemy telephone lines during our assault of the Primasole Bridge over the River Simeto. Thomson had died suddenly and sadly of cancer and was succeeded by the noteworthy H Jones. All succeeding commanding officers of the post-war 2 Para have varied in their attitude towards their wartime predecessors. When the peacetime strength of the regiment was decided on, Ministry of Defence policy was that the three remaining battalions, out of some seventeen, should represent all the battalions and that they should not be considered as the direct descendants of the original 1, 2 and 3 Para. To this end the distinctly coloured lanyards of the battalions were altered and no encouragement was given to particular attachment to the old units. However, tradition is a strange thing. The bearers of a name or number cannot help but wish to feel that they must uphold and share the honour that that name or number has won in the past.

Now H Jones arrived upon the scene and he made every effort to ensure that on the anniversary of the Bruneval Raid, which took place on 27 February, 1942, all the old participants should be traced and invited for a really splendid weekend, based on the aptly named Bruneval Barracks at Aldershot. Indeed and so it was. Among those invited were the Lord and Lady Brabourne, Lady Brabourne's father, Admiral of the Fleet The Earl Mountbatten of Burma, and Professor Jones, who had been the brainbox behind the whole raid.

It was not long after this that the Falklands affair blew up. H, who had been skiing with his family in France at the time, rushed home to fix it so that 2 Para, already loading equipment for a pre-arranged tour of Belize, should be switched and included in the Task Force for the Falklands. Not since the days of the Crimea, when the Earls of Lucan and Cardigan could arrange that their own regiments be preferred for battle, has such a thing been achieved.

I have to confess to having been a doubter. At the time, I thought the whole concept was a most unjustifiable risk. Anyway, I made myself most unpopular by saying so in various places. Then came the news of the campaign which highlighted the performance of 2 Para in capturing Goose Green, after the death of the colonel, in an action which was to win him the VC. The battalion continued to distinguish itself under a new CO, David Chaundler, who had been parachuted into the sea beside the naval Task Force and in the end was to lead them into the final victory.

While visiting the battalion on their return, in one way and another it was arranged that I should write a book about it all and so I did. I was very greatly helped by David Benest, the battalion signal officer, who had himself written a fulsome account of the campaign, but, as he was a serving officer, he could not have it published. I made his account the basis for my book, which was quickly published by a firm called Buchan and Enright. In the rush to get it done, we cut a few corners and as a result there was a considerable hiatus. The Ministry claimed that I had divulged names that they had been withholding on principle and, moreover, had done it without their permission, despite the fact that public relations from Southern Command had told them from the start. Anyway, for a time the whole weight of the media seemed to be after my blood and we had to leave our phone off the hook.

It was a great contrast to the eulogistic reception to my first book and we deliberately kept a low profile. In the event, the book sold like the proverbial hot cakes, no harm was done to anyone and the paperback sales go on and on.

In the village things had been going apace and though most of the developments had been brought about by others, I felt that it was incumbent on me, as Chairman of the Parish Council, to draw attention to these things and that perhaps the best way was to invite the Lord-Lieutenant to come and have a look. The holder of the office in West Sussex was Lavinia, Duchess of Norfolk. There seemed to be no record of such a personage ever visiting our valley in the past, nor do I think that the Duchess had much knowledge of our valley before she came. We certainly had quite a lot to show her and I think that she enjoyed her visit as much as we enjoyed having her. There is quite a contrast between the attitude towards such in England and Scotland. Up there, nearly everyone seems to know and revere the 'Lordy Loo'. Down here, it is more a matter of, 'Who's he?'

Meanwhile, life in the village continues. The commuters rise early to catch their trains or join the tailbacks on the A3 to London or the M25 to elsewhere. The mothers bring their children to school and the local traders make their rounds. The retired gentlemen merge onto the golf course, the farmers make their inspections or tow their equipment to the necessary places, or do all the hundred and one other things that have to be done. The postman comes, closely followed by the newspaperman and milkman. The daily cleaning ladies bicycle through while the housewives set off for their shopping or other engagements, of which there are always a multitudinous variety. It is, in fact, amazing how the village empties during the morning. If perchance you happen to be a purveyor of communications on behalf of some organization, you will often find that most of the premises are deserted, and indeed it can be difficult to find the letter boxes.

The village garage is always a hive of activity. Practically all the families have motor cars and some have several, of which quite a few need constant attention. Alas, our village Post Office and shop is no more, although a Post Office is still extant in another hamlet up the hill. However, we have a choice of places to go to for shopping, all within a few minutes motoring, but a central village shopping precinct is sadly missed, for it is here that so much essential small business is done and even more essential news is exchanged. The village shop is the sounding board of the community, for it is here that people take time to pause, greet each other, be polite, condone and really communicate.

Not long ago there were three pubs in the valley but now there is just one, an ugly edifice at the crossroads, put there by Whitbreads when it was thought that the route of the A3, the main Portsmouth road, would be sited through the valley. It has thus never been a cosy meeting place for the villagers but rather a restaurant for travellers and visitors from elsewhere, despite great efforts on the part of the landlord. There is a saw-mill, a pottery, two builders and also a maker of every type of wooden hut, especially wendy houses. The Tull Brothers were a small family firm of contractors, who could turn their hands to almost anything in the way of roadmaking, drainage, tree felling and clearance generally. There was also a lady who bought up and refurbished old farm implements to be used ornamentally in various places.

Nearly all the precincts from which these activities were per-formed were nicely tucked away, the main exception being the garage. Somehow, these always manage to become major eye-sores. The petrol pumps are the main offenders. How nice it would be if some of the oil kings could produce handsome ones.

I was now asked to speak at a number of functions, usually dinners, among them the Special Forces Club, the Military Book Society at the RAF Club, the Turners Livery Company at the Apothecary's Hall, the 52nd Lowland Division at the Western Club in Glasgow and an American battlefield tour at a hotel near Arnhem in Holland. This I managed to do and return within twenty-four hours. Finally, a luncheon in New Orleans. Here, we were guests of American friends and had time to explore the 'Mardi Gras' city and the glorious countryside, containing many of the mansions typified in the film, Gone With the Wind, and we went searching for a crocodile in the swamps, seated in a rather fragile canoe.

Shortly after this, we attended a reunion of the German Parachute Regiment at Karlsruhe. This was most beautifully arranged. Old friends, Dennis and Mary Rendell, came with us and we had time to do a demi-tour of the Black Forest as well. The old comrades, our old enemies, put on a most impressive show and we felt almost more at home with them than we had with our Yankee-Doodles. Somehow, being European counts for a lot. The outstanding Colonel Rudolf Witzig was the 'king pin'. We were made to feel that we were in the hands of long-lost friends, rather than of old enemies.

Tom Smith, our last fully-trained farm worker, left us in June, 1981, and thereafter Bob Gallagher and I kept things going. We had a number of beef cattle, which we maintained successfully on our grass in the summer months and in the yard during the winter. We no longer reared calves and by degrees slid into the systems of the Jenner family, our next door neighbours, with whom we had come to a share-farming arrangement. Gradually, Bob worked for other local people rather than me and then one day he was run into while riding his moped and killed. Joan, his wife, stayed on in the cottage and continued to give daily help in our house, as she had for several years.

I sold most of our equipment to Robert Jenner, keeping one of the smaller tractors for tidying work. Each year I trimmed the hedges on both our farms and used the ditcher when necessary. I dealt with the mole problems and harrowed and rolled the grass in the spring. There was always much to do in our woodlands, particularly after the great storm of October, 1987, when a number of trees were blown down and many of our oaks were decapitated. Fortunately, I still had all the proper tools to deal with the problems and we do at least have an abundance of firewood for many years to come.

After several years on the Parish Council, of which I had been Chairman for six, I had very mixed feelings when deciding not to stand for re-election. During most of my time, I had been most ably supported by Valerie Porter, as the secretary and Parish Clerk. I had first met her at a small drinks party, where I discovered that she was an able stenographer and was willing to do a certain amount of typing. She was so very obviously competent that when a vacancy for that appointment of parish clerk occurred, I persuaded her to take the job on, and she turned out to be a treasure. From then on, all the background administration was impeccable. On the whole, people, once elected to parish councils, like to remain on them for ever but I felt it important that others should take their turn. The Army trains one to believe that no one is indispensable and I still consider that this is very true. Anyway, I reckoned that I had done all that I could for the village and now new ideas were needed.

I had always felt that the Royal British Legion, with its Poppy Day, epitomized the sacrifices made by the services during the two world wars. I had become elected as President of the Liphook Branch after giving a talk about the Battle of Arnhem some years before but now, for various reasons, it was necessary to build a new war memorial for those commemorated in a dismantled church within the valley. For some years after the last war, there had been a small branch in the valley but it had been allowed to lapse and I now felt it incumbent on me to resuscitate this as a cornerstone for a new memorial.

To my surprise, I found that there were about fifty ex-servicemen living in the valley and most of these were willing to become members, among them three octogenarians living in a residential hotel run by an ex-Polish Lancer. John Booker, our local masterbuilder, elected to raise a simple stone memorial on the site of the altar of the old church if I could produce the stone. Luckily, Viscount Cowdray was willing to provide this, free gratis, and the plan was drawn by a kindly resident, John Hatton. Thus, at relatively minimal cost, we achieved our aim. We had to replace the old standard, for by now the Legion had become Royal, but we were all ready to march on Remembrance Sunday in 1987 from the war memorial to St Andrew's Church at Linch, and later that year to dedicate our new memorial at Iping Marsh.

CHAPTER XX

FINALE

I HAD BEEN A TRUSTEE of the Airborne Forces Security Fund almost since the end of the war. It had been General Boy Browning's firm intention that all those who fought with Airborne Forces should have no immediate financial worries when things went wrong. To this end, during the war he detailed Jock Pearson, one of his staff officers, who was also familiar with the City of London and all its ways, to set up the trust and begin raising money. The whole project had turned out to be a great success. Many of those who had played a significant part with Airborne Forces were invited to be trustees, as were a number of other people whose advice would be valuable when it came to considering investment policy. The organization was ideally suited for working with the other service charities such as the Army Benevolent Fund and the Soldiers', Sailors' and Airmen's Families Association. Whenever a case of hardship or need was reported, it could be thoroughly investigated and no stone left unturned until the maximum sensible help was given. This kept one in touch with the problems encountered by our old soldiers. We nearly always attended the Regimental Day at Aldershot when one of the battalions trooped the colour. Browning Barracks, Aldershot, had been the depot of the Regiment almost since the end of the war and it was here that the recruits were trained to a standard that set an example to the rest of the Army. I was twice asked to take their passing out parade, which was a great privilege. Quite apart from the young soldiers themselves, it was their parents who were so impressive. They had come from all over the kingdom to watch their sons on this day and their pride in their performance was a joy to behold.

In addition to being President of the Para 2 Club, I was similarly honoured by the Southampton Branch of the Parachute Regimental Association and they were of tremendous help in arranging the making and erection of a plaque in memory of C Company 2 Para's raid at Bruneval, which was later unveiled by Prince Charles and President Mitterand jointly, during the fortieth anniversary celebrations. Many of the branches were capable of arranging quite superlative evening occasions. One I shall not forget was with a branch in Yorkshire at Nostell Priory, the home of Lord St Oswald. Nothing was too much trouble here. Meanwhile, the Para 2 Club weekends got better and better and one could not help but feel intensely proud to have commanded such people for so long at the time that I did.

The Army Air Corps gave considerable help in an attempt to record events which took place during the Bruneval Raid, in the shape of photographed descriptions. However, it is almost impossible to reproduce facsimiles of what happened at night in the dark with any degree of realism and we gave it up. Helicopters had landed and taken off from the farm, which caused considerable excitement locally both to man and beast. On the forty-sixth anniversary, the local French authorities renamed the road leading from the village to the radar station, 'Avenue General Frost'. Six of us veterans were flown in great comfort in an Islander to Le Havre airport and back.

A few years earlier, the Ministry of Defence, Army Department, had tried to make a film of the raid as a training aid but it was a complete flop. Similarly, the Regiment commissioned David Shepherd, who had made such a success of his picture of the bridge at Arnhem, to paint one of the Bruneval Raid. We went over there together and he prowled over all the possible viewpoints and then said, 'No, it cannot be done.' He had immediately seen that it was impossible to recapture the drop, the action and the evacuation on one piece of paper, especially as they had all taken place at different times in darkness. He had been hoping to find one viewpoint from which he could depict it all. He was much too honest a man to try to foist a false image.

As I have mentioned, Bob Gallagher, my last full-paid employee, was run into and killed while riding his moped on the A3 on the morning of 20 June, 1985. In fact, he had been working only part time for me because by now our partnership with the Jenners of Hollycombe Farm was well under way. It was nice that so many village people came to his funeral. He never seemed to have many friends, though his wife, who worked for Jean in the house, moved about the village quite a lot. However, his going in such a sudden fashion was a considerable shock. Since the Smiths had gone, we had let that cottage to a vet who had come with a very hefty old hunter and a rather nasty little thoroughbred foal. The old hunter merely had to lean its bottom against any fence or gate to effect its destruction and the foal was bloodyminded. It certainly seemed to us that even a much larger number of bovine animals are far less trouble than comparatively few equine ones.

In September, 1986, we went back to Malta to stay at the Phoenicia Hotel. We had always enjoyed dining and dancing there all those twenty-odd years before and now the management had given us a splendid room overlooking the harbour. However, things were not quite the same. Our old house on the sea front at Tigne had been allowed to fall into a state of the utmost disrepair, with doors and windows hanging askew, paint peeling and roof tiles missing. There were piles of litter everywhere, but most noticeable was the extraordinary number of stray cats. We had been warned that we would get a shock when we saw it and we certainly did. We were also surprised at the clothing, or rather lack of it, now being worn by the women. In our time, all races had been circumspect regarding this but now, even in Valletta, there were shocks for the most hardened.

Nevertheless, our old Maltese friends were just the same and though the polo club was much reduced in numbers it was still going, while the Marsa Club had been much improved, with a delightful swimming pool as its central feature. Our old butler, Frank, and Kitty, our housemaid, came to see us – Frank embracing us both with gusto in the crowded hotel bar. I wrote my name in the official book in the Castille, now the seat of the government. This was perhaps the most impressive building on Malta and had been the Army HQ in our day. I was glad to see that the list of the GDCs remained in position still.

During the night of 16 October, 1987, freak winds swept over parts of the south of England, laying swathes of devastation behind them. The tops of the deciduous trees were still heavy with leaf, which caused many to be broken in half. The actual damage done has never been accurately estimated and much of it has still not been made good, nor could it ever be. We suffered considerably and, at the time of writing, have still not cleared all the wreckage. I rather welcomed some of the results. For instance, we had a row of dark pine trees in front, but some distance from the house. Half of these were felled, which meant that we had to remove the rest and we now have a very much more attractive view. Practically all the exits from the valley were blocked for a time, which gave the commuters a cast iron excuse for not going to work, anyway for one day. We now have enough firewood to keep us going for at least a decade.

1988 saw the appearance of my ex-ADC, Geoffrey Kent, as captain of a polo team, which included HRH Prince Charles. Two New Zealand players were the stars but Geoff and his wife, Jorie, had left no possible stone unturned towards total success during that season. Indeed, it was almost achieved. It was an enormous pleasure to watch an old playmate, for we had been in the army team together in Malta, playing in the highest possible class of this most superlative game. Another ADC, Tim Holderness-Roddam, had married Jane Bullan, a winner at Badminton, and an Olympic Gold Medallist.

In addition to the trips abroad I have mentioned, there were others to Holland, France, Portugal and Spain. Gradually the kerfuffle of getting to an airport or a ferry port, with the subsequent delays and the discomforts involved, has decided me to refuse further such movement as far as is possible. I have felt perfectly happy for Jean to make her own plans with her own friends and have learnt to cope at Northend without her for short periods and this arrangement seems to give us both what we want. I fear that pilgrimages or suchlike will have to be attended as long as can be. One had rather hoped and expected that the fiftieth anniversary celebrations of the Hitler War battles would see the end of such. But, by now, these have come to mean so much to so many people that it seems likely that they will continue even after all the original participants are dead.

Jean and I attended the forty-fifth anniversary at Arnhem in 1989.

This was to be a rather special year, in that far more emphasis was to be placed on the bridge itself. When the pilgrimages began soon after the end of the war, the premier place was given to the bridge. This was, after all, the main objective of the 1st Airborne Division and it had been considered vital to both friend and foe alike. The first memorial was erected and wreaths were laid here on 17 September, which was the first day of each pilgrimage. All those attending the ceremony formed up, in the evening, near or in the Town Hall to march in silence to the great block of stone, which had been taken from the ruins of the Hall of Justice. After the wreath laying, all the pilgrims were guests of the Municipality of Arnhem in a large building nearby and here we were treated to an excellent supper and entertainment.

In later years, for various reasons, the bridge ceremony had been rather briefly celebrated on the Saturday morning and gradually the numbers attending this dwindled, with the Municipality of Oosterbeek trying to provide what had formerly been done in Arnhem. During the battle, through the inability of most of the division to reach their objectives in Arnhem, most of the fighting had taken place in Oosterbeek, which was on the way, and this had led some of the inhabitants to feel that our battle should have been called the Battle of the Lower Rhine, rather than the Battle of Arnhem. However, the whole world had come to recognize it as the Battle of Arnhem. Perhaps it should be referred to as the battle for Arnhem. In fact, it was the battle for Arnhem Bridge.

I had always been rather dubious that the bridge should bear my name and thought that it ought perhaps to have been called the 'Too Far Bridge' in view of the famous statement by Boy Browning that perhaps Operation Market Garden included a bridge too far. Anyway it was meant to be a great honour and so indeed have I always felt it to be. Several years later, it was decided that the new bridge should be named the 'Nelson Mandela Bridge', after the South African dissident who had been a political prisoner for many years. No sooner was this done than rumours were being spread that the 'John Frost Bridge' had been renamed 'Nelson Mandela Bridge'. When asked to comment on this by the media, I had a ready-made, idiot-boy reply, 'Mandela, I don't think I ever met him. Which battalion was he?'

Anyway, the Burgomaster at that time, Dr Dridjber, asked me over to unveil huge new plaques, which could leave no doubt in anyone's mind that the bridge was securely in my name. I am told that General Harmel considers that it should be the Frost-Harmel Bridge, he having held the other end during the battle.

Dr Dridjber was determined that, for the pilgrimage of 1989, of which I was to be the leader, our old bridge was to have pride of place during the ceremonies. By the time they began, he had been succeeded as Burgomaster by Mr Paul Scholton. The Thursday evening saw the official opening with music, ballet and speeches in the Rhine Hall, a huge building just south of the river, which could amply seat everyone who wanted to come: the evening ended with all the right sorts of refreshments.

We returned to the bridge again on the Saturday evening for the silent procession to, and wreath-laying at, the bridge memorial just as it was getting dark. It was far more impressive than the Saturday mornings of recent years and there were literally hundreds more attenders. The Municipality then hosted a splendid reception in one of the old churches nearby, which had been ideally converted for just such a purpose. To ensure that no one should feel at a loss for the rest of the evening, yet another reception was laid on in the Rhine Hall. It was almost a case of *embarras de richesse*. However, the end was not yet, for on the Sunday evening I was bidden to switch on a new lighting system fixed to the girders flanking the bridge, after which Jean and I, with the Burgomaster, walked along it past hordes of young people bearing lighted torches, who were cheering, clapping and generally shouting hurray. This is something which I shall always remember.

I'm never likely to forget the first time I visited this great bridge in the gloaming of Sunday, 17 September 1944. My 2nd Battalion had had a perfect landing at 2 pm on a large stretch of farmland some seven miles west of Arnhem. We were part of the 1st Parachute Brigade, which were to march to Arnhem using three different routes. The Reconnaissance Squadron, jeep-mounted, were to dash ahead to try to seize and hold the main bridge. My battalion was to move along the most southerly and partially riverside route; capture a railway bridge on the way; pass one company across this; capture a pontoon bridge further on, if it was, in fact, in use; and finally, not only capture and hold the main bridge but also take an enemy headquarters in the western part of the town.

After a scuffle on the edge of the dropping zone with some Germans, who were in a lorry and had an armoured car, we had relatively little trouble until we reached the village of Oosterbeek, where the railway bridge lay across the river. When we reached this populated area we were given a tremendous welcome by all the Dutch inhabitants, who pressed all sorts of good things upon us, but we had no time to stop although we were pouring with sweat under the heavy loads which we all bore. During the afternoon, too, a squadron of Spitfires flew over the town practically unmolested, so it seemed that the RAF contentions as to the strength of the enemy flak were not exactly true. 'C' Company, under Major Victor Dover, moved across to seize the bridge, but after they had actually appeared on the embankment and on the near side of the bridge itself, it was blown up and collapsed into the river. Meanwhile, the leading company, under Digby Tatham-Warter was also having trouble from enemy infantry and armoured cars in the area of a feature called Den Brink. I brought up Douglas Crawley's 'B' Company to circle round to the left and deal with this, which had the effect of freeing the road and allowing Digby to press on. I followed with my headquarter and support companies. He went past the pontoon bridge which had been dismantled previously.

It was getting dark as we saw the spans of the main bridge ahead of us but fortunately we found it undefended. We occupied all the buildings nearby, which gave us control of the approaches. Digby then launched one of his platoons to try to cross to the south bank but fire from a stationary AFV and a pillbox on the bridge made this too expensive in casualties. After dealing with the pillbox, he began to try again with another platoon but now enemy infantry attacked our positions from further east and three lorries loaded with combustible materials tried to force their way across from the south. These were all halted and caught fire so that the flames from these precluded any further attempts to get onto the bridge at all.

I still hoped to be able to get part of my force across the river and I sent George Murray, who was our senior Sapper officer, back to the site of the pontoon bridge but he soon returned, saying that there were no suitable craft available there. By this time Freddie Gough, the CO of the Reconnaissance Squadron, had arrived. His unit had had a most unfortunate attempt to come into Arnhem via the main road, being ambushed by enemy machine-gun fire, and in the end he arrived with only a small number of his unit.

Most important to our future was the arrival of David Clarke, of what was then called the Army Service Corps, with a truck which was full of ammunition. Another most welcome addition was 'Pongo' Lewis's 'C' Company of the 3rd Battalion which marched in along the railway line. Finally came the Brigade Head-quarters with Tony Hibbert, the Brigade Major, but less Gerald Lathbury, the Brigade Commander. I had heard him call off further movement from the other two battalions that night which was most unfortunate, for however difficult the day's advance might have been, it was going to be much more difficult in tomorrow's daylight. The Germans, however good they might be, had a saying, 'The night is the friend of no man'. We spent the remainder of the night improving our positions and making contacts with each other and we also tried to get some sleep. Unfortunately we had been told not to trust the local Dutch people because the Underground had been penetrated. This was a tragedy for it wasn't until much later that we realized how much they were prepared to do for us.

Early on the Monday morning came a cry, saying, 'Armoured cars are coming across the bridge!' I couldn't help thinking that this might be the spearhead of the 2nd British Army coming to our aid but they weren't really expected for at least another day. Soon, however, it was obvious that this armour was hostile. In fact, this was the reconnaissance squadron of the 10th SS Panzer Division, which had crossed the bridge the previous day just before we had arrived, and they were now returning from Nijmegen where they had been carrying out a reconnaissance in force. We had laid a necklace of mines across the bridge for just such an eventuality, but, though some of the enemy got through this, it wasn't long before they came into range of our own anti-tank guns and PIATs, which accounted for some 75 per cent of their total strength, and these vehicles lay in front of us burning for several hours to come.

We were now much bedevilled by the unreliability of all our wireless communications. Nevertheless, we were able to ask the 1st and 3rd Battalion to hasten to join us by the route that we had used the day before, and also to summon Douglas Crawley's 'B' Company, which was in the area of the pontoon bridge. Unfortunately, we could make no contact with our 'C' Company, who were at the German headquarters where they became completely isolated and overwhelmed. Dennis Mumford, the battery commander of our divisional light regiment RA, provided most effective support from his guns which were away back near the river in Oosterbeek. The Brigade Major now asked me to move over to the Brigade Headquarters so as to be able to position the rest of the Brigade if and when it arrived. I therefore handed over to my very excellent second-in-command, Major David Wallis, but unfortunately he was killed during the course of the coming night. From henceforward there were few new decisions to be made. We just had to hang on as best we could until relieved either by the rest of the Division or by the 2nd British Army coming up from the south.

By now we knew that we had walked into the 2nd SS Panzer Corps, quite different from the very minor opposition which we had been led to expect. This formation, although severely reduced after its battles in Normandy, still had many of its personnel and a number of AFVs and guns but also a most effective command set-up. Throughout the day, we could hear the other battalions trying to fight their way through towards us and all day long we were pounded by artillery and mortars. Our wounded began to fill the cellars of the buildings which we owned but as night fell the enemy activity died away, which gave us respite.

On the Tuesday morning we had been expecting to see the Polish Parachute Brigade drop south of the river and I had organized a reception party mounted in two jeeps and two carriers, which was to be led across by the redoubtable Freddie Gough. However, there was no sign of the Poles, whose future dropping zone was changed to some distance away. One strange thing was that during the whole of Monday and Tuesday morning we had heard no sound of the battle we expected to be taking place at Nijmegen, the big town immediately to the south. This was a little daunting, for it meant that the programme of the relieving force must have been delayed. During that morning General Harmel, the GOC of the 10th SS Panzer Division, sent one of our captured NCOs back to us, requesting our surrender as our position was so completely hopeless. We did not deign to reply.

Attacks by enemy infantry supported by tanks continued relentlessly throughout the hours of daylight. Most of the buildings which caught fire, being largely made of wood, continued to burn for several hours. Our stocks of ammunition soon became a problem and I had to say that it should all be reserved for beating off attacks and that there should be no more sniping or pot shots. During the course of the day, two towed 150mm guns were brought to the edge of our perimeter and the rounds from these could pulverize our positions. Luckily, a mortar bomb landed on their ammunition supply, which put them out of commission at any rate for a time. Two Tiger tanks suddenly appeared, much to our discomfort, and these may have caused the final elimination of our most gallant gunners of the 1st Air Landing Anti-Tank Battery. Since the Monday evening small bodies of our troops fighting on the eastern side of the main bridge were cut off from the rest of us who were on the west side but they continued to battle on. Particularly noteworthy were McKay's party of sappers, Pat Barnet's brigade defence platoon and Bernard Briggs' detachment.

During the course of that morning we heard that a fresh attempt was to be made by two battalions of the other brigades, together with the remnants of the 1st and 3rd Battalions, to try to break through to us, but by now the enemy in between ourselves and the rest of the Division was far too strong. Moreover, the attack was to be made in daylight. Experience had shown us that the only hope of defeating the Germans in these conditions was to use the hours of darkness as the enemy usually drew stumps at night and we were given a fairly peaceful time, though the fires from the burning buildings and the crackle of the tortured timber almost turned night into day.

Wednesday morning brought no relief and the battle continued all day long. While I was discussing future moves with Douglas Crawley, both of us were hit by fragments from a mortar bomb which landed nearby. I was immobilized and forced to spend the rest of our time in one of the cellars. During the course of the late afternoon, the final bastion caught fire. By now there was no water nor any means of quenching the flames and, faced with the certainty that some two to three hundred of our wounded lying in the cellars would be burnt to death, we arranged with the enemy to call a short truce to evacuate them. Our SS opponents behaved scrupulously in helping to get everybody out but in so doing they were able to improve their positions, so there was really nowhere left for the unwounded survivors to go. Even so, that night and on the Thursday morning, little bodies of survivors with practically no ammunition left, continued to defend themselves until they were located and completely overwhelmed. The remainder of the Division were able to go on fighting for several more days until some two thousand were evacuated back across the river from the area of Oosterbeek where they had been fighting.

Ever since the battle took place all those years ago, one has been hearing about the 'Failure of Arnhem'. Indeed there was a failure in that the main road bridge was not held until the 2nd British Army could cross the Lower Rhine over it. There are many reasons for this.

Firstly, the planning was based on false information. Although the presence of the 2nd SS Panzer Corps in the Arnhem area was known to many, this vital information was withheld from 1st Airborne Division and indeed the relieving 30 Corps. Secondly, the Air Forces planners misinterpreted the suitability of the terrain near the bridge for a parachute drop or a glider landing. Moreover, they quite wrongly accepted the reported strength of the enemy flak, but, worst of all, insisted that it was impracticable to fly two sorties to Holland from the nearby airfields in the UK on one day.

Lieutenant-General Browning, GOC of the Airborne Corps, insisted on bringing his HQ into the battle area where it could do no possible good and, in so doing, used up the lift of a fighting unit. Moreover, he selected for his location the Groesbeek Heights, which are not really a worthwhile tactical feature, and insisted that the 82nd US Airborne Division make this a priority task, while ignoring the one thing that really mattered which was the bridge at Nijmegen. It was the delay in capturing this that spelt the doom of the 1st Airborne Division at Arnhem. It was barely defended by the enemy at all when the Americans came, yet they had to leave it until it was indeed fully defended.

Even after it was finally captured, although we were holding on to Arnhem bridge only by our eyelids, efforts made by nearly all elements of the 2nd British Army to relieve us were half-hearted and failed. In contrast, the German reorganization after their defeat in Normandy was extraordinary. In the space of two weeks they had built a new army. It was all made up with bits and pieces, but it fought just as well as ever. Their Generalship was dynamic, as opposed to phlegmatic. At this particular time, Winston Churchill and his CIGS were away from the UK in Canada and maybe our own Generals were having a few off days. There were obviously a lot of tea breaks.

Meanwhile, 1st Airborne Division was to be virtually destroyed. Their task had been to take and hold the Arnhem Bridge for some hours and they had done this for nearly four days and then continued to resist for several more. There were other adverse factors, including the weather and the non-function of so much of our radio. In fact it would take a whole book to list all the things that went wrong.

The shortage of airlift on the first day caused the adoption of a defensive plan in that the 1st Airlanding Brigade was committed to guarding the DZs until the arrival of the 4th Parachute Brigade on the second. Thus only one brigade was available for the main task on the first day. However, if both brigades had gone for Arnhem on the first day, they would have secured the bridge much more firmly and indeed all the approaches thereto. The enemy flak north of the river would have been dealt with and the air forces could have dropped the 4th Parachute Brigade immediately south of the bridge with impunity, especially if full use were made of the vast fleet of fighter aircraft available.

Within that divisional sector re-supply could have been safely received and distributed. Moreover, something could have been done to encourage the reluctant heroes supposed to be linking up from the south.

As it was, the airlanding brigade was ineffective to the main task for nearly two days and even after the arrival of the 4th Brigade, which was dropped much further away than was necessary.

Instead of at least one of the brigades making a determined night attack into Arnhem, two separate battalions were dispatched without any co-ordination or proper orders. The main trouble was that General Urquart, the GOC, had left his HQ and gone forward on the first day only to be boxed up, so that he was ineffective until the morning of the third day. On his return to his HQ, he sent a senior officer into Arnhem who was to try to co-ordinate the efforts of the remains of the 1st Brigade and two other battalions who were still trying to get to the bridge. Rather a forlorn hope, perhaps, but anyway poor Colonel Hilary Barlow just disappeared. The general also changed the planned DZ for the Polish Parachute Brigade from immediately south of the bridge to one to the south of Oosterbeek. The Poles were able to achieve little by the change, but might have made all the difference to the force still fighting to hold onto the north end of the bridge. We now know that practically all the German opposition in that area were either fully involved north of the river or else trying to cross by ferry much further to the east.

However, perhaps the most damaging decision during Market Garden, made by the British, was not to use the Dutch Underground, or indeed to take any advice from that source. Prince Bernhard had offered both to Monty, together with request to be allowed to visit the Princess Irene Brigade. Both were turned down, Monty saying 'I do not think your underground can be of any use to us'. Admittedly the underground had been penetrated, but largely through the fault of the British Organisation. Thus we were advised not to take advantage of offers of co-operation regarding communication, local knowledge and even information about the enemy.

We now know that the final aim of surrounding the Ruhr was beyond the capabilities of the resources available at the time and that therefore the concept of Market Garden was unlikely to succeed. What we did need was a really effective port of entry on the left flank. All eyes were fixed on Antwerp in this respect, but the enemy had had ample time to take all the defensive measures necessary to deny this. For some reason the selection of Rotterdam as a most viable alternative seems to have escaped attention. If surplus weapons from the UK Home Guard had been delievered to the Dutchmen in Rotterdam and Amsterdam, and had the impetus after Arnhem been beamed on Rotterdam, all the resources of the Canadian Army which were so expensively used to open up the Scheldt could have been diverted and all the German troops anchored to the Scheldt would have been cut off and virtually ineffective.

Moreover all Holland would have been freed. The V2 sites would have been overrun. The approach into Germany from Rotterdam is even shorter than from Antwerp. With a really secure base building up from Rotterdam, we are almost into the North German plain with no more rivers to cross.

INDEX